Acclaim for Rocco Mediate and
John Feinstein's

Are You Kidding Me?

THE STORY OF ROCCO MEDIATE'S EXTRAORDINARY BATTLE WITH TIGER WOODS AT THE U.S. OPEN

"If you're like me and think that Tiger Woods's win over Mediate at Torrey Pines was the most gripping sporting event of the last twenty years, then you'll enjoy Rocco's version of those five days in June, especially the nineteen-hole playoff on Monday, which depressed trading on Wall Street as stockbrokers gathered in front of televisions to watch.... Feinstein smartly keeps the narration in the third person, and in the opening pages he paints the setting — Torrey Pines, Mediate's career, and the peculiarities of the U.S. Open — in a few masterful strokes.... The book does a nice job of recreating the heady atmosphere of Torrey Pines, where the striking oceanfront setting, the postcard weather, and the two riveting protagonists gave the tournament a movie-like feel.... Feinstein collects enough telling details from Mediate that you'll race through the pages."   — Mike Walker, Golf.com

"*Are You Kidding Me?* covers Mediate's entire life and climaxes with a detailed, inside-the-ropes look at the triumph that almost was."   — Scott Brown, *Pittsburgh Tribune-Review*

"An enjoyable look 'inside the ropes' at Rocco Mediate's improbable 2008 U.S. Open battle with Tiger Woods....In *Are You Kidding Me?* Mediate and sports writer extraordinaire John Feinstein revisit the epic battle that was the 2008 U.S. Open. It unfolds like a made-for-TV movie, with the unlikely underdog facing down the biggest kid on his—or any other—block....It's exciting stuff....The real value of the book is in the perspective. This is Rocco's story. He's the coauthor and his voice (and those of his friends and associates) is heard throughout."

—Golfblogger.com

"What better time to take a look back at last year's amazing U.S. Open golf tournament. *Are You Kidding Me?* does just that and in entertaining and enlightening fashion....You don't have to be a golf or sports fan to appreciate the drama and appeal of this story. What Mediate and Feinstein offer is not just a shot-by-shot recap of the tournament—although the coverage of the event is well done—but rather a better understanding of the person and golfer behind it....*Are You Kidding Me?* provides an interesting snapshot of what it is like to make a living on the PGA Tour. It shows the growth of the tour, and the explosion of purses post-Tiger, but it also highlights all of the myriad decisions and the emotional roller coaster ride that the tour involves if you are not one of the elite players. *Are You Kidding Me?* is a must read for golf and sport fans—and would make a great Father's Day gift. But you don't have to be a fan of the game to appreciate the story. It really is a classic tale of overcoming adversity and giving your best when everything is on the line....Last year's battle at Torrey Pines will be remembered for a long time. And Rocco Mediate and John Feinstein have told the story as no one else can."

—Kevin Holtsberry, Examiner.com

"If you are a golf geek like me, then you remember the 2008 U.S. Open like it was yesterday. This tournament played out more dramatically than the movie *Seabiscuit,* and Rocco Mediate was more likable and easier to root for than Rocky Balboa....John Feinstein is a very accomplished sports writer who has written two of the top bestselling nonfiction sports books in history: *A Good Walk Spoiled* and *A Season on the Brink.* He is to nonfiction sports writing as Stephen King is to horror novels. Through Feinstein, Rocco relives his marvelous five days and his battle with Tiger. You won't find a more likable and greater guy to root for than Roc. I won't give away the ending—you'll have to read the book!"   —Robert Lawrence Ludwig, Zipgolfer.com

"When the reader arrives at the closing, which covers the actual U.S. Open encounter between Rocco Mediate and Tiger Woods, Feinstein livens things up with excellent detail and anecdotes."
     —Michael Thompson, AssociatedContent.com

"In the golf world, it was an epic story, even a tragic one (though more Californian than Greek): bathed in brilliant sunshine and surrounded by cameras, a likable but all-too-human fellow finds himself in combat with a god and is destroyed, but not before he inspires us with his courage and heroism....What Rocco Mediate did on five days last June defined the tournament, the course, and both Woods and himself....The section of the book that is devoted to a day-by-day and, toward the end, a hole-by-hole and even shot-by-shot account of what happened on the course is an exciting read, even for those whose interest in golf is minimal....Feinstein knows how to capture golf's quirky, maddening beauty and drama, and he tells a story vividly and economically."   —Richard Horwich, *East Hampton Star*

Are You Kidding Me?

THE STORY OF ROCCO MEDIATE'S
EXTRAORDINARY BATTLE WITH
TIGER WOODS AT THE U.S. OPEN

ROCCO MEDIATE
and
JOHN FEINSTEIN

BACK BAY BOOKS
Little, Brown and Company
New York   Boston   London

Back Bay Books / Little, Brown and Company
Hachette Book Group
237 Park Avenue, New York, NY 10017
www.hachettebookgroup.com

Originally published in hardcover by Little, Brown and Company, May 2009
First Back Bay paperback edition, May 2010

Back Bay Books is an imprint of Little, Brown and Company. The Back Bay Books name and logo are trademarks of Hachette Book Group, Inc.

Library of Congress Cataloging-in-Publication Data
Mediate, Rocco.
    Are you kidding me? : the story of Rocco Mediate's extraordinary battle with Tiger Woods at the U.S. Open / Rocco Mediate & John Feinstein.
        p. cm.
    ISBN 978-0-316-04910-8 (hc) / 978-0-316-04911-5 (pb)
    1. Mediate, Rocco. 2. Golfers—United States. 3. U.S. Open (Golf tournament) (2008 : Torrey Pines, Calif.) 4. Woods, Tiger. I. Feinstein, John. II. Title.
    GV964.M43A3 2009
    796.352092—dc22   2009006623

10 9 8 7 6 5 4 3 2 1

RRD-IN

Printed in the United States of America

For my boys... Rocco, Nicco, and Marco
—R.M.

For the Rules Guys: Mark Russell, John Brendle,
Slugger White, and Steve Rintoul, who are always
there day and night
—J.F.

CONTENTS

ROCCO'S FOREWORD

NEVER IN MY WILDEST DREAMS did I ever think I'd be involved in a book like this one. Or any book, for that matter. Winning the United States Open, I could imagine. A book? No way.

But after my near miss at Torrey Pines in the Open last June, I started hearing from people that I should do a book, that I should tell my story not only about my duel with Tiger Woods, but about all that led up to it. Literary agents were coming at me with offers and writers, saying they knew just how to tell my story.

I was certainly intrigued, but also a little bit skeptical. Mine is not—as you will learn—a simple story. If it was going to be told, I wanted it told right. One writer showed me a proposal he had put together in which he had me talking to God during the Open playoff. I don't talk to God. I think He has enough on his plate without golfers asking him for an extra birdie or two. Maybe the guy got confused when he saw me talking to Tiger. A lot of people make that mistake.

So there I was in early July with these offers, and I still wasn't sure what to do. That was when Cindi Hilfman (who played a major role in my being able to accomplish what I accomplished at the Open) brought up John Feinstein.

"Do you know him?" she asked me.

Sure, I knew John. I'd known him for years. I'd always enjoyed talking to him, whether it was in the locker room or on the driving range, and I knew that Lee Janzen, probably my best friend on tour, had worked with him on a couple of his books and liked and trusted him.

Cindi, it turns out, is also a fan. Maybe it's the whole Duke thing (she did her postgraduate work in physical therapy there), but she says she's read all twenty-three of his previous books. I haven't. In fact, I'm not sure if I've read twenty-three books period.

Cindi suggested I call John to see if he'd be interested in doing a book. Kelly Tilghman (another Dukie: I think there's a pattern here), who had done some work with me at the Golf Channel, had John's contact information, so I tracked him down during, ironically enough, Tiger's tournament at Congressional.

John asked me a lot of questions, one of which was if I was absolutely sure I wanted to do a book. I remember what he said to me: "These things don't happen by magic. It's work. It will take time, and I may ask you some difficult questions. If you understand that and still want to do it, I'm in."

To be honest, I don't think I completely understood what he was talking about. Now I do. It was a lot of work, but also a lot of fun. I thought there was a story to be told—one that goes well beyond what happened during those five days at Torrey Pines—and working with John, I came away even more convinced that was the case.

John made one other suggestion when we first talked: "Let's

not write this in the first person," he said. He thought that writing in the third person (I didn't even know what the hell writing in the third person was until he explained it to me) would give him more freedom to say things about me and tell the story in a kind of detailed way that first person doesn't allow.

Reading the book, I realized he was completely right. A lot of first-person athlete's books (okay, I *have* read a few books) leave me wanting to know more, because the athlete doesn't want to tell you what he thinks about someone or about how difficult something was to achieve. John did a *lot* of reporting. He talked to all the key people in my life and to people I hadn't even thought about. In some cases, people told him things I didn't even know.

Don't worry, though, I'm not going to pull a Charles Barkley and claim I was misquoted in a book my name is on. I've read it carefully, and everything that comes out of my mouth in the book came out of my mouth when John had his tape recorder on.

I think it's a pretty good story, one that I've enjoyed living—for the most part—and one that I hope you'll enjoy reading.

Overall, the experience was a fascinating one. I learned a lot about myself, my friends, and what goes into creating a book. I have only one regret: I heard a *lot* more about Coach K than I thought anyone could ever want to know.

I mean, the guy doesn't even play golf.

Oh, one more thing: The story John tells in the introduction about the title is true. Don't tell my kids.

Enjoy the book.

—Rocco Mediate

Are You Kidding Me?

INTRODUCTION

IN THE 108 YEARS THAT the United States Open golf championship has existed, there has never been an Open like the one that took place at Torrey Pines Country Club in June of 2008. This was an Open so remarkable it even made the United States Golf Association's stubborn insistence on continuing to stage an 18-hole Monday playoff look smart.

The golf world has become accustomed to Tiger Woods doing things that no one else has ever done before. He won the Masters at the age of twenty-one—by 12 shots. He won four major championships in a row. He changed his golf swing when he was the number one player in the world—and got better. Then he changed it again and, after going 10 straight majors without a win, won five of the next 12. Midway through 2008, he had won 65 times on the PGA Tour—17 short of the all-time record—and he was only thirty-two years old.

But his victory at Torrey Pines was spectacular even by his own spectacular standards. He had undergone knee surgery on April 15, two days after finishing second at the Masters and fifty-eight days before the start of the Open—and hadn't walked a single 18-hole round of golf before he teed it up on day one of the Open. He was clearly still in pain throughout the tournament. Just finishing 18 holes, let alone 72 holes, would have been an accomplishment. To finish 72 holes tied for first place and then play 19 more the next day to win the championship was almost beyond belief.

"I would have to say this is my greatest victory," he said when it was finally over.

And yet, extraordinary as it was, Woods's victory wasn't what made this Open unique. Had he won it in 72 holes by a shot or by two or three shots, it would have simply been another example of just how much better he is than every other golfer on the planet and would have set off another round of "Tiger is the most dominant athlete in the world" stories. All of which would have been correct and appropriate.

What made this Open as thrilling as it was, a golf event watched and remembered by millions of non–golf fans, wasn't Tiger Woods.

It was Rocco Mediate.

The notion of the greatest player in history proving once again how great he is—even doing it on one leg—fits handily into Woods's lore. The notion of the 158th player in the world, a motor-mouthed forty-five-year-old whose career has been plagued by back problems, standing toe-to-toe with the greatest player in history for 91 holes is the kind of stuff that can bring Wall Street to a virtual halt.

And it actually did. According to market analysts, during the four and a half hours that Woods and Mediate were on the golf course on Monday, June 16, trading volume on the stock exchange dropped 10 percent. During the last few holes, according to estimates, it dropped double that amount.

There were all sorts of stories like that one on that Monday. Joan Fay, the wife of USGA executive director David Fay, wanted to stay in San Diego on Monday for the playoff. But she had commitments back home in New York on Tuesday and, as her husband pointed out, changing her flight would have cost an arm and a leg. She arrived at the airport Monday morning comforted by the fact that Jet Blue provides TV service on coast-to-coast flights, so she would at least be able to watch.

While waiting for her plane, she ran into several NBC executives, also flying home because of commitments and the expense of changing a flight. They were completely glum because the airline they were on had no TV service.

"I think there are seats on the Jet Blue flight," Joan Fay said. "I'll bet they'd change your tickets for nothing."

A mad scramble followed and the NBC execs all ended up on Jet Blue. As luck would have it, the plane landed in New York just as Woods and Mediate were playing the 18th hole. It taxied to the gate, the Jetway pulled up, and no one got off the plane.

"No one would get off," Joan Fay said. "I mean no one."

One hundred miles to the north and east, another plane had just landed in Hartford, Connecticut. It was carrying golfers and their families from the Open to the next tour stop, which would take place that week outside Hartford. Everyone on the charter flight had been glued to the playoff, and when the plane landed, it pulled up to a private hangar where tournament officials and volunteers were waiting to help with luggage and courtesy cars and directions, and to make sure hotel reservations were in place.

But no one got off the plane.

"They couldn't have gotten me or anyone else off with a

court order at that point," said Lee Janzen, a longtime friend of Mediate's. "We just told the flight attendants to go inside and let the tournament people know we'd deplane as soon as it was over."

All over the country, people who couldn't have cared less about golf were tuned to television sets or computers, putting work and life aside to see how the playoff would be resolved. The notion that the wisecracking everyman from Greensburg, Pennsylvania, could somehow beat the world's best-known athlete was instant must-see TV. It was Johnny Miller, the longtime NBC analyst, who accidentally summed it up on Sunday afternoon when he said, "Can someone named Rocco actually beat Tiger Woods to win the U.S. Open? I mean, he looks more like he should be taking care of Tiger's pool than competing with him in the Open."

Miller caught a lot of flak for that comment—Italian American groups got upset and he had to publicly apologize—but the point he was making (which had nothing to do with Mediate's heritage) was an accurate one. Like everyone else who couldn't take their eyes off what they were watching, Miller simply couldn't believe what he was seeing.

In the end, someone named Rocco came up one shot short—just inches short—of beating Tiger Woods to win the U.S. Open. But the story he wrote during those five days—and what led to it—was once-in-a-lifetime stuff. No one understood that better than Rocco.

"Johnny called me to apologize about the comment," he said. "There was nothing to apologize for, and I told him that. I understood what he was saying. If I had been sitting at home, I would have been saying, 'There's no way this can happen,' just like everyone else was saying it.

"What people didn't understand was I wasn't afraid of [Woods]. Not because I don't think he's great — I do think he's great. He hasn't got a bigger fan in the world than me. But why would I be afraid of him? I'm always amazed when I see guys go out and play against him and they're afraid. Why? No one expects you to win — he's Tiger Woods and you're not.

"To be in that arena with the greatest player of all time. If you're a golfer, why wouldn't you revel in every second of it? If there's one thing that makes me happy about it all, it's that I don't have to look back and say, 'Gee, I wish I'd been able to enjoy it and savor it while it was going on.' I did do that. Every second of it right until I missed the last putt. I loved it all."

There's proof that Rocco isn't just saying that in the aftermath of the event. Mike Davis, the USGA official who directs the U.S. Open, walked every step of the way with Woods and Mediate during the playoff. He was responsible for setting up the golf course each day, for deciding on where tee markers were placed and where the hole was located on each green. During the playoff he was the walking rules official, responsible for letting the players know what to do if they needed any sort of drop or if they weren't sure about any rule that might come into play during the round.

On the sudden-death playoff hole, number seven at Torrey Pines, Rocco drove his ball well to the left, into an almost unplayable lie in a bunker, meaning he was going to have a difficult time staying alive, since Woods had put his ball in the fairway.

"I was walking off the tee thinking that Rocco was really in trouble and this might be the end of it all," Davis said. "I was feeling bad for him because he'd been so close to pulling the thing off. All of a sudden, I feel an arm around me and I look up and there's Rocco with this big grin on his face. He says, 'I can't tell you how much fun I'm having out here. In case I forget, I want to make sure you know I think you really nailed the setup, not just today but all week.'

"I couldn't get over it. Here he is in desperate trouble, probably about to lose, and he's got this big smile on his face and he's talking about how much fun he's having. I don't think I've ever seen anyone enjoy himself under pressure like that in my life."

Rocco ended up losing the playoff on that hole. Woods walked up to him, hand out to offer congratulations.

"Sorry pal, this doesn't call for a handshake," Rocco said. He wrapped his arms around Woods in a hug, a moment both men were entitled to after what they had gone through.

"Even now, months later, people still act as if I won," Rocco said after his whirlwind second half of 2008. "Sometimes I feel like I have to remind them that I played great, I'm really proud of what I did, but I didn't win. The other guy won."

That's true. Tiger, it seems, always wins. But in this case, there is no doubting the fact that his opponent didn't lose. He won—not the U.S. Open but the hearts of golf fans everywhere, and the hearts of a lot of people who had never heard of him before that week in San Diego.

Tiger Woods is the 2008 U.S. Open champion. His performance was nothing short of amazing. But Rocco Mediate was the champion of all Americans—a true underdog who captured the sheer joy of playing and competing. Together, Rocco and Tiger created a singular moment in sport, and an indelible memory for millions that isn't likely to be matched any time soon.

———

THE FIRST TIME I MET Rocco Mediate was more or less an accident. I certainly knew *of* him, but I didn't know him personally. He had been on tour for seven years and had just won for the second time in his career, at Greensboro, a few months earlier.

I was researching *A Good Walk Spoiled*. One of the people I was working with on that book was Lee Janzen. About a month after Janzen won the 1993 U.S. Open at Baltusrol, he and I were supposed to go to dinner and spend the evening discussing the events of that weekend in New Jersey. Janzen had come out of nowhere to beat Payne Stewart and win the Open.

"Mind if I bring a friend to dinner?" Janzen asked when I called to set up a time to meet.

In truth, I wasn't thrilled. When you are trying to interview someone, a third person is usually a distraction. But Janzen was giving me his time, so if he wanted to bring someone along, I was in no position to object. The third person turned out to be Rocco Mediate.

And his presence made the interview work about twice as well as it would have if he hadn't been there.

Janzen is what we call in my business a good talker. He's a nice guy who knows how to tell a story. But with Rocco sitting next to him, he became a great talker. He was loose and comfortable, and Rocco often reminded him of details as Lee walked me through his pre-Open life and the Open. What's more, Rocco told me exactly where he was and what he was thinking as he watched his friend play the back nine on Sunday.

"I kept thinking, 'This is Lee, my buddy Lee, the guy I spent all those hours practicing with when we were in college,'" he said. "When he was walking up 18, I remembered how we used to talk about what we were going to do when one of us won the U.S. Open and how we'd celebrate. And then it hit me: This is real; he's actually going to win the U.S. Open. I sat there with tears rolling down my face, not believing it was actually happening."

As he told the story, his voice caught at the memory. Janzen was equally emotional: "After I finished and shook hands with Payne, the first person I saw coming off the green was Rocco," he said. "He had tears rolling down his face. That's when I lost it myself—when I saw him."

I told Lee afterward he could bring Rocco along anytime he wanted in the future.

Rocco and I became friends after that night. Sometimes I'd go to him looking for a quote; other times we'd stand on a driving range or sit around a locker room talking about anything and everything. I vividly remember him at the 2006 Masters, sitting in the locker room with his friend and teacher Rick Smith, talking about how cool they both felt with Rocco in contention that year. I also remember the look on his face walking off the 18th green on Sunday after his back had exploded on him earlier that day, when he was tied for the lead.

"I just couldn't quit," he said. "I couldn't quit and I couldn't play. It was a pretty awful feeling."

Like everyone else who follows golf at all—and a lot of people who don't follow golf at all—I watched Rocco through his Open weekend at Torrey Pines waiting for the roof to fall in on him. He was tied for second on Thursday and still in contention on Friday and Saturday. But when Tiger Woods made two eagles on the back nine on Saturday (and chipped in for birdie at 17), there really wasn't that much point in watching on Sunday. After all, once Tiger gets the Saturday night lead at a major, the Sunday scramble is for second place. Thirteen times before, he had led majors on Saturday and thirteen times he had held the trophy the next day.

My hope was that Rocco would play well on Sunday and at least cash a big check. I knew he had struggled for several years, back troubles making it difficult for him to play with any consistency at all. So when he actually took the lead on Sunday, I was delighted. He wasn't going to shoot 80 on the last day—as he had that day at Augusta two years earlier, when his back went out on him—and he and Lee Westwood were actually making Tiger work to pull out a victory.

Everyone knows what happened after that. Rocco played superbly down the stretch, and Tiger had to make a miraculous birdie at the 18th, his 12-foot putt *just* catching the side of the hole and spinning around and in to create the playoff.

When that putt went in, I wasn't surprised, but I was disappointed. My feeling was that Rocco's one great chance to win the Open had just come and gone. After all, over 18 holes in a Monday playoff, what chance did he stand against Tiger Woods? I think most of America felt the same way, a notion that was further enforced when Rocco bogeyed the ninth and tenth holes the next day to fall three strokes behind in the playoff.

Those next two hours left all of us with our jaws slack and our hearts in our throats. Had Rocco somehow pulled out the victory, there wouldn't have been a need for this book: Hollywood would be writing the screenplay right now. As it is, the story is a richer one, even more mind-boggling when one knows the details and all the events that led up to that day.

"I have a poster of Rocky on my wall at home," Rocco says. "It says on it, 'He was a million-to-one shot.' Sometimes when I think about my career and my life and then that weekend, I laugh because in truth I was more like a billion-to-one shot."

There's a lot to that: a high school sophomore who couldn't come close to breaking 80 joining the PGA Tour six years later. A guy who needed disk surgery on his back when he was thirty-one years old still playing on the tour at forty-five. A player ranked 158th in the world, who needed a playoff just to qualify for the Open ten days before it began, pushing the greatest player of this or any generation to the absolute limit, going to places with him competitively that no other player had ever been.

All of which is why it was Rocco who came up with the title for this book. "What should we call it?" he asked me one day. I told him I hadn't really had time to think of a title yet. He laughed and leaned forward and, looking at a photo of him and Tiger standing together on the first tee during the playoff, he shook his head and said in pure Rocco, "I'll tell you what we should call it. We should call it *Are You Fucking Kidding Me?*"

So that's what we called it. Almost.

1

The Dream

Rocco Mediate was actually getting a little bit tired of the dream. He'd had it in different forms for as long as he could remember. Sometimes the dream happened when he was wide awake, practicing. Like almost any kid who ever played the game of golf, he would be locked in a duel with someone — usually his hero Tom Watson — for the United States Open title.

"It would come down to a putt," he said. "If I was practicing five-footers, it would be a five-footer. Sometimes I'd make one from across the green. Sometimes I'd hole one from the bunker."

More recently, the dream had occurred when he was asleep. It was always a little bit foggy — the circumstances changed but weren't ever completely clear — but he was always about to win the U.S. Open. "I love all the majors," he frequently told friends. "But there's nothing like the Open. It's just the *one* for me."

Now it seemed he was having the dream again, only it felt completely real. What was eerie was the detail and the specifics of this dream. He was pacing up and down in the scoring area inside the clubhouse at Torrey Pines Country Club, the municipal golf course outside San Diego where the 2008 U.S. Open was being played. On a television monitor in front of him, Tiger Woods—it had to be Tiger, right? If you were going to dream about beating someone to win a U.S. Open, why would you dream about anyone else?—was on the 18th green, lining up a 12-foot birdie putt. If he made it, there would be an 18-hole playoff the next day: Tiger Woods, the greatest player in history, against Rocco Mediate, the greatest player to ever grow up in Greensburg, Pennsylvania; Tiger Woods, the number one player in the world, against Rocco Mediate, the number 158 player in the world.

Rocco wondered when he would wake up. He wasn't completely certain he was capable of even dreaming this scenario. He was aware of the fact that there was a TV camera on him, watching his every move and reaction as Woods circled the green, lining up the putt from every possible angle.

"He's going to make it," Rocco thought. "He has to make it, right? He's Tiger Woods. He always makes these putts." Then again, he knew how bumpy the 18th green was. After four dry days in San Diego, all the greens at Torrey Pines were bumpy, and he knew that Woods could hit a perfect putt and it might catch one of those bumps and bounce away from the hole.

"He's going to do everything right, I know that," he thought. "He's going to get the right line and the right speed. His hands aren't going to shake. The moment isn't going to get to him, because he's been in this moment like a zillion times in his life. He's not going to choke; he's not going to get so nervous that he hits a bad putt. In fact, he's going to hit a perfect putt.

"But it still might not go in. He's going to do everything he has to do to get the putt to go in, but there are some things—like a bad bounce—that are even out of *his* control. He could, through no fault of his own, miss.

"And if the putt doesn't go in, I'll be the U.S. Open champion."

THROUGHOUT HISTORY, THERE HAVE BEEN unlikely U.S. Open champions. Because the Open is truly an open, almost anyone who can play the game at an elite level can qualify. In 2008 a total of 8,390 players had entered the Open, most of them forced to go through two stages of qualifying to make the 156-man field that teed it up in June at Torrey Pines. Those who entered included players from the PGA Tour, members of the various major- and minor-league and mini-tours around the world, and club pros and amateurs. If you had the $100 entry fee and a handicap of 1.4 or lower, you could sign up to play.

Of course the Open is won most often by the game's most glamorous names. Woods had won it twice, Jack Nicklaus and Byron Nelson four times. Ben Hogan, Arnold Palmer, Gary Player, and Tom Watson were all Open champions. But Sam Snead had never won it. Neither had Nick Faldo, Steve Ballesteros, Phil Mickelson, or Vijay Singh.

But surprises happen. Jack Fleck, a club pro, beat Hogan in a playoff at the Olympic Club in 1955. Andy North, who had won only one other tournament in his entire career, won the Open twice—in 1978 and again in 1985. Steve Jones came through qualifying to win in 1996, and Michael Campbell did the same thing before beating Woods by a stroke at Pinehurst in 2005.

But no Open precedent could have prepared fans for Rocco Anthony Mediate. He had also been forced to qualify, playing 36 grueling holes in Columbus, Ohio, ten days before the Open was to begin. He had birdied his second-to-last hole of the day to get into an eleven-man playoff for the final seven spots. Then he birdied the first playoff hole to make the field.

But that was only part of the story. He was forty-five and had thought his career over because of back miseries on more occasions than he cared to think about. He had undergone major back surgery once and been forced to leave the tour for extended periods several times.

As recently as July of 2007, he had gotten out of his car on a Sunday afternoon at Los Angeles Country Club, planning to play a round of golf with friends, taken one step in the direction of his trunk, and fallen flat on his face, his back completely seizing up. In a scene out of a movie, he had managed to reach into his pocket for his cell phone and, remembering that using cell phones was against the rules in the parking lot, sent a text message to his friends inside the clubhouse.

"In parking lot face down. Help."

He was a long way from that parking lot now, two weeks after qualifying, and he wondered when he would wake up, thinking how nice it would have been to find out if Woods made the putt. It would have been fun—even for an instant—to be the U.S. Open champion, even if it was just another dream.

Only he didn't wake up. He was still sitting there, watching the TV monitor while the TV camera watched him, as Woods finally got over the putt. How long had it been since he had finished his own round? Twenty minutes? An hour? Ten hours? At the very least it felt like an eternity.

Woods stood over the putt for so long that Rocco began to wonder if he was hoping someone would give it to him, like in match play. "That one's good, Tiger; pick it up."

Finally, the putter came back and moved forward in a silky-smooth motion. The ball wobbled toward the hole, bouncing along just as Rocco had known it would. For one millisecond, it looked as if it was going to be just wide to the right side of the hole. But it kept swerving, just a tiny bit, and at the last possible instant, it caught the right corner of the hole, spun around the side of the rim — and dropped in.

Rocco saw Woods go into one of his victory dances — both fists shaking, back arched, screaming to the sky joyously. His caddie, Steve Williams, was screaming too and hugging his boss as if he had just won the Open.

This wasn't Tiger's dream, though; it was Rocco's. The putt, amazing as it had been, hadn't won the Open. It had tied him with Rocco Mediate, son of Tony and Donna, the kid who described his handicap as a high school senior as being "about a thousand."

And so Rocco Anthony Mediate sat there watching Woods and Williams exult, thinking on the one hand that he had been one inch from winning the U.S. Open. On the other hand, he was now going to go head-to-head with the greatest player in history for 18 holes in a playoff for the U.S. Open title the next day.

"No disrespect to Jack Nicklaus," Rocco said. "He was great, but this guy [Woods] is from another planet. He makes shots under pressure that no one else has ever made. If he hits fairways, he wins by 15. If he doesn't hit fairways and puts the ball in impossible places, he still wins. He's the absolute best ever, without any doubt at all.

"But I wasn't afraid to play him head-to-head. I wanted to show him what I could do. I wanted to show *me* what I could do. I wanted to show the world what I could do. When the putt went in, I wasn't the U.S. Open champion. But I had a chance to win it in a way no one would ever have dreamed possible.

"Except me. I dreamed it."

THE VERY FACT THAT ROCCO relished the idea of going head-to-head in an 18-hole playoff against Tiger Woods made him markedly different from most of his colleagues on the PGA Tour. Most dreaded the idea of even being paired with Woods for an ordinary round of golf on a Thursday or Friday at a weekly tour stop. His presence was intimidating, in part because he was without question the greatest player in the world, but also because of the way he carried himself. Every pore of his body oozed confidence, the message always the same from the very first tee: I'm better than you. I know it and you know it and so does everyone watching us.

Only on rare occasions did Woods fail to live up to that message. He had stormed onto the tour in 1996, winning two times that fall at the age of twenty, and then had won his first major as a professional, the 1997 Masters, by 12 shots. "He's a boy among men and he's showing the men how to play," eight-time major champion Tom Watson said that week.

Woods hadn't let up much since that Masters. He had eye surgery and knee surgery, and always seemed to come back better than before. He piled up victories at a stunning rate, especially for the modern era. At a time when any player winning twice in the same year was thought to have had a superb year, Woods averaged more than five wins a year during his first eleven seasons on tour. By 2008, he had already won thirteen majors as a pro, putting him second all-time and well on his way to Jack Nicklaus's record of eighteen. During one extraordinary stretch in 2000 and 2001, he won four majors in a row. Considering the fact that any player who wins three majors in a career is considered a lock Hall of Famer, the four majors in ten months—known in golf circles as the "Tiger Slam," since he won all four of the game's Grand Slam events in succession but not in a calendar year—was arguably the greatest feat in golf history.

"Playing with Tiger is just hard," said Paul Goydos, a veteran pro who, as with most players, liked Woods when he didn't have to compete against him. "Most of it isn't his fault. The galleries are always huge and they're always moving after he hits or putts out. They're noisy. Getting from one green to the next tee can be tough because security is so focused on him.

"He's not unfriendly out there, but when it's important to him and he's grinding—which is almost always—he gets this look in his eyes that tells you he doesn't want to hear any jokes or kid around. You can almost see the intensity radiating off his body, especially if it's Sunday and he's in the hunt."

Which, as Goydos points out, is almost always. In 2007, Woods had had a fairly typical year. He played in sixteen tournaments and won seven times—including the PGA Championship. He finished second three times, including in the Masters and the U.S. Open—results that angered him. In all, he had finished in the top ten twelve times and the top twenty-five fifteen times. That gave him sixty-one victories in his career and 144 top tens in 230 career starts. Some perspective: Phil Mickelson, the number two player in the world, who is guaranteed to be a first-ballot Hall of Famer, went into 2008 with thirty-two victories (a remarkable number by mortal standards) and 130 top tens. He had played in 363 tournaments to accumulate those numbers—133 more than Woods.

It wasn't just the numbers that made Woods scary. Anytime he showed up on a leader board, other players began thinking about what second-place money was worth. When Woods was injured and off the tour, Lee Janzen, a two-time U.S. Open champion, joked that "our purses just went up 18 percent." The winner's share on tour is 18 percent of the total purse.

In fact, Woods didn't even have to be on the leader board to make people nervous. In 2003, when he was going through his second swing change and struggling, Woods had to get up and down from a bunker to make par on his last hole in the second round just to make the 36-hole cut at the Masters. Watching on TV, veteran tour caddy Mark Chaney watched Woods make his par putt. He walked over to Brennan Little, Mike Weir's caddy.

"Well, Butchie," he said, calling Little by his nickname, "I thought there for a second you guys had a chance to win. Tough luck."

Weir was leading the tournament at that moment—and leading Woods by 11 shots. As it turned out, he did win, but not before Woods closed to within a shot of him early on Sunday. Even with his game at its low ebb, Woods still frightened the competition.

It wasn't a coincidence that on all five occasions when Woods had finished second in a major championship, the winner had not been paired with him on Sunday. And even when it appeared he had no chance to win, he still managed to put a scare into people.

In 2002, he trailed Rich Beem by five strokes with four holes to play in the PGA Championship. Then he birdied the last four holes. Beem, playing two groups behind him, managed to keep his composure and win by one. In 2007 at the Masters, Woods needed to hole out from the fairway on the 18th to tie Zach Johnson, who had already completed his final round. With the ball in the air, everyone — including Johnson — held their breath, wondering if Woods could pull off the miracle.

Tiger didn't hole the shot that time, but Johnson said later that "anyone else, you know the odds in a situation like that are very much in your favor. With Tiger, I figured the chances were about fifty-fifty."

No one wanted to be paired with Woods late in a major championship. He had clearly established his ability to intimidate en route to that first dominating Masters victory in 1997, when he had a two-shot lead on European Tour veteran Colin Montgomerie after 36 holes. Montgomerie, one of the best head-to-head players in Ryder Cup history, spoke confidently on Friday night about his experience in big situations and how he thought that would help him playing with the rookie the next day.

Woods shot 65. Montgomerie shot 74.

So much for experience.

The only two players who had withstood the pressure of going mano a mano with Woods in the final round of a major were relative unknowns. Bob May, who had never won on the PGA Tour, had matched 66's with Woods during the final round of the PGA in 2000 before losing to him in a three-hole playoff. And Chris DiMarco had actually come from behind when Woods shockingly bogeyed the last two holes at the 2005 Masters to tie. Woods then birdied the first hole of a sudden-death playoff to win.

Both players had taken a nothing-to-lose approach to playing against Woods. Both knew no one gave them any chance to win. In DiMarco's case, he was facing a Woods who wasn't quite himself. He had gone ten straight majors without a victory during his second swing adjustment and didn't appear as boldly confident as the Woods who had won eight major titles in twenty-two starts between 1997 and the midway point of 2002.

That Masters victory marked the return of the dominant Woods. Beginning with that event, his record in the majors was astonishing: He won five times in thirteen starts. He finished second four times, third once, and fourth once. He had been out of the top ten only twice: a 12th-place finish at the British Open in 2007 and a missed cut at the U.S. Open in 2006, his first tournament back after the death of his father. It was the only time he had missed a cut in forty-five majors as a pro. Again, for perspective, Mickelson, who has a superb record in the majors, had missed seven cuts in fifty-nine majors, including two in 2007. As if to prove what a fluke that was, Woods had bounced back to win both the British Open and the PGA that year.

His presence on the leader board at the 2008 Open was more proof of his greatness. He had undergone knee surgery for a second time in April, soon after finishing second to Trevor Immelman at the Masters. He had not played a single round of competitive golf between the Masters and the Open, and there were rumors almost until the moment that he teed off on Thursday at Torrey Pines that he might withdraw. Even his practice rounds had been extremely limited, and people wondered if he would be able to play anywhere close to his normal level.

For 27 holes the answer appeared to be no. Paired with Mickelson and Adam Scott, the number-two- and number-three-ranked players in the world, Woods looked extremely human.

He was struggling to keep his driver under control, putts weren't dropping, he frequently grimaced after making contact with the ball, and he was clearly still hobbling at times.

He was well behind the leaders midway through his round on Friday, a lot closer to the cut line than the top of the leader board. That he might withdraw to prevent further damage to the knee even if he made the cut seemed distinctly possible.

But then, on his last nine holes on Friday afternoon, Tiger became Tiger again. Making the turn, he was at three over par for the tournament, trailing Stuart Appleby, who would be the leader at the midway point by six strokes. At that moment Tiger was four strokes inside the cut line.

But five birdies on Torrey Pines' front nine—he had played the back nine first—completely turned the tournament around for Woods and changed it for everyone else in the field as well. Woods went from struggling to lurking, just a shot from the lead at the end of the day. One of the people he was tied with on Friday night was Rocco, who had followed up a two-under-par 69 with an even-par 71 to tie for second with Woods and Robert Karlsson.

By Saturday night, there was only one leader: Woods. He finished his day by chipping in for birdie from an awkward lie just outside a bunker on 17 and then holing an eagle putt on the 18th green. That set up a familiar scenario: Woods leading a major after three rounds is as close to a lock as anything in sports. Thirteen times he had led majors going into Sunday; thirteen times he had walked away the winner.

Lee Westwood was one shot behind Woods with 18 holes to play, and Rocco was still hanging around. By late Sunday afternoon, with the golf course bathed in sun and a gentle breeze coming in off the Pacific Ocean, the three men were locked in a battle for the Open title. Only one could win, and most assumed it would be Woods.

"Can someone named Rocco really win the U.S. Open?" NBC's Johnny Miller asked. "He looks more like he should be cleaning Tiger's pool than leading the Open."

But there was Rocco in the lead, late on Sunday afternoon. If the world was surprised, he wasn't. Nor were his boyhood friends watching back home in Greensburg, Pennsylvania, a small town about thirty miles outside Pittsburgh.

"Rocco has always had what I would call an irrational sense of self-confidence," said Dave Lucas, a buddy for almost forty years. "A lot of people dream about playing on the PGA Tour; Rocco always *knew* he'd play on the tour, when there was no logical reason to believe it because he just wasn't good enough. There was no logical reason for him to beat Tiger, which is why I knew he would think he could beat him. It makes no sense at all—unless you're Rocco."

All of which made perfect sense to Rocco. One-on-one with the greatest player in history over 18 holes for the U.S. Open title? "Bring it on," he said Sunday night. "I can't wait."

2

508 Crestview Drive

THE STORY OF TONY AND DONNA Mediate's courtship isn't all that different from most stories about kids growing up in middle-class homes in the 1950s.

They both came from small western Pennsylvania towns. Tony was the son of immigrants: Rocco Santo Mediate (pronounced Meed-e-atay until he arrived at Ellis Island and was told to pronounce it Meed-e-ate, as an American) had stowed away on a steamer bound from Calabria, Italy, to New York and had found work on the railroad in Pitcairn, Pennsylvania. After he had made enough money, he sent for his wife, Maria, and they settled in the tiny town of Wall, which was right across the tracks from Pitcairn.

They had had three daughters previously in Italy, but Anthony was their first child to survive birth. He was small but a gifted athlete, an excellent high school pitcher who once struck out seventeen hitters in seven innings while pitching a no-hitter in a semipro game. Even though he was a Yankees fan—they were baseball's dominant team in the '50s—he frequently made the forty-mile trip on the Ardmore Street trolley to Forbes Field in

Pittsburgh and was even given the chance to throw batting practice to the Pirates.

"I remember pitching to Dale Long and Sid Gordon and, of course, Roberto Clemente," Anthony said. "A couple of times I ran laps in the outfield with [pitcher] Roy Face. One day we were out there and Clemente was lying down on a bench in the bullpen. Face took me over and introduced me. I'll never forget shaking hands with him—his hands were huge. He looked at me and said, 'You want to be a baseball player?' I said I did. He shook his head and said, 'You too small. Go and eat more.'"

Eating wasn't going to make Tony much more than five-foot-eight. What's more, he had a lot more on his life's plate than food. His dad had died of an aneurysm when Tony was thirteen, and he had gone to work selling newspapers to help his mom and his younger brother, Joe. "I made ten dollars a week," he said. "We bought our food with it. We'd go shopping with that money and it bought so much we couldn't carry it all home in those days."

He finished high school while he worked and played baseball. No one drafted him, so he played at the semipro level until his early twenties, when he realized it was time to make a serious living. He had uncles who had cut hair for a living, so he did the same thing—except he decided to cut hair for men and women, knowing there was a good deal more money to be made cutting women's hair than men's. He opened a small salon called Anthony's, in downtown Greensburg, which was the "city" near Wall, having a population of about 40,000.

Tony met Donna Emrick soon after that, one night at a dance club. "In those days everyone went dancing," she said. "That's how we got to know each other. He asked me to dance one night, and we just kept going out to dance clubs after that. He was fun and he was sweet."

She was second generation — German and Irish on her father's side, Italian on her mother's, and the fourth of seven children. She had grown up on a farm on the south side of Greensburg and was just out of high school when she started dating Tony.

They were married in July of 1960, and their first child, Rocco Anthony, was born on December 17, 1962. Soon after that, the growing family moved into Rural Oaks, a new development outside town. It was so new that the Mediates were the first family to move there. The community grew quickly, though, with young middle-class families moving in as the suburbs continued to expand.

"It was a perfect neighborhood for kids," Donna Mediate remembered. "Every family had kids and they all played together. They would play together right there in the neighborhood, and when they were older they could walk to the neighborhood pool during the summer and the ice-skating rink in the winter. It was pretty close to ideal."

Tony and Donna's second child, Vincent, was born in 1964. But unlike Rocco, who was a lively, healthy boy from the start, Vincent was born with brain damage, and as an infant he frequently had seizures. Tony and Donna took him to specialists, finally settling on a doctor in Media, Pennsylvania (near Philadelphia), who ultimately recommended surgery to try to relieve pressure on the brain. It didn't work. Two-year-old Vincent suffered an aneurysm during the surgery and never woke up.

Rocco was four when his brother died and he says now that he doesn't remember much about him or about his death, but it is apparent that his death deeply affected him—and still does to this day.

"I remember my parents coming home without him," he said. "They told me he had died, but I'm not completely sure I understood. My mom took me to the funeral home, and I remember trying to open his eyes. I thought he was just sleeping. He looked so beautiful lying there, and I wanted him to wake up.

"I'm not sure if his death is the reason, but I've never been able to go to funerals. I didn't go to either of my grandmas' funerals, and I know that upset my parents, but I couldn't go. I don't think I've been to a funeral since my brother died. It's just too upsetting for me, I guess. I can't even tell you that I remember that much about him, because he was so young, but I guess it's fair to say that, even though we never talked about it, his death deeply affected my family. I would have loved to have had a little brother; I know that. I don't think my parents ever completely got over it."

At first, Tony and Donna thought they didn't want more children, Vincent's death making it too painful for them to contemplate the idea that something could go wrong with another child. They changed their minds, though, and Nicki was born in 1967, Gina two years later. By then Rocco was seven and spending most of his time hanging out with other kids in the neighborhood.

After his baseball career ended, Tony turned to golf as his sport of choice when he wasn't working. His business was growing, and he joined Hannastown Golf Club, a small nine-hole club not far from Crestview Drive, where the family lived. He had become a good player, a three or four handicapper, and he would frequently take Rocco with him to the club—sometimes to play a few holes, sometimes to caddy.

"He didn't like golf," Tony said. "Sometimes when he would caddy for me we would get to the sixth hole, which is right by the front gate of the club, and he'd just say, 'Dad, I'm going home.' He'd drop the clubs and walk home. It wasn't much different when I let him play. He'd play a few holes and then we'd get to number six and he would be gone. He just wasn't that interested."

The two sports that did interest Rocco were baseball and skateboarding. Long before anyone thought about the X Games or any extreme sports, he and several of his friends built a half-pipe in an empty lot in the neighborhood. "There were about four or five of them who were really into skateboarding," Donna remembered. "They somehow put together six or seven hundred dollars to buy the materials and to build it. After a while, though, some of the neighbors didn't like it, and they had to take it down. It was too bad; they had a lot of fun with it."

No one objected to baseball, and Rocco was decent at it — but not nearly as gifted as his dad. "I still remember my dad would throw us batting practice sometimes, and if he wanted to throw hard — even then — we couldn't touch him," Rocco said. "He would throw his fastball right by us and if he threw a curveball, forget it, we had no chance."

Rocco's baseball career has become the stuff of legend, in the strictest definition of the term — it has been built into far more than it really was. When he is playing golf on TV, the announcers frequently will talk about the "promising" baseball career Rocco gave up when he decided to pursue golf. Sometimes they will talk about what a talented pitcher he was. The PGA Tour media guide says he became interested in golf in high school, "after years of playing baseball."

The part about him playing baseball is true, but that's about it. "What I remember about Rocco playing baseball is that I could never hit a curveball," his lifelong friend Dave Lucas said. "Except for Rocco's. I could hit his curveball."

Which may explain why Rocco didn't make the team as a high school sophomore. "I came home the first day of practice and told my dad I had no shot," he said. "I just wasn't good enough. I was a reasonably good hitter, I had a decent arm, but I wasn't going to be able to play varsity baseball—that was apparent. That was really when I first got interested in golf."

Before that, Rocco and Dave Lucas had been spending a fair amount of time at Hannastown. Their parents would drop them off after school, ostensibly to play golf. "We would get there, go inside, and get something to eat," Lucas said. "We might putt a little, maybe play a few holes—sometimes we didn't play at all. Then we'd call one of our parents to be picked up and go home. Neither one of us was into golf. We just hung out. Golf was pretty much the last thing on our minds."

At fifteen, Rocco looked around and realized that both his baseball and skateboarding careers were behind him. His dad had joined another club that year, Greensburg Country Club, which had 18 holes and excellent practice facilities. By then, Lucas's family also belonged there, and Dave had made friends with several very good players—Arnie Cutrell and Bob Bradley among them.

Lucas began bringing Rocco out to play at the new club every once in a while, and slowly but surely, Rocco got hooked on the game. "What I remember is that he wasn't very good when he first started coming out to play," Cutrell said. "I mean, we were pretty good. Bob and I were single-digit handicappers by the time we were in high school. We were pretty good junior players. Rocco just hadn't played that much. If he shot in the mid-80s that was a pretty good day for him. Dave was about the same as he was. We usually shot in the 70s. After a while, though, it was pretty clear that Rocco had decided he wanted to get better. He began working at it—a lot."

What became apparent to Cutrell, Bradley, and Lucas was what his parents already knew: Once Rocco decided something was important to him, once he decided he wanted to achieve something, he would do just about anything to reach his goal.

"He's never done anything halfway or had an emotion that was mixed," his father said. "When he decided he was interested in watches, he had to have the *best* watch collection. When he decides he likes someone, they can't just be a good person, they are the *best* person. You never hear him say that someone is a good teacher; they're a *great* teacher. I think one of the reasons he's been able to get to where he has in golf is because whatever teacher or swing coach he's worked with, he's believed in what they're telling him completely and worked and worked and worked at doing what they've told him he needs to do."

Though he often uses superlatives, Rocco's description of himself as a high school golfer is typical Rocco too: "I wasn't any good at all," he said. "I was like a thousand handicap."

Not exactly. By his senior year, he was playing number one for the high school team and was breaking 80 on occasion. "He improved a lot and he improved in a hurry," Cutrell said. "You could see the hard work paying off. But it wasn't as if he had gotten so good that any of us thought he was going anyplace as a golfer. He'd gotten good—but he was still a long way from being anything special."

What he had gotten—more than anything—was obsessed with golf. Once baseball and skateboarding were in his rearview mirror, golf became his life every day from sunup until, most of the time, after sundown.

"It was all he did," Donna said. "He didn't date, he didn't go to the movies, he didn't study very much, to tell the truth. He went to school and then he went to the golf course. He would play, he would practice, and then he would come home, stop in the garage to wash his clubs, eat dinner, and go to bed. He would put the clubs to bed, then he went to bed. He would get up the next day and do the same thing. The only time it was different was on the weekends—then he would spend the entire day at the golf course."

The sunup until after sundown routine was not an exaggeration, according to his father. "I would wait until it got dark—pitch-dark—and then I'd drive over to the golf course to pick him up," he said. "The putting and chipping green was next to the clubhouse, so there was always some light there. I would pull up and it would look like it had snowed on the green—it was completely white with golf balls. Sometimes I wouldn't see Rocco and then I'd look and he'd be down in the bunker with a bag of balls at his feet. He'd say, 'Hang on, Dad, I have to hole two more before I can go.' Or he'd just want to finish the bag."

All the work began to pay off, though not that quickly. "It wasn't as if he went from a 15 [handicap] to scratch overnight," Dave Lucas said. "But he was clearly a lot better player as a senior than he had been as a sophomore, when he really started getting into it."

When he isn't insisting that his handicap was a thousand, Rocco will concede that he was probably a five or a six by the time he was a senior. Even so, he had absolutely no idea what he was going to do when he graduated from high school. His grades were uniformly mediocre: He was the classic student who was smart enough to do well in school but never cared enough to do more than get by, and he wasn't a good enough golfer to turn the heads of college recruiters.

Cutrell was the best player in the Greensburg group, and he decided to go to Wake Forest, which had one of the top college golf teams in the country. Lucas was two years younger than the others, so he didn't need to make a decision on his future in the spring of 1980. He would end up playing golf at Penn State two years later and going on to law school.

At some point during his last semester of high school in 1980, Rocco decided the best thing for him to do was to attend college someplace and try to walk onto the golf team. His mother began to research schools and finally came up with California University, a small school in California, Pennsylvania, about an hour west of Greensburg. As an in-state student who had been the number one player on his high school golf team, Rocco was able to get in.

"They actually had a pretty decent golf team," he said. "One of the guys on the team was Todd Silvis, who was the son of the first pro [Bill Silvis] I had taken lessons from as a kid. So I knew they had some good players, which meant that I probably wouldn't be good enough to make the team. That was the reason I wanted to go to college — to play golf. I knew I had to get better if I wanted to do that."

As he often did, Rocco turned to his father for help. The relationship between Tony and Donna Mediate and their oldest son is often volatile. All three are emotional people who do not hold back their opinions on any issue. They get angry with one another often, but there isn't any doubt about how much they love one another. Rocco often says he gets his athletic competitiveness from his dad and his toughness from his mom, and they both appreciated his work ethic.

"Rocco wanted to get better," Tony Mediate said. "He had certainly proven his desire with the time he had put in. I had heard about Bob Toski's golf schools in North Carolina, so I called down there to see if I could get him in. They were completely full, not a spot to be had. I can't remember who I talked to on the phone, but when I said I was calling from Greensburg, Pennsylvania, whoever it was said to me, 'There's a very good teacher not far from you named Jim Ferree. You might give him a call.'"

Ferree had learned the game from his dad, who had been a teaching pro, first at Pinehurst, later at Old Town Country Club in Winston-Salem. He had played college golf at the University of North Carolina and had gone on to a very solid pro career, spending eleven years on the PGA Tour—winning once at the Vancouver Open. Like a lot of pros in the '60s, he tired of traveling all the time while playing for relatively small purses. When he was offered a job at Westmoreland Country Club in Export, Pennsylvania, in 1970, he accepted it.

"I was lucky because when I was in college I had gotten to know Jim Flick—he was at Wake while I was at Carolina," Ferree said. "Jim was working with Bob Toski in North Carolina at the Golf Digest teaching schools and they invited me down. Most of what I learned about teaching the golf swing came from them."

It was the Toski-Flick connection that recommended Ferree to Tony Mediate. Westmoreland was only about twenty minutes from Greensburg. By then Ferree had enough of a reputation as a teacher that he was able to charge $50 an hour. That sounded like a fortune to Tony, but he knew it was what his son wanted. So, as a graduation present, he told Rocco he was taking him to Ferree and they would see how it went.

Rocco and Tony have different memories of that first lesson. Tony and Ferree stood behind Rocco while he hit some balls for his new teacher. "I remember Jim didn't say a word for about twenty minutes," Tony said. "Rocco just hit one ball after another. I was standing there thinking, 'Well, that's fifty bucks wasted; he's never going to say a word.'"

Rocco thinks it just felt that long to his dad because he could hear the meter running inside his head. "I don't think I hit ten balls before Mr. Ferree said something. I remember exactly what he said: 'Son, the first thing we're going to work on is that grip.'"

Ferree remembers that part vividly. "I told him his grip looked like two crabs fighting on a stick," he said, laughing. "It was amazing he could hit the ball at all with that grip. I spent the rest of that lesson just trying to get his hands on the club in the proper way. I told him for the next week he shouldn't hit anything longer than a chip shot, because I knew, with the new grip, if he tried to hit anything involving any distance he wouldn't like what he saw and he'd revert to the old grip."

When the lesson was over, Rocco's first question to his father was "When can I go back?" Tony told him he could go once a week if he wanted to for the rest of the summer. Rocco loved the idea, and he spent the next week working on nothing but the grip.

"When he sat down to watch TV, he took a club and sat there with his hands on it in the proper position," Tony said. "He was going to get it right."

A week later, they returned to Ferree. "I figured he'd be back to the old grip or something like it," Ferree said. "Usually, you show a kid something new like that, it's going to take them a while to get it. Rocco walked on the range and he had the grip *down*. I mean, it was perfect. Every shot, every swing. I was impressed. That told me two things: He was really serious about working on his game, and he had a knack for it."

Ferree was teaching some very good players at the time. John Aber, a friend of Rocco's from Greensburg who is now the pro at Allegheny Country Club, was working with him and so was Missie Berteotti, who went on to play on the LPGA Tour. There were other top junior players too.

"Rocco was well behind them when he started," Ferree said. "But it wasn't long before he started to catch up. He had excellent hands and a very good eye. When I showed him something, he could pretty much imitate what I was doing right away. That's what we did a lot: I swung the club the way I wanted him to swing it, and then he swung the club. He got better very fast."

Within two weeks of starting with Ferree, Rocco decided once a week wasn't enough. He wanted to go twice a week. Then three times a week and finally, by summer's end, he was making the drive four days a week.

"The way I looked at it was it would have cost me a thousand dollars for a week if he had gone to Toski's camp," Tony said. "He probably took about twenty lessons that summer, so I pretty much broke even."

By the time he went off to college, Rocco felt like a completely different player. He had seen a noticeable change in the way he hit the ball and he felt a lot more confident in his ability to create shots on the course. Rocco arrived at California

University, which was a small teachers' college, with one goal: to make the golf team. He tried out for the team that fall and was clearly one of the better players. Coach Floyd Shuler gave him a spot on the team and told him he would be playing someplace in the middle of the lineup. "I was maybe number three or number four," he said. "Nothing special, but good enough as far as I was concerned. I was happy."

He became less happy after an incident that took place one night during the winter of his first year. He was sound asleep in his dorm room at about two o'clock in the morning, when he heard what he initially thought was some kind of explosion. "It was the door being kicked open and broken off the hinges," he said. "I thought I was dreaming or something."

He wasn't. Into the room came four of his teammates, including his boyhood buddy from Greensburg, Todd Silvis. They told him he was about to be put through his official hazing as a new member of the golf team. "I was sleeping in a T-shirt and sweats," he said. "At first they were going to drag me out of there dressed like that. They finally let me put some Docksiders on my feet."

He was dragged into a frigid night, tied up, blindfolded, and tossed in the backseat of a car. "The blindfold was kind of pointless: I knew who they all were," he said. "One of the guys had some kind of knife. It was in a sheath, but he kept poking me in the ribs with it just for yuks. We probably drove for twenty or thirty minutes. It felt like four or five hours to me. Finally, they just stopped, took the blindfold off, kicked me out of the car, and left me standing there in the middle of nowhere. It was twenty-five degrees — at most — and I'm wearing a T-shirt.

"I just started walking. I came up a hill and I saw some lights and I figured that was the town of California, so I started walking in that direction. At one point I came to a farmhouse with a light and I thought maybe someone might let me in to warm up or call someone to come and get me. I got about a hundred yards from the house and this huge dog came charging at me. I ran as fast as I could and had to jump a fence to get away from him. I made it, but I cut myself as I was going over and I tore off this necklace my mom had given me when I graduated from high school that said 'Golf Nut' on it. When I realized I'd lost it, I spent a while crawling around in the mud and the dark trying to find it, while the dog kept barking at me from the other side of the fence.

"The whole thing was surreal."

He finally made it back to campus at about 7:30 in the morning, bleeding and freezing and scared, but more than anything angry—angrier than he had ever been in his life. He went directly to Coach Shuler's office and waited for him to come in to work.

"When he walked in, he looked at me and said, 'What in the world happened to you?' I said, 'I'm going to tell you and then you're going to get those sons of bitches over here right now,' I was *so* angry. I told him if he didn't do something about it I was going to call my uncle Joe back home and he'd do something about it. Uncle Joe isn't Mafia or anything crazy like that, but if he and my dad had heard about it back then there would have been hell to pay. I made sure Coach Shuler understood that."

Whatever Shuler understood, he called the four players into his office. Apologies were made. It was agreed they had gone much too far with the hazing and they promised never to bother Rocco again. But there was nothing they could say that was going to change the way Rocco felt about them from that point on.

"I was done with them and really done with the school from that day forward," he said. "I couldn't get past what they'd done to me. To this day, I'm not sure why they did it. They never did anything like that to any of the other freshmen. Maybe it was because I'd walked on the team and they felt like I was taking somebody's spot. I'm really not sure.

"But I knew I couldn't stay there. I just had to find a way to get out. And a place to go. I was looking for someplace to go from that day forward. I wanted out. I just had to find the right exit door."

3

No Backup Plan

IF THE HAZING INCIDENT WAS the beginning of the end for
Rocco at California University, his new beginning came that
spring at the NCAA Division 2 national championships.

Even though he wasn't happy with his teammates, Rocco
played well enough to qualify for the 1981 nationals, which
were held that year outside Hartford, Connecticut. As luck
would have it, he was paired with a player named Tom Patri, who
was the number one player for Florida Southern College. Patri
would go on to win the individual title that year, and Florida
Southern ran away with the team title.

Rocco was impressed—with Patri and with the way Coach
Charlie Matlock's team approached the tournament. "They were
so locked in on what they were doing and what they wanted to
accomplish. They were so much better than everyone else it
was a joke. We were just happy to be playing. We'd go out every
night, have a big dinner, and have a good time. They were there
to compete and to win. Plus, they all seemed like good guys."

Most of the time, athletes are recruited by colleges. In the case
of Rocco and Florida Southern, it was the other way around.

"He walked up to me on the range, introduced himself,

and just started talking," Matlock said. "I knew who he was because he'd been playing with Tom. I thought he had a lot of potential—even then he was a very good ball-striker."

Even so, Matlock didn't want to talk to Rocco. "He told me how impressed he was with our team and our approach," Matlock remembered. "He said, 'We're just here to have fun. You guys are here to win.' I told him to me fun was working hard to achieve a goal and then enjoying the satisfaction of achieving it. He told me he wanted to transfer and come play for us and could I send him some literature. I told him, 'No, absolutely not. I don't want to get in trouble with the NCAA, and in truth, I shouldn't even be talking to you right now.'"

The NCAA frowns on coaches recruiting players from other schools. Matlock didn't want any appearance of impropriety, even if the player in question had approached him rather than the other way around. He wished Rocco luck and completely forgot about the conversation with the eager young kid from Pennsylvania.

Rocco didn't forget Matlock, though, or Florida Southern. When he got home at the end of the semester, he told his parents he wanted to transfer to Florida Southern. He wanted to leave California University and he wanted to go someplace warm where he could play golf all year round. It was too late to think about transferring for the fall semester, but Tony Mediate remembered a friend whose son was at Florida Southern. He contacted him to get some information about the school and to see if Rocco would have a chance of getting in.

Rocco returned to Cal U in the fall and wasn't any happier, even though he was convinced he would play number one on the team the following spring. He had filled out the application forms for Florida Southern and sent them in. Tony's friend had made a call to the admissions department on his behalf, and Rocco was waiting to hear if he had been accepted. He was thinking that, best-case scenario, he might get in the following fall, and he was mentally preparing himself to finish the year at Cal U.

Then came the epiphany.

"It was late in the semester, sometime in December," he said. "The golf course was closed, obviously, and so was the driving range. I would go down to the football field with my clubs and some balls, clear off some snow, and hit balls. It was a wide-open area, so I could do it. I drove down there with a couple of guys one afternoon. We weren't out of the car five minutes when they said, 'This is ridiculous; it's way too cold,' and took off. I stood there hitting balls by myself for a while and finally said, 'They're right; this is crazy. What the hell am I doing here? I have got to get out of this place.' I called Coach Matlock the next day."

Matlock was in the office that morning by happenstance. The semester had just ended and he had gone in to pick up some paperwork he needed for a recruiting trip to Miami. He was about to walk out when the phone rang.

"Coach Matlock? It's Rocco Mediate calling."

"Do I know you?"

"We met at the national championships last spring. I was asking you about Florida Southern, remember?"

Matlock did remember. Rocco told him he had applied to the school for spring admission but would come the next fall if that didn't work out. He wanted to know if he could be a part of his team. Matlock told him to come and see him if he got into the school and they would talk.

"I thought he had potential," Matlock said. "But I wasn't going to make any promises."

Soon after, Rocco got word from Florida Southern that—apparently thanks in large part to Tony's friend—he had been accepted for the spring semester. Overjoyed, he drove to Lakeland to register in mid-January and went directly to Matlock's office.

"He was waiting for me when I got in that morning," Matlock said. "I said, 'Rocco, what are you doing here?' He told me, 'I want to play for your golf team.'"

Being a transfer, Rocco wasn't eligible to play for the team for two semesters. But he could practice with them. Matlock told him he would be allowed to play in a 10-round—nine holes a day—event. If he was among the top ten finishers, he could practice with the team. If not, he would be on his own.

"The first day I played with Marco Dawson and Jeff Schmucker. I shot 35, which wasn't bad. Marco shot 30, Jeff shot 31. Coach Matlock came up to me afterward and said, 'So, what do you think of my boys?' I said to him, 'I want to be one of them.'"

He ended up making the cut—finishing 10th. The good news was he was part of the team; the bad news was...he was part of the team.

Matlock had been a college football player at East Tennessee State and had coached football until he arrived at Florida Southern in 1972 and was asked to add coaching the golf team to his other coaching and teaching duties. "I didn't start playing until late," he said. "But I got to be a pretty good player."

He was good enough to beat Andy Bean, who would go on to be a ten-time winner on the tour, in his club championship in 1970, and he threw himself into coaching the golf team with great zeal. By the time Rocco arrived, Matlock had worked out a finely tuned practice system that included what he called "boot camp." Players were expected to report to the coach at 6:21 A.M. three days a week—"I always thought if you give them an unusual time, they'll remember it," he said—to run three miles and then follow that with a workout.

"I always told the guys that when they were running they should picture themselves playing 15, 16, 17, and 18 on a hot day," Maltock said. "Because that's what this was about—making sure they still had their legs for the last few holes."

Rocco wasn't thrilled initially with the predawn wake-ups or the early-morning runs, but soon after embraced the Matlock work ethic. It fit in with his obsessive-compulsive approach to golf.

"I would get up in the morning and run, then go hit some balls before class started," he said. "Coach Matlock always told us not to schedule a first-period class so we had time to hit some balls in the morning or chip or putt. I would go to class from eight thirty to one and be at the golf course at one twenty. Then I'd spend the rest of the day playing or practicing or both. After a while, I went into Coach and said, 'Well, I'm playing from sunup to sundown, what do you think?' He looked at me and said, 'Can't you work a little harder?' Maybe he was joking, but I went out and found a driving range with lights so I could hit balls after dark. Nothing was going to stop me."

No one, including Rocco, is sure when he found time to get schoolwork done, but he did—barely. Matlock had a rule that players had to maintain a C average to play, and Rocco did that—barely. Matlock only had four players fail to graduate in twenty-three years at Florida Southern, and Rocco was one of them. "He was only ten credits short," he said, laughing twenty-four years after Rocco finished his senior season of golf. "I guess he's not going to go back and get them at this point."

In the fall of 1983, Rocco's second semester at Florida Southern, Matlock brought in a late recruit named Lee Janzen. He had spotted Janzen during a junior tournament that summer and, knowing he was planning to go to Brevard Junior College in the fall because no four-year school had recruited him, offered him a partial scholarship. Janzen jumped at it because of the school's golf pedigree and enrolled two weeks after Matlock offered him the chance to come to school.

Rocco's roommate that fall was Jim Wilhelm, one of the more popular players on the team. "We used to hang out in Jim's room a lot," Janzen remembered. "When Rocco and I first met, we weren't exactly best buddies. In fact, I don't think we liked each other that much. After a while, though, we started to talk about music and we found we had common ground there. We both loved Rush, and we both knew a lot about rock-and-roll."

Rocco and Janzen spent a lot of time listening to music in each other's rooms, playing a game to see who could identify a song, the artist, and the year fastest. "It was very competitive because we were both good," Janzen said. "There weren't a lot of songs that we didn't know."

They also found in each other a willing practice partner. "Some guys practice because they feel like they have to practice to get better," Janzen said. "Some guys do it because their coach makes them do it. Rocco and I both *liked* to practice. We could go out to the practice green at Lone Palm [the club where Florida Southern played and practiced] and spend three hours practicing shots over a bunker and not even notice how much time had gone by. Then we might go into the bunker and spend a couple more hours there. I can't even tell you the number of hours we spent together just trying different shots and competing, trying to outdo each other."

Janzen soon figured out that he was dealing with a unique character in Rocco. "There is no such thing as good or bad with Rocco," he said, smiling. "Something is either the absolute best or the absolute worst. There's no in-between. He was playing Cobra clubs back then and he convinced me I *had* to have Cobras because they were *so* much better than any other golf club I could play with. Finally, I ordered them. They took forever to arrive. Every day Rocco would call UPS and ask where the clubs were. Finally, one morning they told us they were on their way, should arrive by the end of the day. That wasn't good enough. We had to get in the car, drive around, and find the UPS truck with the clubs. We convinced the guy to give us the clubs and went straight to the course so I could try them out."

Rocco was so obsessed with the game that he charted every shot he played. "I'm not just talking about tournament rounds, I'm talking about practice rounds—every shot he hit, he wrote it down," Janzen said. "There was nothing golf related that was too small a detail for Rocco."

By the spring of 1984, Rocco was eligible to play for Florida Southern, and ready to play well. And he had even bigger goals. Matlock always had his players fill out a form that asked them, among other things, about long-term ambitions. When Rocco filled his out, he wrote, "Play on the PGA Tour."

During a large chunk of the '83–'84 school year, Rocco was making the drive from Lakeland to Hilton Head Island in South

Carolina a couple of times a month to see Jim Ferree and have him check his swing. Ferree, who is now retired and living on Hilton Head, spent his winters there in those days. Rocco's going to see him was fine with Matlock, because Matlock respected Ferree and could see how much confidence Rocco had in him.

"By that time Rocco had met Rick Smith through Lee [Janzen] down at Florida Southern," Ferree remembered. "I had taught Rick as a kid, and a lot of what Rick was teaching people were the same things I had taught him. Rick and I used to joke that I would get Rocco and mess him up so he could fix it, and then he would mess him up so I could fix it."

Smith had also grown up outside Pittsburgh and had taken lessons from Ferree. After playing at East Tennessee State and realizing he didn't have the game to make the tour, he decided to teach. He was only a few years older than Rocco and Janzen, so working with the two of them was a natural for both the teacher and the pupils.

Matlock had coached plenty of players who wrote "Play on the PGA Tour" as their goal. When Matlock first saw it on Rocco's form he almost laughed. But by the end of the 1984 spring sea-son, he didn't think the notion was laughable at all. "He came so far so fast it was amazing," he said. "You could see he had potential, even that first time I saw him when he was playing for California. But he worked so hard that his game was almost transformed by the time he finished his junior year."

That summer, at Matlock's urging, Rocco played in every top amateur event he could find. He hadn't done that the previous summer because he didn't think his game was good enough, but two rounds of golf and a talking-to from Matlock changed that feeling.

The first round of golf took place at Oakmont Country Club on the day the 1983 U.S. Open ended. Rocco had made the short drive from Greensburg to Pittsburgh to see the Open with Dave Lucas and his dad, Ken Lucas, an equipment representative for Ping and a friend of Bob Ford, the longtime golf pro at Oakmont. Rocco spent a good portion of the weekend following Tom Watson, his golf hero, whom he'd had the chance to meet two years earlier during a tournament at Firestone Country Club in Akron, Ohio.

"I was there with a friend whose dad was a member of the club, and somehow we got in the locker room," Rocco said. "Tom was in there, and we walked over and introduced ourselves. I mean, he could not have been nicer. I remember he asked me if I played, and I said yes. He said, 'Are you any good?' And I said, 'Not yet.' He just looked at me and said, 'Keep working; you'll get there.' I was already hooked on him because I loved the way he played and competed, but after that there was no doubt. The next year when he chipped in to beat Nicklaus and win the Open at Pebble Beach, I think I jumped ten feet into the air."

A year later, at the '83 Open, Watson and Steve Ballesteros were in the final group at Oakmont on Sunday. Ballesteros quickly fell out of contention, and the tournament became a duel between Watson and Larry Nelson, who was one group in front. Late Sunday afternoon, with Nelson about to line up a 65-foot birdie putt on the 16th hole and Watson finishing up on the 15th, a thunderstorm rolled in and play was postponed until Monday morning, with Watson and Nelson tied for the lead.

The next morning, Rocco and the Lucases went straight to the 16th green. Watson was waiting to tee off on the par-three and Nelson was preparing to putt. They watched in amazement as Nelson rolled his putt over hill and dale and into the cup for a stunning birdie two. That turned out to be the difference; Nelson won by one shot.

Rocco's disappointment over Watson's loss didn't last very long. Shortly after the awards ceremony, he found himself standing on the first tee with Ken and Dave Lucas. "Because Ken knew Bob Ford, we were actually able to play the course a couple of hours after the Open ended," he said. "It was amazing. Because of the rain the course played about 10,000 yards long and, obviously, it was set up as hard as you can possibly imagine. I shot 72 or 73. Just kept the ball in the fairway all day. I was amazed."

To shoot a couple over par on a U.S. Open golf course is no mean feat, even for a good college golfer. At that point, Rocco wasn't sure he was a good college golfer, since he was still a semester away from being eligible to play at Florida Southern.

About a month later came the second eye-opening round of golf. Rocco was at Greensburg Country Club doing what he did almost every day—practicing and getting ready to play with his friends. He got a message to call Danny Bonar, another of his golf buddies.

"Hey, you need to get over here to Latrobe," Bonar said. "I've got a really good gambling game set up for us."

Rocco has always loved to gamble. Several years ago he became obsessed with poker, playing it on his computer constantly and even in the World Poker Championships in 2005. Back then he was always looking for a good "money game," and had become quite good at making putts with money on the line. So the idea of a good money game was enough to get him in his car to make the twenty-minute drive over to Latrobe Country Club.

"When I got there I said to Danny, 'So who we playing with?' He just started walking me toward the first tee. That's when I saw him standing there."

"Him" was Arnold Palmer, who owns Latrobe Country Club and lives a few miles down the road during the summer months. As soon as Mediate saw Palmer standing on the tee, he panicked.

"No way," he said to Bonar. "I can't play with him. I'm pretty sure I won't be able to talk to him, much less swing a club in front of him. I'm not ready: I can't do it."

Bonar ignored the protests and steered the now shaking Rocco onto the first tee.

"The minute we shook hands and he looked me in the eye and gave me that smile of his, I relaxed completely," Rocco said. "It was as if I'd known him all my life. That's Arnold. He has this way of making you feel like he's been your friend forever. I was still shaking when I hit my first tee shot because, for crying out loud, *Arnold Palmer* is standing there watching me. Once I got that ball airborne, though, I was okay. It turned out to be one of the greatest days of my life."

Rocco shot 69 that day. Palmer shot 70. "My dad still has the scorecard," he said, grinning broadly. "I've probably played with Arnold hundreds of times since then, but that's the round I'll never forget. I mean, I know he was already like a hundred at the time [fifty-three, actually], but think about it: a college kid, me, beating Arnold Palmer? No way."

Thus, when Rocco returned to college in the fall he had the following to report about what he had done on his summer vacation:

- Played Oakmont under U.S. Open conditions and shot 72 or 73.
- Played Latrobe Country Club with Arnold Palmer and shot 69 — to beat the King by a shot.

A pretty good summer's work. Or so Rocco thought.

"You didn't play in any of the big amateur tournaments," Matlock told him. "You want to be a pro, you have to play consistently against guys who are going to be pros. You have to prove to yourself that you can compete with them."

Rocco understood the message his tough-love coach was sending him. He knew that his good play at Oakmont and with Palmer proved something, but it wasn't enough. He began planning to play in big amateur events the following summer. And that spring, finally eligible, he became a key part of Matlock's team, along with Janzen, Greg Gamester, and Jim Northrup. Then, as planned, he went off to play against the best competition he could find.

He began the summer by trying to qualify for the U.S. Open, which was being played that year at Winged Foot. He won the local qualifier and then made it into the Open at the sectional. "In a year I'd come from being thrilled to get to play the Open golf course after it was over to actually playing in the Open," he said. "I thought that was pretty cool." He played respectably at the Open, but missed the cut by three shots.

He played in the U.S. Amateur and won his first-round match against Jay Sigel, one of the best amateur players not to turn pro (he did years later, when he turned fifty and played on the Senior Tour), and reached the quarterfinals before losing. Then, in the Western Amateur, he beat Scott Verplank, who had won the U.S. Amateur. A year later, Verplank won the Western Open while still an amateur. Rocco made the final at the Western Amateur before losing to John Inman.

In all, a pretty good summer. By the time he returned to Florida Southern for his senior year, Mediate had decided to give PGA Tour Qualifying School a shot the following spring. He wasn't at all convinced that his game was good enough to get on tour, but he wanted to try anyway.

"I didn't want to be one of those guys who looked back years later and said, 'Gee, I wonder if I might have made it if I had tried,'" he said. "Plus, to be honest, there was nothing else I was interested in doing. I didn't have any kind of backup plan."

The lack of a backup plan bothered his mom. She kept nudging him to keep going to class and graduate, and he kept telling her not to worry, that he would be fine. He had a superb senior season, making the Division 2 All American team while becoming the best player on Matlock's team. "He played as well that year as anyone who has ever played for me," Matlock said. "And I've had some very good players."

Rocco set a number of records—course records, tournament records—that year, most of which, he likes to point out, were later broken by Janzen. But he finished the year filled with confidence and headed off to the first stage of tour qualifying at Indiana University. For ten years, and through 1981 the tour held Q-School twice a year—once in the late spring, once in the fall.

"Which turned out to be a good thing for me," Rocco said. "Because I bombed out completely, didn't even come close. I was lucky, though, because there was another qualifier a few months later and I got another shot at it."

Before he left for the second qualifier in October, Rocco made a deal with his mom: If he didn't make it to the tour this time, he would go back to school to get his degree. "Now *that* gave me incentive," he said, laughing. "I had no intention of going back to school."

Even so, the first stage didn't begin much better the second time around. He had signed up for a qualifier at the University of Georgia, in part because it was closer to Florida Southern, but also because Tom Gleaton, who had been a couple of years ahead of him at Florida Southern, was going to play up there. The two of them decided to share a hotel room for the week. On the first day, Rocco shot 75 and was so disgusted he was ready to go home.

Gleaton came back to the room and found him packing. "I can't play," Rocco told him. "I'm not good enough."

Gleaton told him he was crazy, that one bad round wasn't that big a deal. "You didn't play that badly," he told him. "You go out tomorrow and play well—not great, just well—and you'll be right back in this thing."

Rocco decided to give it one more shot. Gleaton later told Matlock that he had talked Rocco into staying because he didn't want to pay for the hotel room—$36 a day—by himself if Rocco went home. Rocco knows there was more to it than that.

"He just wasn't going to let me give up on myself," he said. "After that pep talk, I stopped feeling sorry for myself."

But whatever Gleaton's motives, he was right—the next day went better. By the fourth and final day, Rocco was right around the number he knew it would take to get through the qualifier. "I'm not sure why, but you always know at Q-School to within a stroke, maybe two at most, what it's going to take to get through," he said. "You can tell by how tough the course is playing, by the conditions, by how tightly the field is bunched starting the last day. I got to the back nine and figured I needed to shoot two under par to make it.

"I made a couple birdies and came to 18, which was a par-four, figuring that worst-case scenario, if I made a par I would play off and if I made birdie I was in for sure. I couldn't reach the green in two and I ended up with about a 25-yard pitch shot that had to go over a swale to the hole, which was on the back of the green.

"I was standing there with a pitching wedge in my hand, when all of a sudden I decided to hit a seven-iron. I just grabbed it out of the bag and decided I was playing a pitch-and-run kind of shot. The ball goes up over the swale, disappears, runs toward the cup — and goes in.

"I was thrilled. I thought, 'Great, I'm in for sure now, no problem.' I signed my card and found out that by chipping in I'd gotten into a playoff! If I'd gotten up and down, I'd have been out. It was three guys for two spots. I birdied the first hole and made it. If I had known I had to hole the pitch on 18, no way would I have come close."

In those days there were only two stages of Q-School. (These days there are four.) The finals that year were at Greenlefe Country Club, which wasn't too far down the road from Lakeland.

"I'd played the course like a million times," Rocco said, understating things as always. "I knew it blind. Needless to say, I went in there with a lot of confidence. I was convinced I was destined to make it to the tour after what had happened at Georgia. I played very solid golf right from the start."

The finals are six rounds — 108 grinding holes of golf. After five days and 90 holes, Rocco was tied for 28th place. Fifty players would get tour cards, so he was in a good position. Even so, there was reason to be nervous. The margin between 28th place and 51st place was four shots, and stories about players skying to a high number in the final round were (and are) a major part of Q School lore. Like anyone on the eve of the biggest day of his life, Rocco struggled to sleep.

"I remember having a dream," he said. "On the first hole, I hit a driver down the middle and hit six-iron for my second shot — and it went in. I actually woke up with a smile on my face, thinking I was going to be okay."

He felt even better when he walked onto the first tee and saw Lee Janzen and Marco Dawson standing there. They had been playing in a tournament in Jacksonville over the weekend and had made a last-minute decision to drive to Greenlefe instead of back to Lakeland to watch their two ex-teammates (Gleaton was also in good position) try to make the tour.

"We'd gotten up early to drive back to school," Janzen remembered. "We were about halfway back, when all of a sudden it seemed the car wanted to head to Greenlefe. We decided we could miss a day of class to go out there and show some support for Rocc and Tom."

Rocco hit a perfect drive on the first hole and had a six-iron left from the middle of the fairway. "I hit it to two feet," he said. "For a second I thought it was going to go in. That would have been too weird."

He was delighted to start with a birdie and played steadily

all day. The only unnerving moment came at the 16th, a long, narrow par-three with out-of-bounds left of the green. Dave Rummels, one of the other players in the group who was also comfortably inside the qualifying number at that moment, hit a three-iron off the tee, hooked it, and watched it hop out of bounds.

As soon as he saw Rummels's ball bounce past the white stakes, Rocco turned to his caddy and said, "Give me a five-iron."

"But you can't possibly reach the green with a five-iron."

"I know that. Give me the f—— five iron."

For all intents and purposes, he laid up to a par-three. "I hit it short of the bunkers, away from any trouble," he said. "I would have been happy to make bogey. The one thing I didn't want to do was hit it OB and make six or something. I ended up pitching it close and making par."

Standing on the 18th tee, Rocco knew all he really had to do was finish the hole and he would get his card. "I was shaking," he said, laughing at the memory. "I mean, that hole has about the widest fairway in golf and I wasn't sure I could hit it. Once I got the ball on the green I relaxed a little, because at that point I think I could have six-putted and still made it. When I holed out, the relief was unbelievable. I was on the tour—and I didn't have to go back to college."

At that moment, he didn't need a backup plan.

4

Back to the Drawing Board

THOSE WHO HAVE PLAYED for a long time on the PGA Tour will tell you that there are few experiences in golf more bitter-sweet than the first time they successfully climb the Q-School mountain.

At the finish there is elation, exhaustion, and relief. Then comes the understanding that getting to the tour is only a small first step, that there are many golf miles to be traveled before one is considered successful on the tour.

"At some point, no matter who you are, the thought crosses your mind, 'Okay, I'm on the tour, but am I good enough to stay there?'" Rocco has said often. "If you know anything about Q-School, it is that more than half the guys who make it through in a given year are right back there the next year."

Rocco's elation on the last day at Greenlefe lasted a few hours—at most. He received congratulatory hugs from Janzen and Dawson and joined Gleaton, who had also earned his card, for a brief post-round celebration. He called his parents and tear-fully told them he was on the tour. Soon after that he was in his car on his way back home to Greensburg—still thrilled but with no one to talk to about what he had accomplished.

"It was a strange trip home," he said. "On the one hand, I found myself thinking about how amazing it was that I was going where I was going. I thought about the fact that six years earlier, I couldn't break 80 and now I was on the PGA Tour. That part was great.

"But it was also kind of scary, realizing how much work I had already done, but that I had that much more to do to try to compete once I got out there. I wasn't a college kid anymore; I was a professional golfer. It was what I wanted to be, but I knew it wasn't going to be at all easy. I really wanted to talk to people the whole way home, but there were no cell phones and it was the middle of the night anyway. It was just me and all my thoughts."

He didn't stay home for long, heading down to Florida right after Christmas to find some warm weather so he could prepare for his tour debut, which would come in early January at Pebble Beach. This was before the tour began its season with two tournaments in Hawaii the way it does now.

He spent a fair amount of his time in Florida working with Rick Smith. He had met Smith through Janzen, who had grown up playing at Imperial Lakes, the golf course where Smith's older brother was the pro. After Rick left East Tennessee State, he had come home to work for his brother as a jack-of-all-trades around the golf course. He had spotted Janzen, then in the seventh grade, hitting golf balls one day and made a suggestion to him about his setup.

"He told me that I had no chance to hit the ball well setting up the way I was," Janzen said. "I figured I had nothing to lose by making the change he was suggesting. I felt more comfortable over the ball right away. I wasn't very good at that point, so I figured almost anything might help. In almost no time I went from struggling to break 100 to shooting in the low 80s. I was completely hooked. After that, every time I saw Rick, I said to him, 'Give me something to work on.' He always did, and we became good friends and he became my teacher even though I wasn't formally taking lessons from him."

When Janzen and Rocco became friends, Janzen introduced Rocco to Smith. Although Rocco had continued to take lessons from Jim Ferree while in college, he enjoyed working with Smith too. In Smith, he found someone young enough to be a friend and someone as obsessed with the technique of the golf swing as he was. Plus, his teaching methods were not all that different from Ferree's, since a lot of Smith's understanding of the swing came from Ferree. By the time he finished at Florida Southern, Rocco was spending a good deal of time on the practice tee with Smith.

Nervous but excited, Rocco flew to Pebble Beach for his first tournament as a full-fledged member of the PGA Tour. In those days, Pebble Beach was one of the more glamorous events on the tour and drew a stellar field. Rocco walked onto the driving range on Tuesday morning and spent a solid hour just watching other players hit range balls.

"Watson was there and [Jack] Nicklaus and [Greg] Norman and just about anyone else you could possibly name who played golf at the time," he said. "I went up and down the range watching them hit balls—not just the big names, but everyone. I still like to do that to this day, watch other guys hit balls, because I really think I can learn a lot doing that.

"That day, though, I wasn't really learning. I was simply in awe. I watched their swings, watched them hit shots, and walked straight back into the clubhouse without hitting a ball. I called

Rick Smith on the phone and said, 'We need to get together again as soon as possible and *really* get to work, because I have no chance—I mean *no* chance—to keep my card out here this year. There's just no way I'm good enough to play with these guys.'

"I wasn't exaggerating," he said years later. "And it wasn't that I lacked confidence. I was just being a realist. I meant what I was saying. I could just see that these guys were on a different level than I was. That didn't mean I wasn't going to try as hard as I possibly could. I just think I had a very clear idea of what I was up against."

Much to his surprise and delight he made the cut that first week, cashing a check for $1,512. He didn't make another cut until May. But he didn't get discouraged, because he wasn't surprised to find himself struggling. He started to play better during the summer and began to see some progress. He made the cut in Canada and found himself paired in the third round with Greg Norman, who had just won the British Open two weeks earlier.

"That was an experience," he said. "People forget that Greg was Tiger before Tiger, if not in terms of dominance, in terms of charisma and aura. Believe me, back then he had it. I was really pleased with the way I played that day. I think I shot 72. He shot 64 and made it look easy. I'll never forget, though, how nice he was to me. Encouraged me all day and told me he thought I was going in the right direction when we finished. I mean, the guy just completely dusted me and he was telling me how impressed he was with my game."

By then Rocco's game and swing had both measurably improved. He had spent long hours on the practice tee with

Smith, working on making his swing more side to side than straight up and down. "Straight up and down, I could only hit the ball one way," he said. "When I changed my swing I was able to shape my shots. Hit a draw, a fade, choose what I wanted to do."

By year's end, he had made 10 cuts in 27 tournaments, had one top-ten finish—a fifth in Jackson, Mississippi, in an event the same week as the British Open, when most of the top players were overseas—and had earned $20,174, which left him 174th on the money list. And just as he had predicted at Pebble Beach, he found himself going back to Q-School.

"It didn't really bother me, because I had seen it coming right from the beginning," he said. "Plus, by the end of the year I felt I was a much better player than I had been a year earlier. I figured if that player could make it through Q-School, this player should breeze. I went in there with lots of confidence. I knew the guys I was up against just weren't as good as the ones I'd been play-ing against all year. If they had been, they wouldn't have been at Q-School."

The finals that year were on the West Coast, at PGA West in Palm Springs. Rocco was never in trouble the entire week, always in the top ten, never really having a nervous moment, even on the last day. "I was in third place going into the last day," he remembered. "I figured out if I shot 80 I was still going to make it, and I knew I wasn't going to shoot 80."

He shot 69 and ended up in third place behind Steve Jones and Steve Elkington—both future major champions. That sent him back to the tour in 1987, but this time he went with a com-pletely different attitude. The scared rookie had become a con-fident veteran.

"You learn *so* much your first year out there about every-thing," he said. "You learn how to travel, you learn about the golf courses, you learn how to live out of a suitcase, and you learn how not to be intimidated. That was my biggest challenge. When I went out there the second year, I had a lot more confidence in my golf swing and in my ability to compete. I didn't think I was as good as Greg Norman or Tom Watson, but I didn't think I had to be."

During that second year, in 1987, he started to find a comfort zone on the tour. He became close friends with Jim Carter, who was two years older than he was and had made it to the tour for the first time at the 1986 Q-School. Because their caddies were good friends, Carter asked Rocco if he would like to play with him in the team championships, a late-season unofficial event in California. Mediate said yes, and a friendship was born.

"In those days Rocc was a lot quieter than he is now," Carter remembered. "I think when he talks about wondering if he belonged — that's something we all feel when we're first out there and don't know if we're going to be good enough to stay out there. We spent a lot of time together with our wives until kids came along and they stopped coming out as much. Back then, Linda was a lot more outgoing than Rocco was."

Linda Newell had come into Rocco's life in the summer of 1986. He had taken a break from the grind of the tour and come home for a week to visit his family. He had walked into his dad's salon and instantly noticed that there was a new nail techni-cian at work. She was a junior at the University of Pittsburgh–Greensburg and was paying her way through school by working at Anthony's.

"Rocco took one look at her and said, 'Dad, is it okay if I ask her out?'" Tony Mediate said. "I told him it was up to her, not me. He asked, she went, and by the end of the year she was long gone from the salon. They were a couple from that day on."

Rocco hadn't had much time for a social life once he'd gotten hooked on golf in high school. His mother remembers begging him to go to the movies with friends or to a dance and being told there just wasn't time. In college he had a girlfriend for a while, but, according to Janzen, that had ended when the girlfriend had said something along the lines of 'If you want to keep dating me, you have to spend less time at the golf course and more time with me.'

"She had no shot to win that battle," Janzen said. "It was pretty much over after that."

Rocco had met someone earlier that summer at the Canadian Open, but once he met Linda, things happened very fast—for both of them.

"To be honest, I wasn't very interested in meeting him," Linda said. "I had started working at Anthony's in April, and every week starting on Thursday there was, well, hysteria in the place about how Rocco was playing, about whether he could make the cut. If he didn't make the cut, Tony would be in a terrible mood all weekend. If he did make the cut, that was all anyone at the salon talked about.

"My older brother was a good golfer, he had made the state championships on several occasions, but I was never really into golf or sports. By the time he came into the salon that day, I was pretty sick of hearing 'Rocco this and Rocco that' all the time."

Linda Newell had grown up on a farm in the tiny town of Stahlstown, the youngest of four children. "We had an apple tree in the backyard and lots and lots of wheat growing behind it," she said. "It was kind of the classic farm upbringing. The thing I loved to do most was read. I would go to the library and find the biggest book I could find. Or I would throw a Nancy Drew into my backpack and go sit at the Salamander River and read. I wanted to write when I grew up."

Linda's parents separated when she was eight, and finances were never easy after that. When she went to college, she paid her own way, working forty hours a week in the hardware department at Sears. During her sophomore year, her roommate, who worked in a beauty salon, told her that working at Sears was completely uncool and convinced her to go to beauty school. She did and landed the job at Anthony's soon thereafter.

"If you were going to work in a salon in Greensburg, Anthony's was the place to work," she said. "It was the biggest, it was the best, and it was where everyone in town went."

On the August day that Rocco walked into Anthony's—August 21, Linda remembers very specifically—Linda happened to be working on the nails of Susan Lucas, mother of Rocco's boyhood friend Dave Lucas.

"I always worked with my back to the front door so the person I was working on was facing it," Linda said. "I heard Susan say, 'Oh, my God, Rocky's here,' and there was this commotion behind me. To be honest, my first reaction was to roll my eyes. But I remember thinking, 'Okay, let's see what this guy looks like.' So I spun my chair around. He was standing at Tony's station, which is elevated, talking to his dad. I looked at him and, to this day I can't tell you why, but I heard a voice in my head say, 'That's the man you're going to marry.' I immediately started arguing with the voice: 'Don't be ridiculous, you've never met the guy, he's a *golfer,* for crying out loud, just stop it.'

"Susan and I were very friendly; we talked about a lot of things. She didn't like the guy I was dating, so as soon as I turned around, she started waving at Rocco to come over. She introduced us. I was absolutely convinced that everyone in the place could hear what was going on in my head, so I was completely embarrassed. I tried to be very cool. I just said, 'Oh, hi,' and went back to work.

"He went off to talk to a few more people while I finished up with Susan. A little later he was in the back talking to his uncle Joe, and I saw the two of them looking at me and whispering. I loved Uncle Joe; we always kidded around with one another. Now Rocco's talking and Uncle Joe is nodding his head yes, over and over.

"Finally Rocco came back to talk to the woman I was working on at that point. He sat down and said to me, 'My sister and I are going to this place called Tingles tonight. If you're not doing anything, maybe you'd like to come.' Believe it or not, I was planning on going there with a friend, so I said, sure, why not, we'll meet you there."

It all happened very fast after that. Linda remembers being so nervous she spilled three drinks on Rocco's white pants. "This was after I asked him if he was one of those golfers who wore those awful polyester plaid pants," she said. "He said he didn't. We played a video trivia game and we won. He looked at me and said, 'So, how about a kiss for the winners?'

"I said okay and he kissed me. Don't ask me why, but when he kissed me I remember thinking of the *Brady Bunch* episode where Peter has his first kiss and fireworks go off. My friend had been in the bathroom, but when she came back we must have had those stupid, giddy grins you get at times like that on our faces, because she just looked at us and said, 'Oh, my God.'"

They went to lunch on Saturday and that turned into spending the whole day together, including Rocco taking Linda to his parents' house for dinner. The next morning, Rocco had to fly out to the next tour stop in Memphis and convinced Linda to ride to the airport with him and his parents.

"The pump in our well in the backyard was broken and we had no water," Linda said. "I woke up at four thirty in the morning and drove a couple of miles to find a stream so I could wash my hair before I went to the house. I guess I should have realized I was hooked then.

"I do remember Donna being less than thrilled. Rocco had just broken up with someone and had missed six cuts in a row, and she thought he needed to concentrate on golf."

On Monday morning, Linda walked into the salon and found a dozen roses and a card at her chair. There was also a plane ticket—to Memphis. "Of course I went," she said.

She was on and off the tour the rest of the year. Donna's concerns abated when Rocco began making cuts on a regular basis after he and Linda started dating. "We would write to each other when I wasn't out there," she said. "I still have a letter he wrote me two weeks after we started dating in which we began naming our kids. At the time, we were planning on having six."

While Rocco was still in college, Jim Ferree had introduced him to Larry Harrison, a friend of his from Hilton Head. Harrison had liked Rocco enough that he offered to sponsor him on the mini-tours and continued to do so while he struggled to make money that first year on tour.

"It was pretty apparent right away this [Linda] was going to be it," Ferree remembered. "If Linda wasn't out, Rocco would finish up in a tournament and jump in the car to drive back to

Greensburg to see her for a couple of days before the next tournament. I understood what he was feeling, but I did finally sit him down and say to him, 'You know, Larry's put some serious money into helping you play. You really shouldn't be spending all your free time in the car driving back to Pennsylvania to see a girl.' Naturally he ignored me. And naturally it all worked out."

Linda may not have been a golf fan, but she was willing to put up with golf to be with Rocco. She went with him to both stages of Q-School that fall. After he had made it back to the finals, they were in a hotel in Jacksonville Beach. Rocco was going to get ready to play the finals, and Linda was flying north to go back to school and to work.

"The morning I was leaving, he said to me, 'Look, I'm only going to ask this once, but please don't go back to school next semester. Come out and travel with me full-time. If it doesn't work out, you can go back to school in a year.' I knew perfectly well if I dropped out of school I wasn't going back. But I said yes anyway."

After Rocco made it through the finals, he and Linda were a couple on the tour in 1987. The plan was for them to get engaged once he made enough money to clinch his card for 1988. That moment came when Rocco finished second to John Inman in the Provident Classic in Chattanooga, Tennessee. By then, everyone on tour knew what the plan was.

"The guys who did the scoreboard drew wedding bells next to Rocco's name after they posted the final scores," Linda remembered. "That was a fun time to be on tour. It was much smaller and everyone knew everyone—players, officials, everyone. It was before people traveled everywhere on their private jets."

They were married the following spring. By then, Rocco was

playing well enough on tour and making enough of a living that they were able to buy a house in Ponte Vedra, Florida, right near the tour's headquarters at the TPC Sawgrass.

All the work with Rick Smith and the year of experience on tour had started to pay off during 1987, that second year on tour. Rocco began to make cuts on a more consistent basis (19 of 32) and found himself playing later and later on Saturdays and Sundays. The second-place finish behind Inman at the Provident Classic in July—he lost by a shot—was worth $62,000, more than triple what he had made in all of 1986. He finished the year with $112,099 in earnings, which was good for 91st place on the money list.

"It was such a great time in my life," he said. "Every day was a learning experience on the golf course, on the practice tee, in the locker room, away from the golf course. I was just a kid trying to figure things out. For me, the PGA Tour those first few years was like going to golf college. A lot of guys went out of their way to help me, which I've tried never to forget. Now when I see young guys out here with that wide-eyed look I'm sure I had twenty years ago, I try to help them whenever I can."

And it wasn't just his golf swing that needed refining. One morning Rocco walked into the locker room at Muirfield Village Golf Club, the site of Jack Nicklaus's Memorial Tournament. It was pro-am day, and he was wearing a pullover sweater and comfortable pants. "They were kind of puffy," he said. "Not all that sloppy, not like painter's pants or anything, but not exactly dressy."

"Hey, kid, come over here," he heard a voice say, and looked up to see 1973 British Open champion Tom Weiskopf waving at him.

Dutifully, Rocco made his way over to Weiskopf's locker.

"Do you think the people who paid money to play with you today want to see you looking like that?" Weiskopf said. "You want to be a pro, you have to look like one. You need new pants—real pants."

He handed Rocco a card. "Call this guy. Tell him I told you to call. Get him to make some good pants for you."

Rocco did what he was told. Since then he has worn nothing but tailor-made pants on days when he goes to the golf course on tour. In fact, he's become a serious clotheshorse. He has a huge collection of belt buckles and gets his belts made too.

Other more experienced players also took him under their wing. Curtis Strange was the number one player in the world when Rocco arrived on tour and didn't play with him much, since they were in different categories when pairings were made, but Strange remembers frequently running into Rocco early on.

"You may not play with a guy, but you do run into people on the practice tee and in the locker room," Strange said. "Rocco was quieter then, but you could just tell he was a good kid. A lot of young guys show up on tour and act like the world is supposed to be at their feet. Rocco was never that way. You could tell he thought he was lucky to be doing what he was doing, and he loved a good story—whether he was listening to one or telling one. The Rocco people see now was always there; it was just a matter of him getting the confidence to show it."

Arnold Palmer was seeing a lot of Rocco too. He wasn't playing very much in those days, but whenever Rocco went home, he would go over to Latrobe and play with him.

"I probably lectured him too much," Palmer said, smiling, years later. "I saw so much potential in him. By the time he had been on tour for a couple of years, he had a very good golf swing and had become one of the best ball-strikers I'd seen in a long time. Plus, I knew he had the kind of personality that would make him a star and someone who would be very good for golf if he started to win with some consistency."

But Palmer had concerns too. "I worried about him. I saw his weight going up at a young age and didn't think that was a good thing. I thought he needed to spend more time on the putting green because at times he putted very well but at other times not as well. With the way he hit the ball, I thought he should be scoring better."

Weight was starting to become an issue as Rocco became established on tour. "People look at him now and they forget there was a time when his shoulders were wider than his hips," Janzen joked.

Of course Rocco knew that putting on weight wasn't a good idea for any golfer. He had been in good shape at Florida Southern because of Matlock's boot camps, but living on the road, especially after he started to make some money, he found it tough to keep weight off.

"I was probably like any guy in his twenties who was making money for the first time," he said. "Plus, I was away a lot. Linda was there some of the time, but not all the time. It wasn't as if I was out partying all night; if I had been I wouldn't have been able to play. But I definitely liked to eat. After a while I got to be a pretty big boy."

At six-foot-one and 190 pounds in college, Rocco was in good shape. By the time his first son, Rocco Vincent Mediate, was born late in 1990, his weight had ballooned to close to

250 pounds and his waist size was a forty-two. The extra weight didn't affect his stamina, but it did start to affect his back.

He had played steadily in 1988 and 1989, still not winning but maintaining his playing privileges without any problem. In 1990, he began to turn a corner and become a player people noticed.

"I think at that point it was just experience kicking in," he said. "I knew the golf courses, I knew which hotels to stay in, I knew how to get the best fares and upgrades on planes. [These days the tour has a travel office and a travel specialist who works out of the locker room, booking flights and hotels for players; back then they were on their own.] I was completely comfortable. Plus, my swing was really good. When I putted well, I could really score."

That has always been the book on Rocco: excellent ballstriker, streaky putter. "He always hit the ball very high and he always had that draw," Carter said. "He never lacked confidence with a driver or an iron in his hands. It was the putter that kept him from winning those first few years."

In his fifth year on tour, he became a consistent contender. He finished second at the Greater Hartford Open and had a third and a seventh. By the time the year was over, he had made a career high $240,625 and was 62nd on the money list. He still hadn't won, but he felt he was getting very close to that breakthrough.

Late that year, back pain prompted Rocco to begin using a long putter. Only a handful of players—most of them on the Senior Tour—were using a long putter at that point, but Rocco decided to try it for two reasons: He thought it might help him putt better and he hoped it might take some pressure off his back.

"My back wasn't bad at that point, but I had put on some weight," he said. "If I had been a great putter I never would have changed, but I wasn't a great putter so I thought it was worth a try. As soon as I picked it up I felt comfortable with it, so I just kept on using it."

In the early 1990s, a long putter on the regular tour was usually a sign of trouble. "Old guys were supposed to use them, not young guys," Strange said. "If you saw a guy with a long putter or putting cross-handed or doing anything that wasn't conventional, the first thing you thought was, 'This guy has issues.' Rocco was probably the first guy on the regular tour to use the long putter and actually have serious success with it."

Rocco was using the long putter at Doral the following March when he made back-to-back birdie putts on the last two holes to get into a playoff with Strange. "I guess that was a pretty good clue that he was putting well," Strange said, laughing, years later. "I remember I had finished ahead of him and had played well down the stretch. I thought I was in pretty good shape even when he made the birdie at 17, because birdieing the 18th at Doral to get into a playoff is a pretty tall order. But he hit a great second shot (to about 10 feet) and made the putt, and my thought was 'Good for you.'"

Because of a rain delay, the playoff was held the following morning, meaning Rocco had to sleep knowing he would need to come out firing the next morning, since the playoff was sudden death. On paper, the advantage had to belong to Strange, who had won 17 times on tour—including back-to-back U.S. Open victories in 1988 and 1989.

"I felt pretty good about it, to tell the truth," Strange said. "On the other hand, Rocco had finished hot by making the two birdies to tie me. In sudden death, it's really a matter of who comes up with a shot first. We both came up short of the green in two because it was playing dead into the wind, and we both hit good chips to set up makeable birdie putts."

The first playoff hole on tour is almost always the 18th. TV likes it that way, and it is easier on fans who don't have to go sprinting to another hole to get into position for a playoff. Even the Masters, which for years started playoffs on the 10th hole, now sends the players back to the 18th tee.

But this was 1990 on a Monday morning, and neither TV nor fans were a factor. So Strange and Rocco played Doral's par-five first hole. Rocco's wedge shot was just inside Strange's, so Strange putted first—and missed. That left Rocco with an eight-footer for his first win. He drained it.

"I still remember him dropping the putter before the ball got to the hole," Strange said, laughing. "I thought, 'Okay, that's inexperience tempting fate like that.' To be completely honest, I was disappointed not to win, the way you're always disappointed when you have a chance like that and don't win, but I was really happy for Rocco. I'd seen how much time he spent on the practice tee and how hard he worked at his game. Plus, I liked him. There are guys I could lose a playoff to and walk away really angry about it. Not Rocco. He earned it too—it wasn't like I just gave it to him. He birdied the last three holes he played. That's good golf."

The Doral victory wasn't exactly the way Rocco had pictured his first win: Because it was Monday morning, there were only a handful of spectators around. There was no post-victory TV interview, and the awards ceremony was all but held in private. Still, after five years, the feeling was overwhelming.

"When he called he was just about crying," Tony Mediate said. "Remember, it was Monday morning, so there was no TV and there was no Internet back then. We were just sitting there waiting for the phone to ring. As soon as I heard his voice, I knew he had won."

The win was worth $252,000, which was just $10,000 less than he had made total in the 91 tournaments he had played in during his first three years on tour. It also meant that he was exempt from having to qualify through the end of 1993 and it gave him a huge boost of confidence.

"There's a difference between staying on tour and winning on tour," he said. "My first five years I was good enough to stay on tour. I played okay and I was always aware of how much money I needed to make to keep my card for the next year. That's what it was about—staying on tour.

"Winning makes you feel completely different. For one thing, you get the two-year exemption, so for the rest of that year and the entire next year you don't have to even think about the money list—you just play. Beyond that, though, you feel like you really belong. You're playing with better players on Thursday and Friday [tournament winners are paired together the first two rounds at each tournament], and guys look at you differently in the locker room, on the range."

Or, as Loren Roberts put it after his first tour win in his tenth year on tour: "Until you win, you feel like you're a day worker out here. Once you win, you feel like you really belong."

Rocco was in his sixth year on tour when he won at Doral. He probably had as many friends among the other players as anyone out there and he had become quite popular with the fans. But he had never felt as if he really belonged.

"I always felt like an outsider in my early years on tour," he said. "It wasn't because I didn't have friends—I did. It wasn't because a lot of the older guys weren't great to me—they were. I just felt as if I wasn't normal. Maybe it was because I didn't have any pedigree as a junior golfer. I never really did anything until college, and then it wasn't until I was a senior.

"I remember Davis [Love] saying to me once, 'You went from nowhere at fifteen to the tour at twenty-two—you realize, don't you, that nobody does that?' He said it to make me feel good, and I get how amazing it was that I was able to do what I did. A lot of guys go back to Q-School multiple times when they're young. I went back once and that was it.

"I still remember watching those guys on the range at Pebble and being awed. Even later, when I'd established myself on tour, there were times when I would watch the other guys and say, 'Can I possibly play well enough to compete with them?' There was always doubt in my mind, even after I'd been out there four or five years. I wondered if I would ever play well enough to get noticed. I've always liked to perform, to show off. I didn't know if I'd ever get to a stage like that where I'd have that chance."

Winning a tournament—and beating Strange, a two-time U.S. Open champion and a former number one player in the world, to do it—was certainly a step in that direction. Stardom appeared to be looming on Rocco's horizon. Unfortunately, it wasn't the only thing heading his way.

5

Down for the Count

AFTER THE WIN AT DORAL, Rocco became a second-tier star on tour. He wasn't in the same category with Greg Norman or Nick Faldo or Fred Couples or Nick Price, who had supplanted Norman by then as the world's number one player. But he was one level down, a solid player who had won on tour and was well-liked by golf fans and other players.

He signed a lucrative contract with Titleist in 1990 and became a media favorite. Buoyed by his victory, he gained more confidence when talking to the media and in his interactions with fans.

"People just liked him," Jim Carter said. "He always had time for people — he was that way early on, when there weren't many demands made on him, and he stayed that way even after he became better known. Rocco was the guy people could always go to for a quote or to help out with a clinic or to spend extra time signing autographs. I think he's one of the few guys who actually enjoys all that. A lot of players see it as a burden. Rocco saw it as fun."

He was easily recognizable too, in part because he was always talking and smiling, but also because of the long putter.

"Long putters had always been thought of as being for old guys," he said. "I was twenty-eight when I won using it. It definitely got me attention I wouldn't have gotten otherwise. But that wasn't why I was using it. I felt comfortable with it and I putted better with it. Then, when my back started to bother me, it made my life a lot easier because I didn't have to bend over to putt."

As he got older and put on weight, Rocco began to experience occasional back pain, but it wasn't anything he was that concerned with, because all professional golfers experience soreness in their backs at some point.

"The body just isn't meant to spend hours and hours making the motion we make when we swing a golf club," said Raymond Floyd, the four-time major champion who was another of Rocco's early mentors. "It's a lot like pitching. The arm and the shoulder just aren't designed for the kind of pressure pitchers put on them when they throw a baseball, which is why so many pitchers have shoulder problems and elbow problems.

"It's the same with golfers and their backs. The twist and the torque and the thrust you put into a swing just aren't good for your back. One of Rocco's strengths as a young player was always his desire. He loved practicing, loved going out there for hours and hours and hitting balls. It's why he kept getting better. But it isn't easy. I've always been able to keep my weight at a pretty good place, and my back would hurt anyway after long practice sessions. You throw in the added weight with all the time he spent practicing, it was almost inevitable that he was going to get hurt somewhere along the line."

Strange and Carter both played with Rocco enough after his back troubles began to know how much pain he was in.

"I know enough about bad backs to know that it's tough to get out of bed in the morning when your back hurts, much less try to swing a golf club and walk 18 holes," Strange said.

Carter could often see that his friend was in pain even when he didn't talk about it. "Sometimes you could just tell by the look on his face," he said. "Later in my career, I tried to play through shoulder problems and I know how awful that was, so I think I have a sense of what he was going through back then."

Back miseries are commonplace on tour. Today, most players go into a fitness trailer that travels from tournament to tournament to be stretched at length before they hit a single practice ball. Many work with back specialists and chiropractors to try to ward off back pain. Players like Fuzzy Zoeller, Fred Couples, and Davis Love III—among others—have been forced to change their practice patterns and have missed considerable playing time because of back troubles.

For years now, Couples has rarely practiced for very long because he doesn't want to risk his back. In 1994, he was in contention on the last day at Doral when his back went into spasm on the driving range while he was warming up. He collapsed, screaming in agony, and had to be carried into the fitness trailer. Players who were on the range that day still vividly remember Couples crying out in pain and the sight of him on the ground.

"Worst pain I've ever felt," Couples said years later. "When it happens that way, it's as if someone has stuck a knife in your back. You're on the ground before you know it."

It didn't happen exactly that way to Rocco, but it wasn't all that different. His victory at Doral in March of 1991 springboarded him to his best season yet on tour. He finished the season with $597,438 in earnings, having finished in the top ten seven times and the top 25 fourteen times in 25 events. For the first time in his career, he qualified for the season-ending Tour Championship (only the top 30 players on the money list get to play), and he finished fifteenth on the final money list.

His life had changed completely since he first arrived on tour and either drove from tournament to tournament or searched out the cheapest airfare he could find when he had to fly. He and Linda had moved into a new house in Ponte Vedra, and his friends joked about how fast he spent money.

"We used to say that Rocco's money must be on fire because he had to spend it before it burned up," Lee Janzen said. "I can remember him telling Linda she needed to spend *more* than she was spending. How often does a husband tell a wife that? She was always very careful about money. Rocco wasn't. It just wasn't his way."

A year later, Rocco didn't play as well as he had in 1991, but he still had a solid year, finishing 49th on the money list. Not happy that he hadn't finished higher than third in a tournament and that he had not played nearly as well as he expected to, he rededicated himself to the practice tee in 1993, and the work paid off.

In March, he finished tied for second at Bay Hill behind Ben Crenshaw, which was a thrill because it was Palmer's tournament. In 1985, during Rocco's senior year at Florida Southern, Palmer had given him a sponsor's exemption into the tournament. Rocco had shown up with a Florida Southern bag and no caddy, and when Palmer spotted him playing a practice round carrying his bag (college players almost always carry their own bags in tournaments), he sent one of his caddies out with a Bay Hill bag and instructions to carry that bag for the youngster for the rest of the week.

Having a chance to win Palmer's event meant a lot to Rocco. A month later at Greensboro, he won his second tournament, again in a playoff. This time it took four holes and his victim was Steve Elkington, one of his good friends on tour. Rocco finally birdied the fourth hole of the playoff to win.

By the time the tour got to Las Vegas, the last full-field tournament of 1993, Rocco had made more than $600,000 and was comfortably qualified for the next week's Tour Championship, which was being held at the Olympic Club in San Francisco.

Since he was one of the bigger names in the Vegas field, he was asked to participate in that week's Merrill Lynch shootout. The shootouts were held on Tuesdays to try to entice bigger crowds to come to the golf course on practice days. Ten players participated over nine holes, with the high score on each hole being eliminated until two players were left to play the last hole. Ties were broken by chip-offs or shots from a bunker—anything to entertain the crowd. They were lighthearted games, with CBS's Gary McCord usually playing the role of MC and a couple of players wearing microphones so they could interact with McCord or chime in with wisecracks. Naturally, Rocco was one of the miked players.

The shootout was being staged on the back nine that day, and there were four players left—including Rocco—when they got to the 16th hole, which is a reachable par-five over water.

"I hit a three-wood for my second shot and got it onto the green," Rocco remembered. "I handed the club to my caddy, took about two steps, and felt this spasm of pain like nothing else I had ever felt. It wasn't the first time I'd had back pain, but nothing, I mean *nothing*, like this had happened before.

"I'm not quite sure how I walked onto the green, but I remember saying to my caddy, 'I can't move.' I had to quit right there, couldn't even think of putting. They took me straight to the fitness trailer, and the guys worked on me and gave me a lot of Advil. It loosened up that night, and I was able to play the first three days even though it was still pretty sore."

In those days, Vegas was a 90-hole event with the cut coming after 54 holes. Rocco somehow made the cut. But on Saturday, playing the 12th hole, he felt the pain again. Not wanting to miss playing in San Francisco, he withdrew immediately and went back to the trailer for more work. Again, the boys in the trailer and lots of Advil helped. He took a couple of days off and then tried to play a practice round at Olympic the day before the Tour Championship started.

"I was out there early by myself and it felt okay for a while," he said. "But then it went again. I was on the 15th hole, which is a par-three, and I tried to hit a seven-iron. There's a bunker in front of that green that's about 120 yards from the tee. I couldn't reach it with my seven-iron.

"There was no one around, so I started to walk in because we weren't that far from the clubhouse. There's a big hill that leads up to the 18th green, and I couldn't get up it. I kept going down, getting up, and going down again. Finally I ended up crawling up the hill to get to the clubhouse. I probably should have sent my caddy in to get a cart for me, but I was being stubborn. It probably took me an hour to go the last 300 yards."

He was determined not to withdraw. For one thing, it was a prestigious event that he had worked hard to qualify to play

in. For another, since there were no alternates, Steve Elkington, whom he was scheduled to play with on Thursday, would
be left to play alone. And for another, there was no cut in the
tournament, and if he finished 72 holes, the worst he could do
was cash a check for $48,000—which was not exactly money to
be laughed off.

Rocco's most vivid memory of the next day is Elkington. "He
picked my ball up out of every single hole," he said. "He figured
my caddy had enough to do trying to get me around."

He somehow managed to play all 72 holes—"and didn't finish last"—but he flew home very concerned about the state of
his back. "I was hoping, to be honest, that a good long rest would
be all I needed," he said. "The guys in the trailer had given
me some rehab exercises to do during the off-season and they
politely suggested I try to lose a little weight. I worked hard on
the rehab and came out for '94 hoping the rest and rehab would
be enough. They weren't."

Rocco was not the only member of his family dealing with
health issues—in fact, his problems were relatively minor
compared to what his mother had gone through during 1993.
Donna Mediate had been diagnosed that summer with multiple
myeloma, cancer in her bone marrow. The prognosis was, in a
word, terrible.

"I still remember everyone who knew my mom going on about
how awful it was and wailing and crying," he said. "I understood
all that, but I honestly didn't believe that was the best way to
help her. My mom is a strong woman. A lot of my toughness
comes from her.

"When I found out what was going on, I sat down with her
and told her, 'Look, I know this is rough and it's unfair. But you're

going to get better. You are going to deal with the treatments and whatever else you have to deal with, but I know you can handle it. I honestly believed that if all she heard from people was how terrible it was and that she was going to die, she would die. I told her she wasn't going to die and she needed to look at this as a fight and just go and win the damn fight.

"I upset some people by saying all that, because they thought I was being cavalier about it. I wasn't being cavalier. I thought if I told her she should feel sorry for herself, she would. If I told her to go get better, she would."

Donna ended up going to the University of Arkansas for a bone marrow transplant and treatment. She and Tony made the trip more times than either can remember, but a year later she was cancer free.

"Rocco was tough on me," she said years later. "The things he was saying weren't necessarily easy to hear, but they were probably good for me to hear." She smiled. "The bottom line is I'm still here."

Eight years later, Donna had a second bout with cancer. This time it was lymphoma. There was no surgery, but there was more chemo and more radiation. Once again, her son more or less ordered her to get through it. Once again, she did.

"If only," he said years later, "I was as good at ordering myself to get healthy. I might have won four or five majors by now."

ROCCO BEGAN 1994 BY PLAYING in five early-season tournaments. Even though he was still hurting, he managed to make four cuts. By spring, the pain was so bad that after being forced to skip the Masters, he went to see Dr. Arthur Day, a noted back specialist, in Gainesville.

"He told me I had a choice: I could do surgery right away to repair my disk or I could do surgery later to repair my disk. 'You're going to have to have surgery, especially if you want to keep playing golf for a living,' he told me. 'It's not a matter of if, it's a matter of when.'"

Rocco knew that surgery would means months of rehab and time away from golf and the tour. He also knew that the U.S. Open was only a few weeks away and it was at Oakmont—the golf course where he had first started to wonder how good he might become after playing there following the last round of the '83 Open.

"Plus, it was a home game for me, and I knew it was going to be Arnold's last Open and I might get paired with him because the USGA does stuff like that," he said. "I decided to wait at least until the Open pairings came out."

David Fay, the executive director of the USGA, still did the pairings in those days. He always liked to put together threesomes for the first two days that made sense for one reason or another: It could be three past U.S. Amateur champions or two players who had once met in an Open playoff.

In this case, Fay wanted to put together a threesome for Palmer that would be meaningful, since it would be his last U.S. Open. He chose John Mahaffey to be one member of Palmer's group because Mahaffey had won the PGA Championship at Oakmont in 1978 and thus had history with the golf course, just as Palmer did.

Then, looking through the names in front of him, Fay came to Rocco's. "It was a natural," he said. "Pennsylvania kid, grew up near Oakmont, plus I knew that Arnold had been one of his mentors."

As soon as he heard who he was paired with, Rocco was going to play if he had to be pushed around the golf course in a wheelchair. "I had to try to play," he said. "I mean, Arnold's last Open, being paired with him? Come on. There was no choice."

For 27 holes, the back held up and Rocco was on the leader board, only a couple of shots behind leaders Ernie Els and Colin Montgomerie. But on a steamy, humid day—the temperatures reached record highs that week in Pittsburgh—Rocco felt the back go again as he, Palmer, and Mahaffey walked to the 10th tee.

The two days had been remarkably emotional. Palmer was cheered every step of the way, every swing, every putt, every tipped cap. Rocco could see how emotional Palmer was getting as the day wore on and he told himself he had to hang in and at least finish the round. He wanted to walk up the 18th fairway with Palmer, to be on the green to hear the cheers, and to give him a hug when he finished. What's more, he didn't want to take away from Palmer's moment by having to leave him to finish in a twosome with Mahaffey.

So he fought his way through the last nine holes. At the 17th, a short par-four that some players can drive or at least come very close to the green off the tee, he hit a five-iron.

"Why'd you hit an iron there?" Palmer asked, as they walked down the fairway.

"Because I can't make a full swing," Rocco answered through gritted teeth. "I'm just trying to finish."

Fortunately the 18th hole was playing downwind, and Rocco was able to half-swing a driver and get a five-iron onto the green.

The hole was playing so short that day that Palmer, who had been hitting fairway woods well short of most of the par-fours all day, was able to reach the green in two.

As the three players began their walk up to the green, Rocco and Mahaffey hung back for a long moment to allow Palmer to walk onto the green alone. The cheers were absolutely deafening. It seemed as if all thirty thousand spectators on the grounds were ringing the 18th green. On the 10th tee, a few yards from the green, Strange and the other players in his group stopped to applaud and to watch as Palmer walked onto the green. He was crying by then, the tears streaming down his face.

Mahaffey and Rocco made sure Palmer was the last one to putt out. "Can you imagine what it would have been like, putting after Arnold had finished?" Rocco said. "I mean, are you kidding? No way."

After Palmer holed his last putt, Rocco wrapped his arms around him. Both men were crying by that point. "All of this," Rocco said to Palmer, gesturing in the direction of the thousands of people around the green, "is because of you."

Years later, Palmer remembered that moment and that comment. "I think I said something like, 'I hope just a little bit of that is true,'" he said. "That was one of my more special moments because of where it was and the way the fans acted, but also because of what Rocco said on the green after my last putt."

Rocco was talking about Palmer's importance to the growth of the game and the fact that his popularity and charisma had taken the tour from being a minor league sport to a major league sport. Tiger Woods would arrive in 1996 to take golf to another level, but Palmer had been the Man long before anyone used the phrase.

As he walked off the green, trailing Palmer and the myriad cameras following him, Rocco's back was killing him. He had managed to hang on and make the cut, but he wasn't certain he would be able to play on Saturday, much as he wanted to.

"It was the U.S. Open, for God's sake," he said. "You don't WD [withdraw] from the Open if you can walk. I could walk—it just hurt like hell when I did."

He managed to make it around the golf course Saturday but shot 77, feeling pain every time he swung the club. "At best I was taking a half-swing most of the time. The doctor had told me I wouldn't make it any worse by playing, but I was beginning to wonder."

After he had signed his scorecard, he walked very slowly up the steps to the locker room. There was no air-conditioning in the Oakmont clubhouse except for one area off the locker room, which had been air-conditioned for the week. It was supposed to be the players' dining area, but it had become, for the most part, the players' cooling-off area, since the rest of the locker room was as steamy as it was outside.

Rocco walked in, collapsed in a chair, and saw his friend Fuzzy Zoeller sitting a few feet away, also recovering from 18 holes in the brutal heat. Zoeller, who had been through back surgery several years earlier, looked at the younger man sympathetically.

"You look awful," he said. "You look worse than I do, and I can barely stand up I'm so tired."

"I'm in pain, serious pain," Rocco said. "I can't play golf like this."

"You're right, you can't," Zoeller said. "And it isn't going to get better on its own. It's going to get worse."

"What do I do?"

Zoeller shrugged. "You get the surgery done as soon as possible. Get it over with. The sooner you get it done, the sooner you start getting better."

Rocco knew he was right. He withdrew from the Open, flew home, and called Dr. Day, asking him how soon he could have surgery done to repair his bulging disk.

The date for the surgery was July 12, 1994. "Eight o'clock in the morning," Rocco remembered. "It took about four hours. When it was over, the doctor came in and said, 'Now the work begins.'"

The immediate aftermath of the surgery was extraordinarily painful. "It took me two days to get out of bed to go to the bathroom," he remembered. "I finally got up when the doctor came in and threatened to put a catheter in me if I didn't get up in the next five minutes."

Five days after the surgery, Rocco went home. Then, as the doctor had explained, the work began. "I became a rehab junkie," Rocco said, laughing. "As soon as I was able, I was in rehab every morning. I worked for hours and hours. It was a little bit like when I was a kid and all I did from sunup to sundown was play golf or practice golf. Now, all I did was exercises to strengthen my back and workouts so I could lose weight. If I wasn't working out, I was resting to get ready for my next workout."

His goal was to come back and play golf at the start of 1995. In September, two months after the surgery, he walked onto his back porch with a wedge in his hand and decided to try to hit a couple of balls and see what happened.

"First one, I went down," he said. "I mean, went down. Fortunately I didn't hurt myself. I really think it was just my balance—or lack of it. I got up, took a couple more swings, half-swings, really, and I was okay. It was a step. It really felt good just to have a club in my hand again and hit a golf ball."

The time at home was enjoyable in one sense—he got to spend some extended time with his family. By then, Nicco, a second son, had been born, and Rocco Jr. was old enough (almost four) to really enjoy seeing his father for weeks at a time instead of days at a time.

"In truth, that was probably the best year of our marriage," Linda said. "That's not to say it wasn't stressful; it was. I had to be the positive one all the time even though I was just as scared as he was about whether he was going to be able to come back or not. I watched him go through that rehab and put in the hours and hours of work, and I was truly amazed. He knew he had to get in shape, he knew he had to lose weight, and he knew he had to do the rehab on the back. Once he made up his mind to do it, there wasn't anything that was going to stop him from doing it.

"The best part, though, was that he was *there*. I think he really enjoyed having that time with his children and I think it strengthened our relationship, because he wasn't living out of a suitcase —there one week, gone the next. In many ways, it was a wonderful time in our lives."

But there was also a good deal of fear. On the day of the surgery, Rocco woke up convinced he would never play again. It took him a while to get past that feeling.

"I couldn't help but wonder if I'd be able to play again," he said. "I don't mean play as in go out and swing a golf club, I mean play at the level I'd been at before I got hurt. The margin for error on the PGA Tour is so tiny. I had to deal with the idea that

I might not make it all the way back. When I thought about that, I'd catch myself thinking, 'I'm thirty-one years old; I'm married with two young children. If I can't play golf, what will I do?'"

Just as when he finished college and went to Q-School, there was no backup plan.

But he smiled. "Whenever I got to that point, I'd just tell myself, 'That's it. Stop thinking that way. You're going to make it back. There's no other option.'"

By December he felt good enough to play in a team event in California with Lee Janzen. "We even played okay," he said. "Won a couple matches. I still wasn't 100 percent, but I felt good. I had lost a bunch of weight and I felt stronger. I started the next year thinking I was just going to keep getting better.

"Except I didn't."

The 1995 season was probably the most difficult of Rocco's career. At times, the back felt okay. At other times, it hurt and he had a hard time playing at all, much less playing well. It was one step forward, two steps back. He made the cut at the Players Championship — finishing 55th — but had to take a few weeks off afterward.

"Every time I got to a point where I thought I was turning a corner, the pain would come back," he said. "It wasn't anything as dramatic as when I first hurt it, but it was really hard to play golf. It was frustrating as hell. I called Dr. Day and said, 'What's going on?' He said, 'Keep doing what you're doing; these things take time.' But it wasn't working. I knew I had to take a break and rest it again. Playing wasn't doing it any good."

Since he had won a tournament in 1993, Rocco was exempt through the end of 1995 but not beyond. He had played in only six tournaments in 1994 and he had played in eighteen in 1995 before deciding he had to stop. The combined twenty-four starts were fewer than he typically played in a year. Since his Doral victory had earned him a two-year exemption, Rocco thought he should be entitled to extend his exemption through 1996, making that, in essence, his second year. He decided to take his case to the tour's policy board.

"Before they met, I talked to the players on the board and they all told me they thought I was right, that I had a good case," he said. "I met with the board at the Western Open [in late June] and explained that my injury had basically cost me a year of my two-year exemption. They listened and said they would let me know."

The policy board has nine members—four players, four businessmen who are tour sponsors in some way and are handpicked by the commissioner, and the president of the PGA of America. Many players don't like this system because it means if there is an issue in which the players oppose the commissioner, the four players can be outvoted by the five nonplayers.

This wasn't one of those issues. The vote was unanimous—to deny Rocco's request for an extension. The board's reasoning was simple: There were rules in place that allowed an injured player to receive a medical exemption, but not for an entire year—unless he didn't play at all for an entire year. Rocco had played in eighteen tournaments in 1995. Since he had played in twenty-four tournaments in 1993, his last healthy year, he would be given a six-tournament exemption at the start of 1996.

He had made $105,618 in the tournaments he had played in 1995. At year's end, the 125th-ranked player on the money list would earn slightly more than $142,000. That meant, under the tour's rules, that Rocco would have six tournaments to earn enough to exceed the difference. If he did, he was exempt for the rest of the year. If not, he would be a nonexempt player who would have to hope tournament directors would give him sponsor exemptions.

It was Commissioner Tim Finchem who walked out to the range, where Rocco was chatting with friends, to give him the news that his request had been turned down. "I knew he wasn't going to be happy," he said. "I'm the commissioner. It was my job to tell him and explain to him why we really didn't have the option to give him anything more than what the rules for medical exemptions allowed."

He never really got the chance to explain. "He got about as far as 'The vote was nine-zero against you' before I exploded," Rocco remembered, shaking his head at the memory. "I just went nuts, screaming at him, telling him what I thought of the decision and what I thought of him. I was over the line—out of line—but I was really hot. I had no idea what kind of shape my back was going to be in at the start of the next year. To be honest, I was scared because who knew if I would be able to play well at the start of the year? I hadn't played very much good golf since the surgery, so there wasn't really reason to have much confidence at that point.

"Even so, the way I spoke to him was wrong. I knew it as soon as he walked away."

Rocco flew home from Chicago the next morning. A couple of days later, he called Finchem's office and asked if he could come by to see the commissioner. "I walked in and told him I was sorry for the way I'd behaved on the range," he said. "I said

I still disagreed with the decision, but that was no excuse for my behavior. He was cool about it. He said he understood and there were no hard feelings."

The rest of the year was spent back at the rehab drawing board. "I really didn't play at all for months," Rocco said. "I was just working to try to make the back stronger, doing the exercises the doctor had given me. I was losing weight, getting into really good shape again. It was almost like right after the surgery. I started hitting some balls and playing again a little bit in the fall. I wanted to come out of the box ready to play because I knew I only had six events to make my money."

He decided to start his season in Phoenix, a tournament he had always liked on a golf course—the TPC of Scottsdale— he liked. "I felt good physically and mentally going in there. The back felt strong. I'd hit a lot of golf balls and felt ready. I knew I had to make, like, $40,000 [actually a little more than $37,000] and I wanted to do it as quickly as I could just to get that pressure off my back—so to speak."

He was in contention the entire week at Phoenix. There is no tournament on the tour with bigger, louder crowds than Phoenix. Being loud and drunk at Phoenix is considered the right way to behave as opposed to other tournaments, where it is likely to get you removed from the grounds. Some players have trouble dealing with the Phoenix crowd mentality; Rocco—naturally—thrived.

"I love it there, always have," he said. "Hey, golf is supposed to be fun for everyone—players, fans, all of us. As long as they don't yell in the middle of my backswing, I'm fine. Hey, if I was watching I'd be yelling too."

With the crowds very much in his corner, Rocco put together

four solid rounds, 68–67–70–69, to finish in sixth place. That finish earned him $42,088—almost five thousand dollars more than he needed to clinch his playing privileges for the entire year. "I felt good all week," he said. "The 68 the first day was big—gave me a confidence boost. I think the fans knew I'd been hurt. They were great every day.

"What a relief that week was," he said. "It meant I could make my schedule for the rest of the year, my travel plans—everything. Plus, I didn't have to worry about asking people for a spot in their events. I've had friends who have gone through that, and it's no fun. You don't like to be dependent on anyone else to have the chance to do your job. After Phoenix, I felt like I had my job back."

He did his job extremely well for the rest of that year. At the Players Championship in March, he was having a reasonably good tournament, heading for about a 30th-place finish on Sunday, when he suddenly got hot on the back nine. He birdied the last six holes—the first player ever to accomplish that feat on the TPC Sawgrass—and jumped into a tie for fourth place, three shots behind winner Fred Couples. Since the Players has the biggest full-field purse of the year (in 2008 it was $9 million, with $1,620,000 to the winner), the tie for fourth combined with the sixth at Phoenix meant that Rocco had clinched his card for 1997 before the end of March 1996.

The rest of that year went about as well as Rocco could have hoped—except for the fact that he didn't win again. He played twenty-one times—dropping a few tournaments from his normal schedule to rest his back—and was in the top ten almost half the time (10). He earned a little more than $475,000 for the year, which put him a very solid 40th on the money list. The sleepless nights wondering if his back would ever be strong enough for him to compete on tour again were in the past. He and Linda had had their third son, Marco, in 1995, and all was well in Mediate Nation.

6

The Good Life

Rocco's comeback year, 1996, was his eleventh on the PGA Tour, although almost two years had been lost because of his back troubles.

"Even when I played in '94 and '95, I couldn't really play," he said. "I was just trying to get through tournaments without falling flat on my face — literally."

He had made a total of 12 cuts during those two years and finished in the top ten three times, never coming close to contending. He had gone from a hot young player to a player whose future appeared to be in doubt. He had gone from averaging just under $500,000 a year in on-course earnings from 1990 to 1993 to making about $150,000 combined during those two injury-plagued years.

"Money became a concern during that time," he said. "Really, what saved me was that Titleist stuck with me. They kept paying me even when I couldn't play and certainly couldn't do anything to promote their product. That and the fact that Frank had talked me into getting disability insurance."

Frank was Frank Zoracki, who had become both a friend and

a business adviser to Rocco through the years. Zoracki was a couple of years older than Rocco and they had met quite by accident one afternoon at Greensburg Country Club.

Zoracki had joined Greensburg for two reasons: He had gotten hooked on golf even though he hadn't played it much as a kid, and he thought it was a good place to network. He had graduated from the University of Pittsburgh as an aspiring dentist, but when he didn't get into Pitt dental school he had gone to work for Prudential Insurance.

"I'd become a decent player," he said. "And the golf course, specifically the country club, was a good place to meet people who had money and needed insurance."

Zoracki was playing with some friends in the fall of 1986, when he encountered Rocco and his friends on the golf course.

"It wasn't long after Rocco had gotten his card for the first time," Zoracki remembered. "I was out playing with some friends and I think I had missed a putt on the 15th hole—a par-three—which had put my partner and me down in the match we were playing. I guess I was a little bit annoyed and I was a tad slow walking off the green. As I was about to leave, a ball lands on the green a couple yards away from me.

"I wasn't in the best mood as it was, so I looked back at the tee and yelled something like 'Hey, watch what you're doing.' I remember I got some attitude back, something along the lines of I should be clearing the green faster. I walked off kind of angry, and when I got to the next tee, one of my buddies said, 'Hey, that was Rocco Mediate you were yelling at just now.'

"I knew the name. I'd seen stories in the local paper about him when he was in college and when he got his card. Plus, I had sold some insurance to his parents, so I was familiar with the name. But at that moment, I really didn't care. I was like, 'I don't care who the guy is, he just hit into me.'"

By the time Zoracki had finished his round, he had cooled off. When Rocco and his friends walked into the grill room after they had finished their round, Zoracki went over and introduced himself. There were no hard feelings on either side. A couple of days later, Zoracki was in Tony Mediate's salon getting a haircut, when Rocco walked in.

"I asked him if he had any insurance," Zoracki said. "He said he didn't, and I told him it would be a good idea if he got some."

Out of a shouting match on the golf course and a brief discussion about insurance, a friendship was born. A couple of months after buying life insurance through Zoracki, Rocco ran into him in West Palm Beach, when he was getting ready to start the new PGA Tour season.

"We played together a couple of times," Zoracki said. "I was down there on a golf trip, and one of the guys I was with was Arnie Cutrell, who was one of Rocco's buddies. So we hung out quite a bit."

Eighteen months later, after Rocco and Linda had gotten married, he asked Zoracki to put together a medical-insurance plan for him. While he was at it, Zoracki suggested he buy disability insurance.

"Waste of money" was Rocco's first response.

Which made sense. After all, he was a twenty-five-year-old golfer. What was the likelihood that he was going to become disabled and unable to continue playing golf?

Zoracki kept after him. "It wasn't an easy sell," he said. "To begin with, the only company that would even write disability insurance for a golfer was Lloyds of London, and it was expensive—several thousand dollars a year. Rocco kept telling me it was crazy, but I kept after him. Athletes get injured. He was planning a family. I thought it made sense. He finally did it, but every year when he had to write the check to pay the premium, he would scream and yell at me about wasting his money."

There was no more screaming and yelling in 1994 and 1995. It took a while for Lloyds to be satisfied with all the paperwork needed, but once the claim was settled, Rocco got about $25,000 a month in disability insurance while he was off the tour.

"It was a lifesaver," he said. "Anything else Z does the rest of his life, I'll be grateful to him for that."

The two are now close friends and Zoracki, who left Prudential after ten years to go work for Northwestern Mutual Life, is now a money manager, handling all of Rocco's finances and acting as his agent most of the time in recent years. He has also become Rocco's bad cop, the guy who delivers the bad news to people when Rocco has to say no—or, worse, has to turn what was a yes into a no.

"I've kind of pleaded with him for years to say no first when he's not sure about something," Zoracki said. "I've told him it's a lot easier to turn a no into a yes than the other way around. He hates saying no to people, and I get that; it's part of what makes him who he is. But sometimes because he doesn't want to say no, he'll say yes to an outing or a speech and then when he thinks about it and realizes he can't do it, he'll just say something like, 'Z, you gotta get me out of this.' That isn't always pleasant for me."

Zoracki does it because, like most of the people in Rocco's life, he is intensely loyal to him. "Rocc is Rocc and that takes in a lot of territory," Zoracki said, laughing. "He is, first and foremost, a lot of fun to be around. What you see is what you get. He's not phony at all. The guy people see on TV who they like so much is the same guy you see when you're with him a lot.

"But he does have an obsessive personality. He's always been that way from what I can tell. He can't just have a Mercedes, he has to have the best Mercedes. A restaurant isn't just good, it is the absolute best, and when you go in there with him he's going to order for you and you damn well better like it. He never just likes anything. He either loves it or hates it. There's no inbetween. If you ask him about a round of golf, he'll almost never say he played okay. He'll tell you, 'I shot a million,' or 'I shot nothing.' There's nothing ordinary in his life."

The years between 1996 and 2002 were better than ordinary for Rocco but short of extraordinary. He won for the third time on tour in 1999 at Phoenix, the place where he had announced his triumphant return to the tour in 1996. One of the players he beat down the stretch on that Sunday was Tiger Woods, who ended finishing third.

"The rest of my life I can tell people I had a chance to beat Tiger on a Sunday and did it," he said. "What's more, I did it head-to-head, paired with him Saturday and Sunday. It was nice to do it — at least once."

He won again the next year at the Buick Open and two years later won Greensboro for the second time. That gave him five wins on tour, and after sixteen solid years — injuries notwithstanding — he had pieced together a very good career.

"Think about what it means to play fifteen years and win five times — especially dealing with coming back after the surgery," said Curtis Strange. "What that means is that the guy wasn't just a player who could get hot on occasion and play well. It means he was a very good player—a consistently good player—who, when his putter got going, could play with anybody. Those may not be Hall of Fame numbers, but they're very good ones."

Not long after Marco's birth, Rocco and Linda built a very big house at the TPC Sawgrass. It was, as his friends would say, "typical Rocco."

"The in-home theater was like nothing you'd ever seen in your life," Lee Janzen said. "It was amazing."

Life was good during this period. The arrival of Tiger Woods on tour had sent purses skyrocketing and it coincided with Rocco playing the best—and healthiest—golf of his life. The difference in purses can be seen in microcosm through Rocco's annual earnings. In 1996, the year that Woods joined the tour in August but had no influence on purses, Rocco finished 40th on the money list and earned $475,940 for the year.

Three years later, after the tour had renegotiated its TV contracts in the first year A.T.—After Tiger—and demanded that title sponsors increase their purses to reflect the sport's newfound popularity, Rocco finished two places higher on the money list—38th—and made more than double the money he had made in 1996, finishing with $963,075 in earnings.

Everyone on tour recognized that Woods was making them all into wealthy men. Even so, there was some initial resentment among many players about Woods's transcendent fame and the tour's willingness to do backflips to keep the new star happy. Some players half-jokingly began referring to their workplace as the TGA Tour—Tiger Golf Association Tour—and wondered if all of those flocking to pay homage to Woods had ever heard of Hogan, Palmer, or Nicklaus.

Woods and his entourage were demanding and, at times, arrogant—especially early on. Woods turned pro after winning his third straight U.S. Amateur title. Like any rookie pro, he was entitled to up to seven sponsor exemptions for the rest of 1996. Unlike many rookies, he quickly found there wasn't a tournament on earth that didn't want to give him an exemption, since he was the biggest draw in golf the instant he turned pro. Woods's initial goal was to avoid going to Qualifying School, which a handful of players had been able to do in the past. He needed to win as much money as the 125th-ranked player on the money list in his seven tournaments to avoid Q-School.

The suspense didn't last long. After finishing in a tie for 60th place in his debut in Milwaukee, Woods went on to win in Las Vegas and at Walt Disney World. The first victory guaranteed him a two-year exemption and eliminated any thoughts of having to go to Q-School. A few days later, having accepted a sponsor's exemption to the Buick Challenge in Callaway Gardens, Georgia, Woods withdrew, saying he was exhausted. He also skipped a dinner honoring him as the college player of the year that had been scheduled in Callaway Gardens for the night prior to the first round, specifically because he had planned to play that week.

Two weeks later, after his win at Disney, Woods told the locker room security guards to keep the media outside while he was cleaning out his locker. PGA Tour rules are very specific about media access to locker rooms, and a tour official, Wes Seeley, stepped in and told the guards that the media should be allowed inside.

"The tour makes the rules for everybody," he said. "The locker room is open when Palmer's in there, when Nicklaus is in there, when Watson is in there, and when Tiger Woods is in there too. The kid isn't the fifth Beatle."

Seeley's approach was both correct and admirable. Of course, years later friends couldn't resist pointing out to him that he had been right: Woods wasn't the fifth Beatle. He was John Lennon.

These incidents were simply part of Woods's celebrity learning curve. There were others: After winning the Masters by 12 shots in April of 1997, he turned down an invitation to join President Bill Clinton and Rachel Robinson at a ceremony in New York marking the fiftieth anniversary of Jackie Robinson's breaking baseball's color line. Although he defended the decision for a while afterward, Woods later wrote a letter to Mrs. Robinson, apologizing for not being there.

While some players snickered at Woods's occasional off-the-golf-course errors—there wasn't much they could criticize on the golf course—Rocco never went that route. He understood from the beginning what Woods was going to mean to golf and to all those who played the game. Plus, as he put it, "I liked the kid."

Woods was initially shy around his peers, in part because most were older than he was, in part because he understood the resentment some of them felt. But the more he got to know other players, the more comfortable he became. And the more comfortable he became, the more they found that they liked him.

"Tiger is a guy's guy," Rocco said. "He likes to tell bad jokes and talk about ball games and give everyone a hard time. Plus, he can take it when he gets it back. Once people got the chance to know him, they liked him."

Not surprisingly, Rocco was one of the players who went out of his way to make Woods feel comfortable early on. "To be honest, I try to do that with all the young players," he said. "I remember how intimidated I felt when I first came out and how much it meant to me when guys like [Raymond] Floyd and [Tom] Weiskopf and Curtis [Strange] went out of their way to try to help me out. I try to encourage guys, point them in the right direction when I can.

"With Tiger it was different. He had all sorts of people giving him advice, whether it was his dad or his agents or his swing coach — whoever. He didn't need me or anyone for any of that. But I tried to make him feel like he was one of the guys. The way you do that is you give someone a hard time, joke around with them. I think he always appreciated that about me."

Woods always enjoyed the handful of people on tour not intimidated by him. Rocco was one of those people — along with good friends like Mark O'Meara and John Cook — and Tiger felt comfortable with him, on the golf course and off it.

"We were friends almost from the beginning," Woods said during the 2008 Open. "Rocc was always a guy who was easy to be around. He's been a good friend, a real friend almost since the day I got out here."

While Woods's career was skyrocketing, Rocco's was doing just fine. His victory at the Buick Open in 2000 helped him win more than $1 million in a season for the first time: $1,320,278. He made even more than that over the next three years, peaking in 2002, when he made $2,040,676. Those winnings were once again a reflection of the post-Tiger boom in purses. Just eleven years earlier, Rocco had made just under $600,000 for the year and had finished 16th on the money list. The $2 million–plus he made in '02 landed him 21st on the money list.

In 2001, Rocco seriously contended in a major for the first

time. As consistently as he had played for most of his career, he had never been able to play well in the majors. During his first fifteen years on tour, he had played in twenty-five majors and had only finished in the top 20 twice: a tie for 16th place in the 1991 PGA Championship and a tie for 18th in the 1996 British Open.

"I actually had a chance for three rounds at the [U.S.] Open at Pebble in '92," he said. "But then, that last day when the wind blew so bad, I shot 80-something [84] and dropped way back. I think I finished a millionth." Close—he was tied for 44th after a day in which more than half the field shot higher than 80 in gale-force winds.

It always bothered Rocco that he hadn't played better in the majors. Like every golfer, he cherished the majors and had grown up dreaming about playing in them and playing well in them.

"I love them all for different reasons," he said. "I mean, the Masters is great—the golf course, all the traditions, the green jacket—I love going there. The British Open is *so* different than anything we see all year long. I love the golf courses and the wind and the way you have to play the ball on the ground. The PGA is probably the fairest test of the four—the golf course is always hard but never brutal.

"But the [U.S.] Open has always been my favorite tournament. It's our national championship, and that means a lot to me. I still remember watching Watson chip in at Pebble Beach [in 1982] to beat Nicklaus and jumping out of my chair screaming. That was so exciting, I almost felt like *I'd* chipped the damn ball in.

"I've always liked the fact that when you go to the Open you know, you just know, it's going to be ridiculously hard. I don't mean that to sound like it's unfair. Sometimes, yes, they've let it go too far. That's the tough thing about what they do. You can push the golf course right to the brink and it's absolutely great, or you can go over that brink by just a little bit and then people start screaming.

"I thought Tom Meeks did a really good job when he was setting up the golf courses for the USGA. Wonderful man. I really like him. But I also like—no, I love—what Mike Davis has done since he took over the last few years. When I go to the Open I always feel like a little kid because I'm so excited to be there."

The 2001 majors season got off to a great start for Rocco when he finished 15th at the Masters. He actually got to within four shots of the lead, held (surprise) by Tiger Woods, on Saturday after shooting a 66. That put him in one of the late groups on Sunday afternoon and gave him an outside chance—really outside—to win. He shot 73: disappointing but not devastating.

"I would like to have played better, obviously," he said. "But it was really the first time I'd played late there on Sunday, so it was a new experience—a good one, but a new one for sure. Plus, I think I'd have had to shoot 59 to catch Tiger, so it wasn't like I blew a chance to win by not playing well."

Actually, a 64 would have caught Woods, but no one else in the field came close to that score—one shot higher than the course record—that afternoon. So Rocco walked away feeling pretty good about his performance. Not only was that his highest finish ever in a major, but it guaranteed him a spot in the Masters in 2002 regardless of how he played for the rest of the year, since the top 16 finishers in each Masters are guaranteed a spot in the tournament a year later.

He arrived in Tulsa for the 2001 U.S. Open at Southern Hills feeling good about his game. He liked the golf course and he liked the setup. He didn't even mind the hot weather. "Could have been worse," he said. "It was hot, but not crazy hot."

There was just one problem: his back. "It would still hurt me periodically," he said. "It hadn't gotten to the point where I fell down or couldn't play at all for a good long while, but some days it would just be cranky."

On Wednesday, as Rocco was hitting balls on the range with Rick Smith watching, the back was very cranky. "I told him he should withdraw," Smith said. "I mean, he was in real pain. The first couple of days he was practically chipping the ball around the golf course. How he did what he did I'll never know."

Unable to take a full swing, he still played solid golf for two days. By Friday night, after a lot of Advil and time in the fitness trailer, he felt better. The hot weather no doubt helped too. On Saturday—just as at Augusta—he really got rolling, shooting a three-under-par 67 to pull within one shot of coleaders Retief Goosen and Stewart Cink going into the final round. That put him in the second-to-last group on Sunday, and he went to bed Saturday night knowing he had a legitimate chance to win the U.S. Open. Not only was he one shot out of the lead, but Woods—having one of his rare off weeks—was nowhere in sight of the leader board. Rocco would be competing against other mortals on Sunday.

"I loved the way it felt to know I had a real chance to win," he said. "A lot of times you go to bed on Saturday night at a tournament thinking, 'If I can go real low on Sunday I have a chance.' And there are times when that happens, but it doesn't happen very often. To go to bed knowing you can just go out and keep playing the way you've been playing and it can be good enough to win is exciting."

He played well again on Sunday, continuing to find fairways and greens consistently. But his putter failed him in the clutch. Two three-putts on the back nine doomed his chances. He ended the day shooting a respectable 72. That left him alone in fourth place, two shots behind Goosen and Mark Brooks, who played off the next day for the championship, and one shot behind Cink.

"Obviously I'd have loved to have had those three-putts back, but I wasn't exactly the Lone Ranger that day," Rocco said, referencing the fact that Goosen and Cink both three-putted the 18th green, Goosen from five feet to create the playoff with Brooks. "I was happy with myself in that my swing held up in the heat and I hung in there and had a chance. Most of all I came away feeling like I wanted to be there again—to have that chance to win, at any major but especially at an Open."

Even though he continued to play well the rest of the year, the back still flared up periodically, getting stiff and tight and making it hard to take a full swing. Four times he was forced to withdraw from tournaments—including the British Open—after the first round. "That was a huge disappointment," he said. "To go over there, to be playing in a major and not be able to tee it up, to be honest, it just sucked."

But he had reached the point where he accepted the fact that his back was going to give him trouble at times. He had a surgically repaired back, he was in a constant battle to keep his weight down, and he played golf for a living. That was his life.

"Do I wonder at times what kind of career I might have had

if I hadn't had the back problems?" he said. "Occasionally. But not too often. For one thing, there's no point; it doesn't change things. For another, I know I'm lucky to have played as much as I've played for as long as I've played and to play as well as I've played."

He had another top ten finish in a major in 2002, finishing sixth at the PGA Championship, five shots behind winner Rich Beem. That performance, along with the win at Greensboro, helped him put together his best year on tour, which, as he pointed out, wasn't a bad thing, with his fortieth birthday falling that year in December.

"Things were good during that period," he said. "I was healthy, I was playing well, I was able to take enough time off during the year that I had a chance to be with the boys and got to watch them grow up. I never pushed them to get into organized sports. I always thought if you did that it meant they would be running in different directions all the time. If they wanted to play a sport, that was fine. But I didn't want all our family time spent in cars going to different ball games every weekend when I was home.

"They're pretty good athletes. They play some golf. But none of them is obsessed with a sport the way I became obsessed with golf. To be honest, I think that's a good thing."

Linda was traveling far less now with three children at home, but Rocco still felt as if the marriage was on solid ground. "At the very least, we were both very devoted to raising our children," he said. "Maybe I was a little selfish at times because I spent time with the boys and with my friends but not as much time as I should have spent with her. But I don't think it caused any problems back then. She was very patient with me."

Linda remembers those years—after the birth of Marco, when Rocco was healthy and playing well—as quite happy.

"It's never easy when your husband is away a lot or when your father is away a lot," she said. "And I really didn't travel at all after Marco was born. But Rocco was happy, and that made things better for everyone when he was at home. Plus, I actually had time to get to know people in the community and to feel as if I was a part of it. The first few years we were married I traveled so much all my friends were people on the tour. That changed when I got off the road. I really felt comfortable living where we were living."

The following year, 2002, was a lot like 2001. Rocco played well, but the back continued to flare up at times. When he asked Dr. Day about it, the doctor told him that was the way it was going to be as long as he played golf. His back was healed, but it was never going to be as strong or pain resistant as it had been before he was hurt—especially playing golf for a living. There was nothing as dramatic as the three-wood at Vegas in '93, just some nagging pain. He worked on his rehab exercises, made sure he got stretched in the trailer before he played, and felt fine on the golf course more often than not.

It was also that year that he and Linda—"really me, a lot more than her"—decided to move south to Naples. The winter weather there was warmer than in north Florida, there were more good golf courses, and Rocco had heard the schools were excellent. He bought a piece of property near the water and began building a house almost as big as the one in Ponte Vedra.

"Looking back, it was a mistake," he said. "I thought the golf would be better, the schools would be better, everything would be better. In the end, the schools were worse—we ended up putting all three boys in private schools for a while—and the hassles involved with moving and building a house and maintaining a house like that weren't worth it. We had a comfortable, familiar way of life in Ponte Vedra and we left it all behind. If I had thought the thing through more thoroughly, we probably never would have moved."

Of course, it isn't Rocco's way to sit and think things through in great detail. Once he knows an idea makes sense, he acts on it instantly. He is the kind of person who never tells a waiter in a restaurant he needs a few minutes to look at the menu. He walks in knowing exactly what he's going to order.

Which is why Linda knew it was pointless to argue with him when he started talking excitedly about moving to Naples. "When you are an athlete's wife, you have to understand that in the end it is all about them," she said. "I knew that for a long time. When he wanted to go to Naples, it wasn't something we were going to debate, it was something we were going to do."

Rocco didn't win again that year, but he finished second twice—at the season-opening Mercedes Championships and then in September at the Deutsche Bank Championships. He went into the last full-field event of the year needing only to make the cut to qualify for the Tour Championships—and didn't make the cut. That was a disappointment. Even so, he finished the year with $1,832,656 in earnings—a good thing given the cost of the new house. By then he had signed with Callaway and was making good money off the golf course too, since he was frequently asked to do corporate outings as a well-known player with a reputation for being outgoing and friendly.

"He was a good Monday guy," Zoracki said. "Outings are held on Mondays, and Rocco's reputation was as a guy you wanted at your outing. He learned a lot from Arnold about making people feel comfortable when he was with them."

That year also produced one of the bigger thrills of his career even though it came at an event watched by almost no one that meant almost nothing. Having turned forty at the end of 2002, he was invited to play in something called the UBS Cup—a corporate-run Ryder Cup–copycat event that matched players over the age of forty from the U.S. against a "Rest of the World" team of players over forty.

The event was staged by IMG, the management giant that represents, among many others, Tiger Woods and Arnold Palmer, and it was held in Sea Island, Georgia—one of the more scenic places on earth.

Palmer was the U.S. captain. Getting to play on a team headed by Palmer was a big deal in itself for Rocco. Getting to represent the United States in an event that wasn't the Ryder Cup or even the Presidents Cup was also exciting. But the best part of the weekend was getting to be Tom Watson's teammate for one of the matches.

"I actually went to Arnold and said to him, 'Can I please play with Tom one day,'" Rocco said, laughing. "I was like a little kid. All the years I'd been on tour I had never even been paired with him. The thought of being his teammate was almost more than I could handle. In fact, it was more than I could handle. I played terribly. I was so nervous."

That weekend was a tough one for Watson. His close friend and caddy Bruce Edwards was in the latter stages of ALS and was caddying for him (in a cart) for what he knew would be the last time. "If anyone could have cheered me up under those circumstances, it would have been Rocco," Watson said. "He certainly tried. The problem was, neither one of us played very well."

"Yeah, let's blame the loss on him," Rocco said. "But in truth, that isn't fair. I was so nervous I could barely swing a club."

A couple of weeks after the UBS Cup, Rocco was at home playing with Mark Murphy, a friend he had met in Ireland while playing at Waterville in 2000. Murphy was a pro who played on the European Futures Tour—the equivalent of the U.S. Nation-wide Tour.

"I went down again while we were playing," Rocco said. "It didn't seem to be that bad at first, but by the time we got off the course and got home, Murph practically had to carry me into the house. It got better after I rested it, but I wondered if I was in trouble again."

The trouble wasn't as bad as it had been ten years earlier. He hadn't ruptured anything, and Dr. Day told him he didn't think he needed any more surgery or, for that matter, that surgery would do any good. "He just said the same thing to me again: You have a bad back—period. When you cut on one part, even after it gets strong again, there's always going to be extra pres-sure on other places in the back. Sometimes it will feel okay. Other times it won't. Basically he said I had to live with it—keep doing what I was doing with my exercises, keep my weight down because that was always going to be a factor—and hope that I could play pain-free more often than not.

"I'd had a good run with only occasional flare-ups of pain— seven years. But I wasn't getting any younger—I was forty-one, and that's a time in life when guys who have played a lot of golf and have good backs sometimes run into trouble. In a way, it was almost predictable."

So were his struggles in 2004. He was on and off the tour throughout the year, and even when he played, he didn't play well. He got to play in only 19 tournaments and made only eight cuts all year—his lowest total since 1995, when he had sat out the second half of the year. He only finished in the top 20 twice—a tie for 16th in his first tournament of the year, the Bob Hope, and a tie for 15th at the International, in August.

In many ways, '04 was like '94 and '95 had been. Week to week he didn't know if his back was going to allow him to play. He had to withdraw from Bay Hill when the back went on him during a practice round. He only got to play in two of the four majors—the Masters and the PGA. By autumn he knew he was in serious danger of falling out of the top 125 on the money list for the first time since his rookie year.

"I tried to play the last four [tournaments] that year because it was a matter of pride for me to try to get into the top 125," he said. "I knew I had the top 50 list to fall back on, but I didn't want to do it. I wanted to save it in case I needed it for later."

The top 50 list is the tour's list of all-time-leading money winners. It is, needless to say, top-heavy with today's players, since purses today completely dwarf those of the past. To get a sense of how ridiculous today's money is compared to that of the past—even the recent past—consider the career money totals of three of the greatest players of all time: Sam Snead, Arnold Palmer, and Jack Nicklaus.

Snead won 82 times on tour—still the all-time record—and won a total of $487,000 in prize money for his career—which is less money than a player receives these days for a second-place finish in one tournament. Palmer, fifteen years younger than Snead, won 62 times during his career, good for $1,861,857. That haul—he teed it up in 734 tournaments—would have placed him 45th on the money list for the 2008 season. Nicklaus, ten years younger than Palmer, had the most dominant career in history until Woods came along. He played in 594 tournaments and won 73 times. His earnings were $5,734,322—meaning his career earnings would have placed him third on the 2008 money list.

Through 2004, Rocco had earned a little more than $11.3 million in his career. That put him in 47th place on the all-time money list, largely on the strength of that five-year period from 1999 through 2003 when his lowest money total for a year was $963,075. The tour allows any player who is in the top 50 on the career money list a one-year exemption if he finishes out of the top 125 at the end of a year. Most players who are in the top 50 like to hold on to that exemption to use when they get close to age fifty and their game falls off a bit and they are waiting to be eligible for the Champions Tour.

"I would have preferred to never need it," Rocco said. "If I was going to need it, I'd rather have needed it when I was forty-nine. I was forty-two. But I had no choice. I knew I couldn't get any kind of medical, especially since I had played the last four tournaments of the year, even if my total starts had been six less than my usual number. I had to use the top 50 exemption and hope I was healthy enough to play well the next year. If I couldn't do it, then it would be time to start thinking about alternatives."

He smiled. "I told my mom that at least if I needed a fallback plan it would come twenty years later than she had thought it would."

Donna Mediate laughed when the subject of Rocco's fallback plan came up late in 2008. "I still like to think he's going to finish college," she said. "But I think I know better by now."

7

The Slide

LOOKING BACK NOW, ROCCO CAN SEE that his life was not in especially good shape in 2004, 2005, and 2006.

The back pain had become more persistent, and he was worried about his golf career. The move to Naples had been expensive and had not gone terribly well in any sense: The kids had struggled with the move and with their new schools. Linda wasn't happy because they weren't happy and because she could see that Rocco wasn't happy. Rocco was also drinking more than he could remember drinking in the past.

"I didn't like taking too many painkillers," he said. "I mean, I tried all different kinds of prescriptions and they helped at times, not so much at others. After a while, when I was home and the pain was bad, scotch became my painkiller. It masked a lot of the pain, but, looking back now, I realize it was masking more than just back pain."

The Mediates had been married for almost twenty years. They had worked hard to raise their three boys, but the combination of Rocco's travel and his back woes had caused them to drift apart. To say that this happens often to players on the PGA

Tour is a little like saying that 2008 was not an especially good year for the economy.

Golf is probably tougher on marriages than any other professional sport. In team sports, players are home for half the season and there is usually an off-season that lasts at least four months. It can still be tough, but there are long stretches built in where players are home, and even in-season, they are never away for more than two weeks at any one time — usually less than that. Football players have by far the best life in that sense. Other than three weeks of training camp, they make no more than a dozen road trips — all of them, with the exception of a Super Bowl, overnight.

Golfers might get one or two home games in a year if they happen to live in a city that hosts one or, in the case of a couple of Florida cities, two PGA Tour events. The tour season begins in early January and stretches for most players into early November. Some players in need of extra cash will then play "Silly Season" events — unofficial late-year tournaments where the money doesn't count toward the official money list but does count toward paying bills.

Because golfers tend to have their peak years later than most athletes, they are often away playing while their families are growing up. Team sport athletes are frequently retired by thirty-five — if not sooner — and thus home in most cases by the time their kids are old enough to go to school. Tennis players, the only other major sport athletes who don't have a home-and-away schedule, are usually retired by thirty.

"It's a good news, bad news story," said Davis Love III, who was a comeback story in 2008 when he won a tournament for the first time in two years after suffering a serious ankle injury at the end of 2007. "On the one hand, it's great that I can still realistically be out here competing when I'm forty-four years old. On the other hand, I have a daughter who is now in college and a son who is in high school, and I've spent long chunks of time away from home working at my job while they've been growing up."

It takes a strong marriage to survive all that time away, especially when the wife is left home alone for lengthy stretches to take care of school-age children. "Even in the summertime, when in theory your family can be out on tour with you, they really don't want to be there," Rocco said. "Why should they? They have friends at home and activities and it's a lot more fun than schlepping around from one hotel to another. Even if you have enough money to rent a house at times or stay in a really nice hotel suite, it isn't the same as being at home and being with your friends. If I were them, I'd rather be home too."

Some players travel the tour in RV's to try to make it easier for their families to come with them. Others, as Rocco says, spend the money to rent houses for a week at tour stops rather than putting their families through life in a hotel. But most understand that, in the end, they are going to have to spend long periods of time on the road without their families.

Family life for those who play on the tour was best described years ago by 1992 U.S. Open champion Tom Kite. "When you're at home," he said, "you feel like you're missing something by not being out on tour. When you're out on tour, you know you're missing something by not being at home."

What makes those gaps in family life bearable for those who

play the tour is the fact that they are being paid—quite hand-somely when they play well—to play a game they love. They enjoy the camaraderie of the locker room and they revel in the competition and the chance to test themselves from week to week.

"It's like anything else," Rocco said. "When you're playing well, the weeks fly by. You look up in September and say, 'Where did the year go?' But when you're struggling or when you're hurt or—God forbid—you're hurt and you're struggling, every week feels like a month out there."

That's the way it was for Rocco for most of three years. What made it worse was that he understood that he wasn't doing all that good a job at home either. "I was so focused on the idea of getting better, of figuring out a way to be healthy and to play good golf again, that I probably wasn't paying as much attention to the kids when I was home as I should have been. And I know for sure that I wasn't paying enough attention to my marriage."

A struggling player can easily find his life becoming a vicious circle: He is miserable on tour because he's playing poorly; then he's miserable at home because he's brooding about his play and he finds no solace in his family, which is a lot more interested in his role as husband and dad than golfer. It is a large part of the reason why the divorce rate on the PGA Tour is extremely high. Second marriages are so frequent that players often refer to their second wives as "mulligans."

"I don't think I was brooding during that period so much as I just wasn't there emotionally," Rocco said. "I was usually doing one of two things: trying to find a way to get the pain to go away or, if I couldn't do that, drinking scotch to mask the pain. Either way, it wasn't exactly ideal."

He was also playing a lot of online poker. He had started playing when he was at home and couldn't do anything except sit around the house and hope the pain would go away. "There were days when I was home where I had nothing to do for seven, eight hours because if I tried to walk down the hall, I risked falling down," he said. "I was bored, so I started playing. For a few years I was hooked on it, playing it for hours and hours. After a while I realized I needed to stop. It was like anything you get addicted to—it was something I needed to stop. But it took me a while to get to that point."

Life was equally difficult for Linda. She understood that Rocco was in pain and that he was upset about his golf. But the drinking, understandably, bothered her. So did the obsession with poker.

"If he wasn't playing with people in the house, he was playing online," she said. "It was as if he needed that, since he couldn't compete the way he wanted to compete on the golf course."

Discovering poker as an outlet wasn't all that different for Rocco than discovering golf as a teenager had been. He wanted to play all the time, compete all the time, and try to get better. In 2005, he made it to the World Series of Poker's Main Event—held in Las Vegas—and finished 600th out of 5,619 players. That was the good news. The bad news was that the time spent playing poker was more time away from the family and, unlike golf, was not exactly a moneymaker for him.

By the end of 2004, Rocco was in a state of near panic about his golf future. At the urging of Leonard Thompson, one of his tour buddies, he went to see Jimmy Ballard in Miami. Ballard has a reputation not only as one of the top teachers around—he has worked with, among others, Curtis Strange, Steve Ballesteros, Sandy Lyle,

Peter Jacobsen, and Hal Sutton—but as someone who teaches a swing that relieves pressure on the back. That's why Thompson recommended that Rocco go see him.

"It was one of the better moves I've ever made," Rocco said. "Rick [Smith] understood. A lot of what Jimmy does is similar to what Rick and Jim Ferree teach, but he has this 'connection' theory that relieves pressure on the back."

Ballard believes that if Rocco had come to him early in his career, he never would have had back problems. "First time I saw him was when he won at Doral in '91," he said. "He had a very good golf swing, but I could see it was putting pressure on his back that was going to cause problems."

Ballard learned his theory of the golf swing from Sam Byrd, who was once Babe Ruth's backup on the New York Yankees. Byrd is still the only man to play Major League baseball and win a tournament on the PGA Tour, and he lost to Byron Nelson in the final of the PGA Championship (it was a match play event then) in 1945.

"Sam got the yips that day," Ballard said. "Otherwise he'd have won."

The Byrd-Ballard swing does take pressure off the back. Rocco adjusted his swing and it helped his back. "Didn't cure me, because I was already hurt," he said. "But if I hadn't gone to Jimmy and hadn't changed my swing when I did, I probably would have been done by the end of the next year, because it was getting nothing but worse. He saved my career."

He still goes to see Ballard and in 2008 took Paul Azinger to see him when Azinger's back problems flared again. "Because of the guys I've worked with—Ferree, Smith, Ballard—and because of how much I've studied the swing through the years,

I know a lot about the golf swing," he said. "Usually I would tell you that any player on tour who goes to another pro [which happens frequently] for help with his swing is crazy—but I knew Jimmy could help Zinger."

Listening to Rocco and Ballard discuss the Sam Byrd theory of the golf swing is a little bit like listening to Swahili. They are speaking another language, but it is one they are both quite comfortable speaking.

Playing on his one-time top 50 exemption in 2005, Rocco continued to struggle the first half of the year, with the exception of a good week in Los Angeles, when the back held up and he managed to tie for 13th place. Everything else was either bad or worse. He had to withdraw two weeks in a row in May, first in New Orleans and then in Charlotte. His spring résumé looked like this: WD–WD–Cut–Cut–T65.

The T65 in Washington was the first time he had played on a weekend since March. "Believe it or not, it gave me some confidence," he said. "It wasn't so much that I played well as I played four straight rounds of golf on a good golf course [Congressional] without any serious pain."

That brief feel-good moment took him to Pinehurst for the U.S. Open. He opened there with a 67, which was good enough to tie him with John Daly for the lead. He played solidly the last three rounds and even though he was never in serious contention to win, he was thrilled to finish tied for sixth place. It was good for his confidence and it was good for his bank account. Unlike the previous year, he had no fallback if he didn't finish in the top 125. The thought of going back to Q-School a few weeks before turning forty-three didn't thrill him.

"All I could do was hope the pain would stay away," he said.

"The Open told me that when I was healthy, or even semi-healthy, I was still plenty good enough to compete. The key was being able to walk 18 holes every day and take a full swing at the golf ball. That doesn't sound like much to ask, but for me at that point it was everything."

The 2005 Open turned his year around. He ended up making 12 of his last 14 cuts and had to withdraw only one more time, and that wasn't until October in Greensboro. As a two-time champion, he felt bad about having to pull out, but he wasn't going to take any chances. By then, he had made enough money to preserve his spot in the top 125. He finished the year with $696,250, which was good enough for 121st place on the money list. Hardly spectacular, but Rocco wasn't complaining.

"I had kept my job for another year," he said. "I understood that given my age and my back, that was no small thing for me."

Unfortunately, the first half of 2006 didn't go as well as the second half of 2005 had. The early part of the year was again a struggle. He missed his first three cuts and four of his first five, a tie for 48th place at Doral being the only check he cashed prior to the Players Championship, where he tied for 58th. His goal in the spring was to be healthy for the Masters. Even though he hadn't been in the top 100 on the money list for two years, he was still exempt into the Masters because of his sixth-place finish at Pinehurst. He arrived at Augusta, having taken the week off prior to the tournament, feeling rested and ready, he hoped, for a good week.

"Other than '01, I had never really played very well there," he said. "It wasn't because I didn't like the golf course, because I did. It could have been because putting is so important there, and for a long time I wasn't a great putter. But really, if you think about it, striking the ball there is extremely important because if you don't drive the ball to the right spots on the fairway, you have almost no chance of getting close to the pins. You have to be in certain places to have a chance. That part of my game has always been a strength."

He got the week off to a good start on Thursday by shooting a four-under-par 68. The golf course had been lengthened to more than 7,500 yards by the Augusta National membership as part of a redesign that began soon after Tiger Woods shot an 18-under-par 270 there in 1997, so any under par round at Augusta National was now a good day. Winning scores have been consistently higher in recent years at the Masters, topping out in 2007, when Zach Johnson won at one-over-par 289 after a week in which the winds blew every day.

In 2006, the tournament was plagued by rain delays. By the time darkness closed in on Saturday, most of the leaders were still in the early stage of their third rounds. Rocco, who had shot 73 in the second round to stay within striking range of the leaders, had played only four holes. The players had to return to the golf course to resume play at 7:30 the next morning, meaning about a 5 A.M. wake-up call for most.

Rocco continued to play well Sunday morning. He was three under par for the tournament, trailing Phil Mickelson by only two shots, when he arrived at the par-five 15th hole. He hit a perfect drive down the right side of the fairway and had a three-iron to the green

"The ball was a little bit above my feet, but it was still a shot I felt good about," he said. "The ground was still wet from all the rain. When I swung down at the ball, my foot slipped."

Rick Smith, who was out walking with Rocco, saw his foot

slip and saw him reach for his back. "I knew it was trouble right away," he said. "I'd been thinking I'd have both my guys in the last group for the afternoon [Smith was also working with Mickelson back then], and then I saw Rocco grab his back. My next thought was, 'Can he finish the round?'"

He finished, still in contention at two under par, tied for fourth place just two shots behind Mickelson, who had made a late bogey to fall to four under. Rocco went straight to the fitness trailer to be worked on before he had to tee it up for the final round.

"We had a couple hours," he said. "By the time I got out of there, I felt a lot better. I thought I might be able to make it through the round.

"So much can happen there on Sunday afternoon," he said. "Even with all the changes to the golf course, you still have holes where you can go low and you can go high. I was as excited going into that last round as I think I've ever been at a golf tournament. I thought if the back would hold up I had a legitimate chance to win."

He felt exactly the same way standing on the ninth tee that afternoon tied for the lead. The ninth hole at Augusta National is a short but extremely difficult par-four. Players drive the ball straight down a hill and then must play their second shot straight up a hill to a green that tilts back to front. The Sunday pin placement is always near the front of the green. Any shot that lands pin-high or below the pin almost always rolls off the green and back down the hill, leaving a difficult pitch to try to get close enough to salvage a par.

In 1996, still leading Nick Faldo by three shots playing the ninth hole, Greg Norman hit a second shot that landed no more than a foot from the hole. But the ball spun back off the green and halfway down the hill. Norman made bogey; the lead, which might have jumped back to four shots had he hit his second shot a few feet farther, went to two shots; and Faldo ended up winning by five shots as Norman completed one of the most famous final-day collapses in major championship history.

Ten years later, Rocco hit a perfect drive down the hill but knew he had a problem when he got to his ball. He was on a sidehill lie, and he was afraid that when he swung he might slip again. "I tried as best I could to stay absolutely still over the ball," he said. "The amazing thing is I hit a hell of a shot."

The nine-iron shot flew directly at the hole and hit the bottom of the flagstick. It could have dropped in or it could have stopped near the hole. It did neither. If it had just missed the stick, it might have settled close to the hole. Instead, it bounced backward off the green and halfway down the hill. At that moment Rocco didn't really care where the ball was. His back had gone on him again the instant he followed through on the shot.

"I hit the ball pretty much exactly the way I wanted to hit it," he said. "For a second I thought it was perfect. In a sense, it almost was. But I knew my back was gone. I could barely get up the hill to where my ball was. For an instant I thought I might go down, which I certainly didn't want to do with all those people around the green, not to mention all the people watching on television. Sunday at the Masters—how many people do you think are watching? A billion, a trillion?"

Certainly millions. Rocco managed to make it up the hill to his ball and, under the circumstances, made a miraculous par, chipping the ball to four feet and making the putt. But as he walked off the green, he knew he was in serious trouble.

"I'd felt that pain enough times in my life that I knew exactly what it was and exactly how badly I was hurt," he said. "If I hadn't been so high up on the leader board, I would have walked straight off the green and into the clubhouse because, realistically, I knew I was done. But given where I was, I had to at least try. I was about 99.999 percent sure I wasn't going to win. But I was hoping I could somehow get through the back nine and still finish at least in the top ten."

He couldn't. Walking down the hill on the 10th fairway was murderous, and by the time he reached the 12th tee he was one over par on the back nine (having just missed making a five-foot par putt at the 11th), in extreme pain, and fading fast.

The 12th hole at Augusta National is a tiny little par-three that is listed on the scorecard as being 150 yards long. It is the middle hole on the treacherous three-hole swing dubbed "Amen Corner" by the great Herbert Warren Wind because players in contention on Masters Sunday pray they get through these holes — water is in play at each of them — unscathed.

The 12th at Augusta has frequently been the hole where Sunday dreams come to die at the Masters. Although players rarely hit more than a nine-iron off the tee — often only a pitching wedge is called for — they must carve a precise shot over Rae's Creek to a tiny green. Miss short and you are wet. Miss long and you are in a bunker or a flower patch, aiming your second shot downhill in the direction of the creek.

"Any time you are in contention and you stand on that tee, you get the shakes," said Fred Couples, the 1992 Masters champion who may have caught the luckiest break in Masters history on 12 the year that he won the tournament. His tee shot came up short of the green and seemed destined to slide back into the water. Somehow, the ball got stuck on a tuft of grass and stayed there, allowing Couples to chip up, make par, and win by two shots. "I knew when the ball stayed up it was my day to win," he has often said when the subject of that shot comes up.

Rocco wasn't shaking standing on the 12th tee—his back hurt too much for him to be nervous. He took an eight-iron even with the hole playing short and he hoped he could take an easy swing and have enough club to clear the creek.

"I almost made it," he said later. "When the ball was in the air, I thought it might get to the front of the green and I'd be okay. Then I could see it was short and I was hoping it might somehow stay dry."

It didn't. It came up just short of clearing the water. The silence as the ball hit the water was deafening. Rocco walked to the drop area, hoping he could get his wedge close enough to salvage a bogey. Instead, he went into the water again. The all-time record for turning the 12th into a nightmare is a 13, set by Rocco's onetime mentor Tom Weiskopf in 1977. Rocco didn't get to the record, but he came close. He hit three balls into the water from the drop area.

"I was honestly beginning to think I might never get the ball on the green," he said. "In fact, the thought crossed my mind, 'Am I going to run out of golf balls?' If I did, that's it, I have to walk back in, I'm done. Fortunately I had a dozen balls in the bag. The fourth shot from the drop area I actually hit pretty well."

He got it to five feet and made the putt for 10. Any hope for a top ten or even a solid finish drowned in Rae's Creek.

"If I'd been smart, I'd have walked in right then," he said. "But I didn't want to look like I was quitting because I'd made a mess of 12. At that point, like it or not, I had to find a way to finish."

He did, actually playing respectable golf on the last six holes to shoot 45 on the back nine. That was nine over par, seven of those nine shots coming on the tiny 12th. He signed for an 80, which left him tied for 36th place, and went home knowing he wasn't going to play golf for a while.

"Hilton Head [the week after the Masters] is usually one of my favorite events," he said. "There was no way I could play there."

He went home to rest and get the back treated. He wasn't sure what was more upsetting, getting hurt again or getting hurt at a moment when he had a real chance to win the Masters. He was beginning to wonder if he was ever going to be healthy again.

"Dr. Day had told me this was the way it was going to be," he said. "I didn't have a ruptured disk like I'd had when he did the surgery. I still had a bad back. It's the kind of thing where if you don't play golf for a living, it can be annoying and at times painful, but you can function. But if you play golf for a living, there are going to be times when you can't. And you never know when it's going to happen. That was probably the worst part of it."

He came back to play a month after the Masters in Charlotte. He managed to make the cut there—finishing in a tie for 59th place—but the rest of the year was a lot like 2004: stops and starts, the back flaring up, the back feeling a little better.

"If I'd been smart I would have just stopped playing," he said. "I would have rested it for a long time and maybe gone to see someone about a different kind of rehab program because clearly what I was doing wasn't working. There were times when I would be home alone and I would walk down the hall to get something and I would just go down. I would have two options:

Lie there until someone came home to help me, or crawl to a chair or into my bed. At times I felt like a complete cripple.

"The pain wasn't even the worst part; the frustration was. I had the feeling this was something that was never going to go away, that I had probably been lucky to play healthy for as long as I had and this was it. I really thought there was a good chance I was done—especially since it didn't look like I was going to make enough money to keep my card."

He ended up playing only ten more tournaments after the Masters. He shot a 68 the first day at Westchester but had to withdraw because the back went on him again. This time he was out for six weeks trying to get healthy. He attempted to play the Buick Open, a tournament he had won in 2000, and had to withdraw again. That led to another six-week break before he was finally able to play in five events in the fall. He managed to make four straight cuts, but except for the tournament at Jackson—a second-tier event that was played at the same time as a lucrative World Golf Championship tournament—he never finished higher than 50th. He was 16th at Jackson, but with the purse not as high as most weeks, that was worth only $39,400.

When the painful year was finally over, he had entered eighteen events and made eight cuts. His winnings were a paltry $145,899, by far his lowest total since he had returned from back surgery in 1996. He finished 227th on the money list and found himself asking the tour for a medical extension at the start of 2007.

This time the tour was generous. Because he had been forced to withdraw from three tournaments, the board deemed Rocco to have played only fifteen times. He had averaged between 23 and 25 starts a year when healthy, so he was given ten tournaments at the start of 2007 to make a little more than $450,000—which would give him combined earnings of more than $660,000, which had been the total earned by Darren Clarke, who had finished in 125th place on the 2006 money list.

Rocco was relieved to be given a reprieve at the start of 2007, but he knew it wouldn't do him any good if he continued to feel the same kind of back pain he had felt through most of 2006. For the first time in his life, he found himself thinking in terms of a backup plan.

"I thought resting for a couple of months, really resting, might help," he said. "But I'd taken a couple long breaks in '06 and had come back and still had problems. It was better in the fall but not good enough. I had to be realistic: I needed to play well in the ten tournaments they'd given me or I was going to be reduced to asking for sponsor exemptions. I had to think about an alternative if things didn't work out."

As luck would have it, just when he was thinking about an alternative, one came along—at least a temporary one. New TV contracts had been negotiated by the tour beginning in 2007. Included in the package for the first time was the Golf Channel. ESPN had opted out of most golf coverage, since it was paying Tiger Woods prices to televise tournaments that almost never included Woods. USA Network, which televised Thursday–Friday rounds of numerous tournaments, also opted out.

That opened a door for Golf Channel, which had previously been allowed to televise Champions (Senior) Tour events and Nationwide (Triple-A) Tour events but never the PGA Tour. Under the new deal, Golf Channel had the Thursday–Friday rights to every PGA Tour event and would televise the entire week of all the Fall Series events and the first three tournaments of the year: the Mercedes Championships, the Sony Open in Hawaii, and the Bob Hope Chrysler Classic. Those three January events were on weekends when the NFL was televising playoff games, and none of the networks wanted to compete with that.

The new deal meant Golf Channel needed to hire a lot of people. Networks that televise golf are constantly looking for ex-players who can translate their understanding of the game to a microphone. For every one who can, there are at least a dozen who can't. Knowing that Rocco's playing future was murky after his injury-riddled 2006 and knowing that he had always been glib and comfortable in front of a camera, Golf Channel offered him the chance to work the first three tournaments.

"I figured why not give it a shot," he said. "I wasn't in the Mercedes anyway and I didn't usually play Hawaii. It was a chance for me to see if I was any good at it and to maybe give myself a fallback position if the back didn't get any better."

It was, in effect, a tryout for both sides.

The three weeks went well. Rocco enjoyed himself, the Golf Channel people liked what they saw. There was definitely a sense that this could be something Rocco could do when the time came for him to stop playing.

He still wanted to play. But as he headed to Phoenix to return to playing the game rather than talking about the game, he knew he might be ten tournaments away from asking for a more permanent chance to wield a microphone.

"The thought that I might be done—I mean really done—crossed my mind. I'd been scared after the surgery but convinced

I would work my way back and be able to play again. Now, though, there was no reason to believe that was going to be the case. I'd done the work. I'd had the best care. I'd tried everything and I was still struggling.

"I didn't know what was going to happen next."

8

Cindi

BACK ON THE GOLF COURSE with his clubs rather than a microphone, Rocco didn't start 2007 any better than he had ended 2006. In fact, he started worse.

"At least at the end of '06 I was making cuts," he said. "Out of the box in '07, I couldn't crack an egg."

He hadn't played in a tournament for three months when he teed it up at the FBR Open in Phoenix. Perhaps it was just rust, but he missed the cut by, as he likes to say, "a million." Actually, it was by three shots. A week later at Pebble Beach, a place where he had made the cut as a rookie when he was convinced he wasn't good enough to play on tour, he missed the cut again—this time by a whopping nine shots. He had eight tournaments left to make the money he needed to remain an exempt player.

During those first few weeks on tour, Linda and the kids had traveled with him. Linda had decided at the end of 2006 to take the kids out of school, enroll them in an online homeschooling program, and bring them on tour with Rocco.

During 2005 and 2006, Rocco and Linda had talked at times about divorce. According to Linda, she was the one who initiated the conversations, wondering if separating might make them both happier. Rocco, she said, wouldn't hear of it.

Linda had been so unhappy during that period that she went to therapy. She finally decided that maybe—just maybe—if the entire family was together on the road for an extended period of time, it might bring them all back together.

"To be honest, it didn't work," she said. "Rocco was miserable. Whether it was because he was playing poorly or because he wasn't used to having us on the road, I'm not sure. But having all of us there was clearly too much."

After Pebble Beach, Linda and the kids went home. The experiment was over.

The Nissan Open in Los Angeles was next up. Rocco decided to go from Pebble to L.A. to spend a couple of days hanging out with his friends Bill and Brad Shaw before the tournament began on February 15. He drove to Los Angeles on Sunday morning—the cut at Pebble comes on Saturday because it is after 54 holes—and, since the back felt okay, he told the Shaws he would meet them at Los Angeles Country Club to play.

It was that afternoon that Bill Shaw asked him if he might want to get his back worked on the next day to see if it might help him play better that week.

"Sure, why not?" Rocco said. "Who have you got in mind?"

"Cindi Hilfman," Bill Shaw said.

"Who's she?" Rocco asked.

Bill Shaw shrugged his shoulders. "She's a physical therapist here in town. She works on a lot of guys who play at L.A. Country Club. She's very good.

"Oh, and she's very sick; she may be dying from kidney disease."

Rocco still remembers his friend saying those words. "He said it matter-of-fact, like, 'And she has blond hair,'" he said. "I don't think he meant it to be cruel or to sound like he was being casual about it. I think it just struck him as one other thing he knew about Cindi to tell me before I met her.

"I didn't know what to think. I was certainly willing to meet her and let her take a shot at my back. I had nothing to lose. But I almost expected her to be wheeled in or something or look incredibly feeble when she showed up. To say she wasn't what I expected is putting it unbelievably mildly."

The Shaws put in a call to Cindi Hilfman. Cindi not only knew who Rocco was but had told Brad Shaw almost a year earlier that she thought she could help him with his problems.

"I was actually sitting watching the Masters with Brad," she said. "I saw what happened to him when his back went again that day. I could see what the problem was watching on television. I mean, to me, it was so obvious I could see it even through his clothes.

"The problem was in his lower back—in his pelvis. It had nothing to do with the disk he'd had surgery on. His pelvis was asymmetrical, out of balance. I could see it when he tried to swing the club. I remember saying to Brad, 'I can help that man. You have to tell him I can help him.'"

When Brad Shaw called that Sunday afternoon, she said she would come to the house the next morning. Rocco was sitting in a chair, feet up, talking on the phone to Frank Zoracki when he heard the doorbell. A minute later a face peeked around a corner.

"I saw this smile," he said. "It was the kind of smile that lights up a room. I remember thinking, 'If this is Cindi, she certainly doesn't look to me like she's dying.'"

It was Cindi. She was forty-one and she wasn't dying, but she had been sick most of her life. Shortly before she turned four, she was rushed to the hospital with what doctors thought was an appendix problem. An appendectomy was performed, but it didn't make her better. Eventually, after numerous tests, she was diagnosed with an extremely rare autoimmune kidney disease—medullary sponge/kidney disease, which, among other things, causes kidney stones to form in her system constantly.

"On average I pass somewhere between seven and ten a month," she said. "The first time I obstructed, they thought it was my appendix. When the appendectomy didn't make me better, they ran more tests and that's when they discovered the problem was in my kidneys."

The disease causes cysts to form in both her kidneys, which leads not only to the kidney stones but to blockages and to difficulty getting the kidneys to drain. Through the years she has had stents put in to open up the kidneys and one transplant attempt—which failed.

The disease is so rare that Cindi has never encountered anyone else with her specific symptoms. "A lot of the doctors I've dealt with have told me they studied it in medical school and that they know of it, but I've never met someone who treated anyone other than me," she said. "The guess is there aren't more than thirty or forty people in the country who have it. It isn't genetic; it's probably caused by some kind of birth defect."

Even though she was always frail because of the kidney problem, she grew up a self-described tomboy. "I lived in a neighborhood surrounded by boys," she said. "So I played a little bit of everything, including golf."

She was also a superb student who wanted to go to medical school. Even though her grades in college (South Dakota) were plenty good enough to get into med school, her doctors and friends told her that her health would make it impossible to get through the rigors of residency. So she applied to Duke's master's program in physical therapy and spent three years there.

After graduating, she and a friend from back home, Jeff Booher, talked about starting their own clinics specializing in golf-related injuries. Booher went off to work in the fitness trailer on the PGA Tour while Cindi went to work for the veterans administration, dealing often with people who had undergone transplants and were trying to rebuild their bodies. In 2003, Booher left the tour and started Fitness Golf, in Lincoln, Nebraska, where he had gone to live. Soon after, Cindi opened a Fitness Golf franchise in Los Angeles.

"We worked mostly with amateur golfers, a lot of them really good players—college golfers, elite amateurs, that type of player," she said. "I never worked with anyone on the tour even though I had met some of the guys when I went to visit Jeff while he was still working out there."

She had actually seen Rocco in the fitness trailer on a number of occasions, but they had never spoken—even though Cindi knew Rocco was friends with the Shaws.

After Rocco and Cindi were introduced, she sat down and began asking him questions about his back. Cindi eventually asked Rocco if he would lie down so she could take a look at his back. He complied.

"First place she touched me—with one finger—I jumped about ten feet straight into the air in pain," he said. "I remember hearing her say, 'Just as I thought.'"

She worked on him for about two hours that day, isolating a trigger point in his lower back that was about the size of an egg and caused him pain every time she touched it. By the time she was through for the day, it was closer to the size of a marble.

"If you want," she said, "I can come back tomorrow."

"Please," he said.

For the next three days she worked on him. On Wednesday he played in the Pro-Am and was pain-free, feeling as if he could swing the club without hurting for the first time in three years. "Honestly, I felt like I could do cartwheels," he said. "I felt as if someone had willed me a new back."

He shot 71 the first day and got hot with his putter on Friday, shooting 66, easily the best round of golf he had played since the Masters the previous April. "It was nice to make a cut with room to spare," he said. "It was even nicer to play completely pain-free for the first time in about a hundred years. I felt liberated."

On Saturday he shot 71, which put him in position for his first top ten finish since the 2005 U.S. Open—*if* he could play well on Sunday.

"Yeah, *if*," he said. "I went out and was tight on the front nine Sunday, really tight. I was trying too hard. It had been a while—other than Augusta—since I'd played late on a Sunday. I was struggling when I got to the 11th hole. I hit my second shot, and I heard a voice a few yards away say, 'Nice shot, Rocco!' I turned around and she was standing there."

Cindi Hilfman had been at the Shaws' house that afternoon. Rather than wait around and see how her new patient was doing in small snippets on TV, she decided to go out and see for herself.

"Rest of the day I didn't miss another shot," he said. "She gave me a real boost."

He ended up shooting 68, which jumped him into a tie for ninth place. That was worth $135,200—a major step toward making the money he needed to, as he put it, "keep my job."

More important than any of that, though, was the way his back felt and the way he felt about the way his back felt.

"It was as if I had discovered the fountain of youth or something," he said. "All the people I'd been to, talked to, all the work I'd done, had produced nothing. Now I'm with this woman for one week and I think I can dunk a basketball—which I couldn't do before I had back problems."

He was flying home to Naples on Monday, but before he did he talked to Cindi one more time. "Look, you've performed a miracle here," he said. "I would really like it if you would think about coming out on tour to work on me on occasion."

She said she would think about it and let him know. He told her he was playing in two weeks at the Honda Classic and then going to Tampa and then on to Bay Hill—Arnold Palmer's tournament.

"I flew home as excited as I had been in years," he said. "I told myself it was only because of the way my back felt, but deep down I probably knew it was more than that."

Later that week, Cindi called. "I think I can make it to Tampa if that works for you," she said.

"Absolutely, it works," he said. "I'll see you there."

ROCCO PLAYED REASONABLY WELL at the Honda Classic, making the cut and finishing in a tie for 39th. The back didn't feel as good as it had in L.A., but it held up. He was very happy that Cindi would be coming to Tampa.

As soon as she arrived and started working on his back, it began to feel better again. "What was amazing was that after all the years and all the people I'd gone to, she seemed to have figured out what needed to be done to relieve the pressure so that I could play pain-free," he said. "It was nothing short of a miracle."

Cindi also worked on Paul Azinger that week—at Rocco's urging. Azinger has dealt with on-and-off shoulder problems since undergoing radiation treatment in his shoulder for cancer in 1994. "He was about to withdraw, and Rocco suggested to him that he let me take a look at him," Cindi said. "I worked on him and he ended up making the cut. Rocco didn't."

Rocco missed the cut by one shot, in part because he was so excited about everything that was going on in his life all of a sudden. He was amazed by how his back felt, and seeing what Cindi was dealing with made his problems seem simple.

"How she deals with it day after day I will never know," Rocco said. "But she never complains. She just does what she has to do and moves on. She is absolutely amazing."

Initially, Rocco simply saw Cindi as someone who made it possible for him to play golf, and whose friendship quickly became important to him. Cindi saw Rocco as someone who needed help.

"I saw a lot of pain when I first met him," she said. "It wasn't just the physical pain—that was obvious. But the fact that his body had failed him at critical times in his life clearly bothered him, especially what had happened at the Masters. Even when the back didn't hurt, he was convinced it was going to happen to him again. That clearly weighed on him even though he kept saying, 'It's no big deal.' It *was* a big deal."

Frank Zoracki could hear the newfound happiness in his voice when they talked.

"Rocco being Rocco, he was already convinced that Cindi was the best friend he'd *ever* had—that much I could tell," Zoracki said. "He kept saying, 'Frank, I've never met anyone like this in my life.'"

Cindi continued to come out on tour, and as time went on, she became a part of Rocco's group. "She did become my best friend very quickly," he said. "I could talk to her about anything."

That was the way he introduced her to people—as his back therapist and his best friend. He was, at the time, telling the truth.

IF ROCCO'S LIFE WAS COMPLEX off the golf course, it was finally headed back in the right direction on the golf course, even though he had missed the cut in Tampa by bogeying the last two holes on Friday. "I think in a way I was just too excited about everything that week," he said. "I was so happy to feel healthy and to feel happy. It had been a long time since I had felt those two things at once."

Next came Bay Hill. Most of the time, a player who had fallen to Rocco's spot on the money list wouldn't have been playing Bay Hill, since it is an invitational, with a limited field. Normally only players who finish in the top 70 on the money list are guaranteed a spot. But because of his friendship with Palmer, Rocco was given a sponsor's invitation.

He took full advantage. He shot 66 the first day to trail leaders Tiger Woods, Vaughn Taylor, and Paul Casey by two shots. The next day he blew by everyone in the field, shooting 65 to take a stunning three-shot lead.

"I simply could not believe the way I felt," he said. "I had no pain — at all. I was on a golf course I knew, playing in front of great crowds. I could not have felt better. Problem was, on Friday night I started thinking about how cool it would be to win again. I let it all get to me."

It got to him on Saturday, when he shot 76 to slide down the leader board. At 207, he was three under par and trailed Taylor by five shots. He was still in the top ten going into the last day and thinking he might at least cash a big enough check to get close to clinching his exemption for the rest of the year.

"I never really thought about winning on Sunday," he said. "I was just trying to shoot as low a number as I could and see where it got me."

Only two players who started the last round in the top ten broke 70 on that brisk Sunday afternoon. One was Vijay Singh, who shot 67 to win the tournament by two shots over the runner-up. That runner-up was Rocco, who also shot 67 to blow by everyone else.

"Looking back, there's part of me that will always be disappointed because I really lost my chance to win on Saturday," he said. "Being Arnold's tournament, that's one of the ones I always really wanted to win. But what I knew was most important was the money I made by finishing second. It took all the pressure off me that I had been feeling at the start of the year."

It was his highest finish in a tournament since he had finished second in Boston in September of 2003. Second place was worth $594,000, which was more than enough to put his '06 and '07 earnings well past Darren Clarke's. Just as he had done at the start of 1996 with his finish at Phoenix, Rocco had earned his job back. He made it with four tournaments to spare.

"I can't tell you how I felt that Sunday night," he said. "The first thing I did was call Cindi to tell her what had happened, because I felt she'd had as much to do with it as I had. I just felt fantastic about everything at that point. I didn't have to worry about the money list anymore, not just for one year but for two, because the second-place finish, combined with what I'd done in L.A. [where he had made $135,200] and Honda, put me at $700,000, meaning that if I kept breathing for the rest of the year I wouldn't have to worry about keeping my card for '08.

"But what really felt great was I was pain-free. I could swing a golf club. I wasn't worried that I was going down at any minute. I felt like I had a new life—in so many ways—at the age of forty-four. All of a sudden I thought I was twenty-one and starting all over again when anything seemed possible."

That feeling took a hit a few weeks later at Hilton Head. Rocco hadn't been in the Masters, so he had been home the previous week. On Monday night he went to Jim Ferree's house to speak to a group of junior golfers who were in Hilton Head as part of an annual event that matched juniors from Hilton Head with juniors from Dornoch, Scotland.

"We do it every year," Ferree said. "One year our kids go over to Dornoch and play, and the next year their kids come to us. Rocco came to the house and spoke to the kids and they loved it. He told us he was playing a practice round at seven the next morning and if any of the kids wanted to come out and walk along, he would be able to talk to them throughout because there wouldn't be anybody around. They thought that was great.

"We got there at a little before seven and went to look for him. Someone said he was on the putting green. We walked over there, and he was lying on the ground."

"I got there about 6:30 in the morning, hit a few shots, and went over to the putting green," Rocco said. "There was nobody around because it was so early. I hit a few putts, walked over to pick a ball out of the hole, and—boom!—I went down again."

He managed to get to the fitness trailer, where the tour's trainers worked on him and got the back loose enough that he could get up and walk around. They recommended he not try to play that day and see how he felt in twenty-four hours.

"I decided to just go home," he said. "I wanted to know what had happened before I pushed it again."

He called Cindi, who immediately offered to fly east. He told her no, but she was insistent. She flew to Florida and worked on him for two days.

"She had me up and running again in twenty-four hours," he said. "If I had stayed at Hilton Head, I probably could have played on Thursday. She explained to me that I was never going to have a good back again, that the key was trying to keep the muscles from getting so tight that I couldn't play or couldn't walk. She was still trying to figure out exactly how to get that done. I was a work in progress."

The back held up well after Hilton Head, even through 36-hole qualifiers for the U.S. Open and for the British Open. Rocco didn't qualify for either event but was encouraged by the fact that he was able to play—and walk—36 holes in a day pain-free.

He played extremely well at the inaugural Tiger Woods tournament, held at Congressional Country Club outside Washington, a past and future U.S. Open course. He shot 66 on the last

A young Rocco in a rare moment of quiet contemplation.

The swing in its early stages.

Ball-striking was never an issue. Putting often was.

Rocco and his hero-mentor Arnold Palmer. COURTESY TONY AND
DONNA MEDIATE

The fact that Rocco
could get down on
his knees to look at
a putt was proof that
his back was healthy.

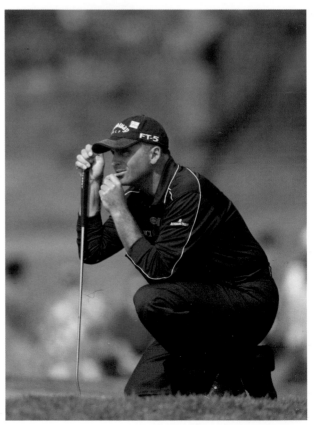

Rocco was part of an impressive weekend leader board at the 2008 U.S. Open at Torrey Pines. COURTESY U.S. GOLF ASSOCIATION.

As the week went on, the ovations grew louder with each made putt.

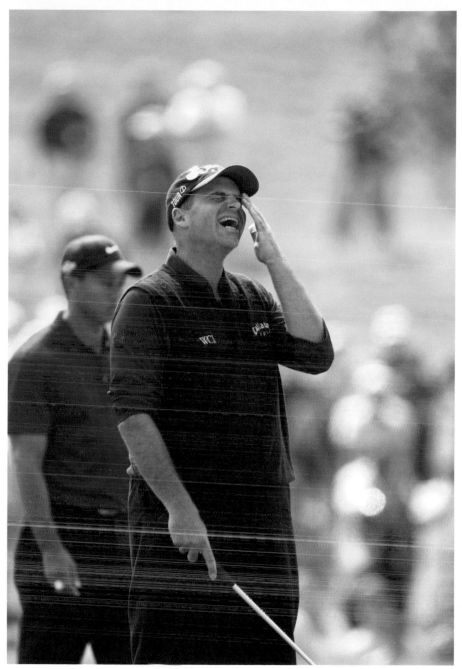

So near yet so far...Rocco understood how much every miss meant in the playoff.

"We were two friends playing golf—and trying to kill each other."

Rocco sits down by number 18 to sign his card while Tiger checks his. They were still tied after 90 holes of golf.

Rocco: "This calls for a hug." Tiger: "Great fight." COURTESY U.S.

Tiger with the trophy, Rocco with the medal (in his pocket). "I didn't even want to look at the trophy. It wasn't mine."

day to tie for sixth, which put him over $1 million in earnings for the year, the first time he had hit that figure since 2003.

"Interesting the three courses I played really well on the first half of that year," he said. "Riviera, Bay Hill, and Congressional — all very tough courses, places where you have to strike the ball well to have a chance. Riviera and Congressional have had majors, and Bay Hill is probably good enough to have one if they wanted to go to the trouble.

"That's always been me when I'm healthy: I strike the ball as well as anybody. It had been a long while since I had felt as if I could do that. At Bay Hill, I led the field in one category: greens hit in regulation. When I'm playing well, that's what I do — I hit greens. If I make a few putts, not even a lot of putts necessarily, just a few, then I score."

He was disappointed that he didn't qualify for the U.S. Open, because it was at Oakmont and he very much wanted to play there. But his outlook was so positive at that point that he didn't get down about it. "I just knew good things were coming," he said. "I could feel it. Cindi was a big part of it, not just because she was keeping my back working, but because she had so much confidence in me. Every time she told me I could do something, I believed I could do it."

Cindi had played a good deal of golf (to a handicap of about 15) before her health had forced her to give it up, and her understanding of the game made it easier for Rocco to talk to her about ups and downs in his game — completely separate from their discussions about his health.

"I had a comfort level talking to her I hadn't had in a long time," he said. "It was as if my whole career was starting over again."

———

ROCCO PLAYED WELL FOR A ROUND at the Buick Open at the end of June, leading after 18 holes before falling back to finish tied for 62nd. Still, he was feeling good about his game and decided to take a week off before the PGA Championship, which was being held at Southern Hills, the same golf course where he had finished fourth in the Open in 2001.

"I was really excited about playing there," he said. "My kind of golf course, plus I knew I could play well there under pressure, because I had done it before."

He flew to Los Angeles ten days before the PGA was scheduled to start and, on Sunday morning, drove to Los Angeles Country Club to play golf.

"I got out of the car and was about to walk into the clubhouse, when I remembered that I had left my coffee in the car," he said. "I turned to get it, tried to stand up after I had reached for it, and it happened again. I went down; I mean, I did a face-plant right next to the car. It was amazing I didn't really hurt myself just on the fall.

"I was lying there and realized I wasn't going to be able to get myself up. I reached into my pocket for my phone, and all of a sudden, for some reason, it occurred to me that you weren't supposed to use cell phones in the parking lot. So I somehow texted my buddies inside to come and get me."

They came and got him up and managed to bring him back to Riviera, where he was staying for the week. He didn't want to bother Cindi at home on a Sunday morning, but she called him. When he told her what had happened, she told him to come over to the house right away. He said, no, he wasn't coming on a Sunday morning. She insisted.

"The first problem was getting to my car," he said. "It was about seventy-five yards from the front door to where I was parked, and I swear it took me an hour to get there. It was really bad—by far the worst it had felt since she had started working on me.

"I didn't really feel right going over there, especially on a Sunday morning," he said. "She worked on me for a couple of hours and said something was seriously wrong and she thought we needed to go see a doctor. I told her, 'No, you'll just work on it again tomorrow and I'll be fine.'

"Well, she did. I went to her clinic, and when I left it felt okay. Then it went again that afternoon. I called her and said, 'Make an appointment with the doctor.'"

The next day Rocco went to see Dr. Tom Knapp, who did an MRI on the back. "Cindi was convinced I had some kind of tear in there and that was why she couldn't fix it," he said. "Sure enough, the pictures come back and I've got something called a transforaminal disk herniation at L1 in the side of the back. As soon as she saw the picture, I could see her getting upset. It was exactly what she had thought it was when she worked on me on Monday."

"I thought he was going to need surgery," she said. "It had nothing to do with his disk; it was in a different spot than his previous surgical level [which had been at L2/L3]. But Tom [Knapp] seemed to think it might be treatable with a shot. Other than the pain of getting the shot, there was nothing to lose by trying."

The next morning Rocco was given the injection, which was painful enough that he was given a local anesthetic beforehand.

"I remember I practically jumped off the table when he put the needle in," Rocco said. "He told me he had to shoot the steroid into me right on the spot where the tear was, and that meant the needle had to go in right on that spot. He actually felt around with the needle until he found the spot that made me jump and he said, 'That's where we need to go.'

"He gave me the shot in the morning, and that afternoon I wanted to go hit balls. [Cindi wouldn't let him.] I knew, long-term, the thing I needed to do was rest and let the tear heal. But I really wanted to play Southern Hills, so we flew out there so I could give it a try."

He lasted 27 holes. On Thursday, he played well, shooting 71. But playing the back nine to start his round on Friday, he began to feel some pain. "I was still around the cut line, but Cindi saw something she didn't like," he said. "On the 17th hole she walked over to me and said, 'You're done. We need to get you out of here before you hurt yourself.' I told her I wanted to at least play the 18th hole. So I did and I chipped in for birdie. At least no one could claim I walked off because I was mad or not playing well. At that moment I was inside the cut line.

"Still, I hate walking off in midround, especially at a major. Cindi said to me: 'We now have a new goal: to keep you from ever having to walk off a golf course again.'"

The reason Cindi wanted him off the golf course that day had more to do with his knee than his back. "I knew his back was okay," she said. "But there was a muscle memory problem. He was still compensating in his stance, *thinking* he needed to even though he didn't. He'd been having a meniscus problem with his knee, and I was afraid he might really hurt it if he kept compensating on a hard golf course like that."

They flew back to L.A., where Rocco rested and Cindi continued to work on his back every day. A few weeks later, he was able to play in the first three events in the new FedEx Cup playoffs, which he had qualified for with his play during the year. He was hardly brilliant—finishing 75th, tied for 52nd, and tied for 30th—but the back held up through twelve rounds of golf in eighteen days, which was a good sign.

He finished the year with $1,166,294 in earnings, good for 78th place on the money list. That meant he would begin 2008 as a fully exempt player and, he hoped, with a fully healthy back.

"I figured if I could stay healthy for an entire year, I could still play very well," he said. "I'd only been healthy in spurts in '07, and even with that I had played better than any year since '03, which was the last time I'd been able to really play a full schedule.

"I was excited to start '08. I thought it might be a special year."

9

Not So Special

For all the high hopes Rocco brought to the start of 2008, there was also a good deal of pressure.

His contract with Callaway, which had provided him a nice chunk of off-course income ($250,000 annually) for many years, was up at the end of the year. He knew with the golf economy tightening that all the manufacturers were looking to cut costs.

"When that happens, they don't cut back on Tiger Woods or Phil Mickelson," he said. "They cut back on the middle-class guys — like me."

Rocco had the advantage of being well-liked by the Callaway people, and he also knew that they didn't look at him as just another middle-of-the-road player because of his personality. Still, he knew he couldn't afford an injured year or an off-year if he expected Callaway to re-up, especially for numbers comparable to what he had been paid in the past.

A good start to the year would have been nice. It would have made him breathe easier about Callaway and, obviously, cashing big checks made things a lot simpler.

"So of course I start out the year not being able to play at all," he said. "I never do things the easy way. It just wouldn't be me if I did."

His first three tournaments produced missed cuts. In Hawaii and in San Diego he played well on Thursday—shooting 69 each time—and then poorly on Friday—75 in Hawaii and 77 in San Diego. In between, at the Bob Hope, he was consistently mediocre, shooting six under par for four rounds at an event where the cut, which comes after 72 holes in a 90-hole tournament, is usually no less than 10 under par.

He was most frustrated by the way he played in San Diego, since the tournament site was Torrey Pines, which was where the U.S. Open was to be played in June. "I knew the golf course would be different in June because the weather would be different and because the USGA's setup would be a lot different than what we saw in January," he said. "But it would have been good for my confidence to play well there."

He laughed. "I don't think it hurt Tiger to win there for a sixth time. Even if a golf course is playing differently, it helps to have had some success there. I had never had success there. Of course at that point, I wasn't even in the Open, and the way I was going, it wasn't likely that I was going to have to worry about how I played Torrey Pines in June."

He finally made a cut in Phoenix, on a golf course where he had enjoyed great success, including his win there in 1999. The good news was that he played well on a Friday—shooting 69—but he couldn't get anything going on the weekend. He shot a one-over-par 72 the last day to finish in a tie for 50th.

"I made fourteen thousand," he said. "It felt like a million just because I had a check to cash. I was hoping that making a cut was a start."

Phoenix was also the first event in which Matt Achatz caddied for him. The idea of asking Achatz, who had never caddied on the PGA Tour before, to come out to Phoenix and work was Cindi's.

"I'd met Matt in Naples when he was working at Calusa Pines Golf Club [the golf course where Rocco often played in Naples], and he caddied for me a fair bit there," Rocco said. "I liked him and thought he was good, but it wasn't until after he worked for me at Tiger's event at the end of '07 that the idea of him coming out even came up."

Achatz was thirty-three. He had been a mini-tour player, one of those very good golfers who just wasn't good enough to make a living playing the game. He had been caddying for several years at high-end clubs — East Hampton Country Club on Long Island in the summer and Calusa in the winter.

He had decided at the end of the summer of 2007 to try something different that winter and had landed a job at Sherwood Country Club, outside Los Angeles. When he saw something in the paper mentioning that Rocco was going to play in the pro-am of Woods's event, which was being held at Sherwood, he called him.

"I asked him if he was bringing his regular caddy out," Matt said. "He said he wasn't, so I asked him if he'd like me to work for him. He said yes. But I never thought it would lead to anything."

Cindi liked Matt right away, and when she suggested Rocco ask him to come on tour, Rocco decided to give it a shot. "It was a tryout at first," he said. "But I could see right away that he knew what he was doing, he was going to work hard, and we liked each other. So we decided to make it permanent."

Matt helped him make his first cut, but he wasn't a cure-all. A week later Rocco missed the cut at Pebble Beach. A tie for

62nd in Los Angeles meant that he had played six West Coast tournaments and made a little more than $27,000, which left him 166th on the money list.

"I actually hit the ball better in Los Angeles," he said. "I hit a lot of greens, which is why I made the cut. But I couldn't make any putts at all."

IT WAS AFTER LOS ANGELES that he decided to try the long putter again after almost a year with a conventional putter. "Cindi thought I could afford to try the conventional putter again because my back was doing well," he said. "When I got off to the bad start, I was convinced it was my putting, so I wanted to try something that had worked for me in the past."

He stuck with the long putter through Florida because he wasn't completely convinced it was time to change. Things didn't go much better, though, over the next few weeks: two more missed cuts and then, most disappointingly, a missed cut at Bay Hill, where he had staged his comeback a year earlier with his second-place finish.

"To be honest, I was getting very frustrated and very nervous," he said. "I had never really had a slump like that in my entire career when I was healthy. Most of the time when I missed a bunch of cuts it was because I wasn't healthy. Now the back felt absolutely fine, and I wasn't hitting the ball well. Even when I did hit it a little bit better, I couldn't make anything, and if you don't make putts you can't score.

"What kept me going was that Cindi kept telling me I was going to be fine. She knew I was going to play well sooner or later as long as my back didn't hurt, and she was completely convinced she could keep my back from hurting. Her confidence gave me confidence."

That confidence was being imparted by phone during March. Cindi was in the hospital and Rocco was taking care of his back by himself for the first time in a year. But though the back held up, his game did not.

"I think he'd gotten used to me being there by then—not just to work on his back but being on the golf course, being the one who started every day saying, 'Hey, it's going to be a great day,'" Cindi said. "I might be a little bit Pollyanna at times, but I think he needed that, since he was so pessimistic so much of the time."

Cindi was healthy enough to travel to Hilton Head in April. She had been counseling Rocco all through Florida to think about going back to the conventional putter. "I didn't think his problem had been putting," she said. "He wasn't hitting the ball as crisply as he did when he was playing his best when we were on the West Coast. Plus, he had a lot on his mind. I think that was it as much as anything."

It was after the first round at Hilton Head that the long putter got shelved again. "I hit the ball great all day and I didn't make a thing," Rocco said. "I shot three over [74] and I really should have been more like three under," he said. "I think I had 12 three-putts that day."

That was a Rocco exaggeration but not by much. After the frustrating round was over, Rocco, Cindi, and Matt went to the putting green. "I'm begging you," Cindi said. "You've got that Sabertooth putter in Matt's car. Try it. You can't possibly get any worse."

Rocco agreed. He sent Matt out to the car for the putter. "I put five balls down from 10 feet and made all five of them," he said. "After that, it was a pretty easy decision. Of course the putting green and the golf course are two different things.

"First nine holes the next day I shot 31. Made everything I looked at. The back felt fine; it was no problem—which was especially nice, since it was exactly a year ago I'd had to withdraw because of it. I knew I wasn't going to putt like that every day, but I just decided to stick with it for a while and see what would happen."

He ended up shooting 65 on Friday, reversing what had been the norm for the year—good Thursday, bad Friday—and made the cut with room to spare. He ended up in a tie for 36th place, nothing to throw a party over, but his best finish of the year. "I was still inconsistent from tee to green at that point," he said. "That's always the key to my game. Even though I was putting better, I wasn't getting myself in position to shoot a low number as often as I would have liked. Still, I was starting to feel as if I was pointed in the right direction. I knew, as long as I was healthy, that sooner or later I was going to start to hit the ball better."

He made three of the next four cuts but was spending the weekends eating what the pros call "rabbit food." It's a term players use to describe those who tee off early on Saturday and Sunday—they're good enough to make the cut, but not in serious contention, meaning they aren't going to be making the big money that leads to big steak dinners. Rocco was dining on a lot of carrots and celery in the month of May but was glad that he at least had a seat at the weekend table. Still, when he arrived at Jack Nicklaus's tournament, the Memorial, in early June, the 36th place at Hilton Head was still his highest finish of the year.

"I think I had made about a hundred dollars all year," he said.

In truth, he had made just under $120,000 in fifteen tournaments for the year, putting him in 178th place on the money list. The week of the Memorial was an important one for Rocco. Muirfield Village, the Nicklaus-designed golf course that the Memorial is played on, is one of the tougher layouts on the PGA Tour, which was usually good for Rocco. What's more, on the Monday after the tournament, he would be joining many of his fellow pros in the 36-hole U.S. Open qualifier that would be held on two golf courses not far from Muirfield Village.

"I really wanted to make the Open," he said. "I'd missed it the year before and I'd missed the cut the year before that at Winged Foot. I had no excuses. I was healthy and there just wasn't any reason for me not to play well enough to make it through the qualifier. I knew it was a tough day, 36 holes is always tough, but I'd done it before and I knew I could do it again.

"The *last* thing I wanted to do was miss the cut and have to wait through the weekend to play on Monday. I thought I needed a good Memorial to help my confidence *and* my checkbook going into the qualifier."

On Tuesday, Frank Zoracki made the two-and-a-half-hour drive from Greensburg to the Columbus suburbs to go over some business issues with Rocco and to spend some time with him. Late in the day, the two of them sat on the stone wall that divides the two levels of the putting green just outside the clubhouse, to relax for a few minutes before Zoracki made the drive home.

"I had a dream about you the other night," Zoracki told Rocco.

"That's a little bit scary, isn't it?" Rocco answered.

Zoracki laughed. "I'd say so. In it I saw you holding a trophy, a big trophy. I think it's a sign that something good is about to happen. You're going to start playing well."

"Your dreams to God's ears," Rocco said.

The next day, Cindi flew in to spend the weekend and Monday. On Thursday and Friday, Rocco played solidly, shooting 70–73, which was one under par and put him in contention, since the scores, in windy weather, were high. The 36-hole lead was held by Kenny Perry and Matthew Goggin at seven under par.

There was rain in the forecast for Saturday afternoon and the conditions were tough from the start. Still, that was no excuse for the way Rocco played the front nine. "I was six over after 10 holes," he said. "I was awful. I couldn't hit the ball straight and I couldn't make a putt. If it hadn't rained, I might have shot 100."

But it did rain after he had parred the 11th hole. More important, there was lightning in the storm passing through, and the players were pulled off the golf course. Rocco's mood was at least as foul as the weather when he and Cindi were taken to the clubhouse on a golf cart after the siren blew, signaling a delay.

"I cannot believe I'm playing like this," he said. "It's ridiculous."

"Calm down," she said. "You aren't that far off. You missed one or two shots. You make a few putts coming in and you'll be fine."

"Are you kidding? I'm terrible. I can't play at all."

"I'm serious. Get over yourself. You've got more important things to worry about than missing a few putts today. Monday is what matters. I think the way you're playing right now, you're going to make the Open on Monday."

Rocco laughed mirthlessly. "The Open? The way I'm playing? I'm losing my mind out here, I've made a hundred dollars all year, and you're talking about me making the Open? You know, right now I don't even care about the Open."

"Well, I do," she said. "And I think you're going to make it."

They rode in silence the rest of the way in.

During the delay, Tony Renaud, who runs the annual Skins Game that is played on Thanksgiving weekend, sat down at the table where Rocco and Cindi were waiting out the rain.

"You know, Tony, Rocco could help your event," Cindi said. "He has just the kind of personality that people enjoy in something like that, especially since you mike the players."

"Looking back, it was funny that she would bring it up," Rocco said. "I mean, I hadn't broken an egg all year. But you could almost see something in his eyes, as if she'd planted a seed. If nothing else, it took my mind off how badly I'd been playing."

He was in a better mood when the storm passed. "I don't know if it was something she said or thinking about the Open or just getting a chance to catch my breath," he said. "All I know is I went out and birdied 12, 13, and 14 and made an eagle at 15. All of a sudden I turn an 80-plus into a 74, which keeps me in the ball game. Life went from total darkness to seeing a light in a couple of hours."

The 74 allowed him to stay in position to finish well if he had a good round on Sunday. Because all the scoring was high, he had dropped only from a tie for 11th place to a tie for 18th place. Goggin, the leader, was seven shots ahead of him, so he probably wasn't going to catch him. But a top ten finish was certainly possible.

"When you haven't been in the top 30 all year, being in 18th place after three rounds, it feels as if you have a five-shot lead on the field," he said.

On Sunday he started well and played good golf all day. His three-under-par 69 was one of the lowest rounds of the day, and he jumped from a tie for 18th to a tie for 6th when it was over. That was worth $201,000—far more money than he had made in his previous fifteen events combined—and vaulted him from 178th on the money list to 126th. All of that was nice, but it wasn't the most important thing that happened during the weekend.

"For the first time all year, I felt good about my game for more than just a day. The 69 was great, but being able to hang in Saturday and make those putts on the back nine was just as important. It was the first time all year I had taken a bad round and made it better rather than taking a bad round and making it worse. That was very important in terms of my mind-set going into Monday."

Regardless of his mind-set, Rocco knew without doubt that Monday was going to be a very long day.

EACH YEAR SEVERAL THOUSAND GOLFERS pay $100 to enter the U.S. Open. Anyone who is a registered professional or an amateur with a handicap index of 1.4 or lower can enter. In 2008, a total of 8,390 players entered the Open. The oldest entrant was seventy-nine, the youngest was twelve. A few of them—seventy-two—were exempt into the championship itself. Several hundred more—including Rocco—were exempt from the first round of local qualifying. The rest had to advance through local qualifying to the sectionals. In all, there were 450 players competing in the sectionals for the remaining 84 spots.

Two of the sectional qualifiers are designated as "tour qualifiers." These are sites near a tour stop—one is held on the Monday after a tournament has just been held (in this case the Memorial); the other is held on Tuesday just prior to the next tournament (which was in Memphis). Because there are more spots available at the tour qualifiers, they attract the most players and, naturally, the toughest fields.

In the case of Columbus, a total of 140 players were entered, vying for 23 spots in the Open field. Among those entered were players like Fred Couples, Davis Love III, Chad Campbell (who would go on to make the Ryder Cup team), Jesper Parnevik, and Kenny Perry, who withdrew after winning the day before at the Memorial. The players were split up onto two golf courses, playing 18 holes on one course in the morning, breaking briefly for lunch, and then switching courses for the afternoon. The lunch break was usually no more than thirty minutes because it was assumed there would be a playoff for the final spots at the end of the day and the hope was to finish before dark.

Early in the day it didn't look as if Rocco was going to have to worry about a playoff or making hotel reservations for San Diego.

"First nine holes I hit eight greens and I was two over par," he said. "I couldn't make anything. I was giving away shots and I was getting more and more frustrated by the hole."

Cindi was frustrated too—with Rocco. She thought he was talking himself out of playing well, that he was getting so down on himself every time he missed a putt that he was making it impossible to get something going.

"After nine holes, she was so angry with me she was ready to leave," he said. "I remember her saying, 'I'm going to leave you alone for a while; we're not good for one another right now.' I didn't believe her, but she took off. Instead of walking with me, she ran up ahead."

There are no ropes at qualifiers and almost no spectators. Cindi had been walking in the fairway with Rocco and Matt during the first nine holes.

"I got it up and down for par at the 10th and then I caught up with her on the 11th tee and I said, 'I don't like this. Would you please walk with me?' She said okay, and I birdied 11. After that, things went a lot better."

He managed to get through the first 18 holes on the tougher of the two layouts, Ohio State's Scarlet course, with a one-over-par 72, which put him back in the pack but still in contention. He was calmer in the afternoon, grinding his way around, playing a bogeyless round at Brookside Golf and Country Club. Even so, he knew coming down the stretch that he was right around the qualifying number. "Everyone was saying 140 was the number, so I figured it would take 139 to play off," he said. "Any time you hear a number in those things, you have to figure it's going to be one or two shots lower than that. You don't figure that, you're in trouble."

He birdied the 17th hole to get to four under par for the afternoon and for the day (the golf courses were par 71–72) and tried valiantly to birdie 18, figuring that would give him a safety net. But his birdie putt from twenty feet swerved low, and he signed for 139.

Then he waited.

"That may be the toughest thing about qualifiers—the

waiting," he said. "You finish and then you stand there around the scoreboard and you see guys come in. Anyone smiling, you know that's bad news for you. You see guys you know and ask them how they did, and they say, 'Eight under,' and you say, 'Great!' and you're happy for them, but inside you're dying because that's one less spot for you."

Rocco had finished more than two hours before the last group would finish. That meant he and Cindi and Matt had to wait. Rocco decided to go sit in the car.

"He was sulking," Cindi said. "He was feeling sorry for himself. At one point Matt, who was sick, said, 'I'm going to go into the clubhouse and get some water.' Rocco said, 'I don't need any water.' I looked at him and said, 'Did it ever occur to you that *Matt* might need some water, Mr. I'm-the-Only-One-on-Earth?' He was a little better after that."

When the 132 players who made it through all 36 holes were finished, Rocco's analysis proved to be exactly right: Carl Pettersson, a fine tour player, was the medalist at 131. In all, sixteen players had shot 138 or better, and they were all being handed paperwork to take with them as they headed for their cars — and San Diego. There were eleven players tied at 139 and seven spots still available. That meant a playoff — eleven players vying for seven spots in the Open.

"You're going to be just fine," Cindi told him when it became apparent he was going to be part of a playoff.

"I was exhausted at that point and angry with myself for putting myself in such a hole in the morning," Rocco said. "It was eight o'clock by the time we teed off [since Ohio is on the western edge of the eastern time zone, there is light in early June until after nine o'clock], and when I looked around I realized I was ten years older than everyone else in the playoff except for Tom Pernice.

"They put me in the second group—five guys went off first, and then the six of us went off after them. After we'd hit our tee shots, I waved at the other guys as we walked off the tee and said, 'Come on, children, let's see if we can get this thing finished before your bedtimes.'"

As the six-some headed down the 10th fairway at the Scarlet, word filtered back from the green that no one in the first group had made a birdie. That meant anyone who birdied in the second group would be in the Open.

"I had hit a good drive," Rocco said. "There was a big bunker about 290 yards out on the left side of the fairway. The young guys just blasted their drivers right over it. I had no chance to do that, so I just played away from the bunker and kept my ball in the fairway. The other guys were so far ahead of me I could barely see them when I got to my ball."

Even though Rocco's ball was well back from the others, he actually had an advantage because he was on flat ground. "Over the bunker the fairway dips down and then goes back up to the green," he said. "From where I was, I had a flat lie *and* I could see the flag. A lot of them were on downhill lies or sidehill lies and they were so far below the green they couldn't see the target nearly as well as I could.

"I just checked it off to the wisdom of age."

Regardless of the reason, Rocco found himself with a nine-iron in his hands and a shot he felt very comfortable trying to hit. "I said to Matt, 'Boy, are these guys in for a shock when I knock this to three feet,'" he said. "I hit a nice little cut and it felt absolutely perfect coming off my club."

He was a foot off on his prediction—the ball settled four feet from the flag. No one else in the group got to inside twenty-five feet. One of the five, Justin Hicks, holed his birdie putt, meaning he was going to San Diego. By the time Rocco got over his putt, it looked more like forty feet than four. "It occurred to me that I'd played 37 holes and worked my ass off all day to get to this moment and I better not blow it," he said. "I hadn't been in position to make a putt that was that important in a long time. My heart rate was definitely up. I could feel it. My hands may have been shaking; I'm not sure. Fortunately, I didn't overthink it; I just told myself it was going in and it did."

It was 8:30 in the evening, and the shadows were getting longer by the minute. There were maybe fifty people standing around the green watching, and for a moment, Rocco couldn't find Cindi, who had been hanging back, too nervous to get close at that moment. When he did spot her, he felt as if he had won the Open rather than simply qualifying to play in it.

"She had this huge smile of satisfaction on her face," he said. "I walked over to her and said, 'You were right.'

"She just said, 'I can't begin to tell you how proud I am of you right now.' I told her she should be proud of *us*. It was one of the cooler moments I can remember having in a long time."

Rocco's qualifying to play in his thirteenth Open hardly drew any notice in the golf world. The USGA puts out a blog each year chronicling interesting stories about those who come through qualifying to make the Open. There are stories about the youngest player to qualify, the oldest player to qualify, relatives of famous players who qualify, amateurs who qualify, and occasionally about women who try to qualify, like Michelle Wie in 2006. There was no mention at all of a sore-backed forty-five year old who had made his first Open as a twenty-one-year-old amateur in 1984 returning twenty-four years later after failing to make the field the previous year.

Qualifiers are often a factor at the Open, since very good players often have to go through them. Previous Open champions frequently have to qualify because the Open only gives champions a ten-year exemption. Arnold Palmer played in Open qualifying seven times late in his career. The other three majors are far more generous: British Open and PGA champions are exempt until they are sixty-five, and Masters champions are exempt for life.

The last qualifier to win the Open was Michael Campbell in 2005. Campbell almost overslept on the morning of his qualifier but was rousted out of bed by his wife. Two weeks later, he out-dueled Tiger Woods down the stretch at Pinehurst to win the Open. In 1996, Steve Jones survived a playoff at his qualifier and then beat Tom Lehman and Davis Love III over the last few holes at Oakland Hills to become an Open champion.

Rocco was well aware of both Jones and Campbell. But he wasn't really thinking in those terms as he left the golf course on the night of June 2.

"After I hurt my back in '94 and had to withdraw, I didn't make the Open the next four years," Rocco said. "That really hurt because I love the event so much. With all the talk from Cindi and Frank and others about how I was going to qualify, it occurred to me that, at forty-five, I might not have that many chances left to play in the Open. It certainly doesn't get any easier as you get older. I was thrilled to be back. Torrey Pines had never been my favorite golf course, but that didn't matter. I was in the Open. At that moment when the birdie putt went in, that was as good a feeling as I'd had in the game in years.

"I was psyched to get out there and to play. I couldn't wait. I had a feeling it was going to be a fun week."

10

Welcome to Torrey Pines

TORREY PINES COUNTRY CLUB IS IN LA JOLLA, California, several miles north of downtown San Diego, a few miles off I-5 if you are driving north to Los Angeles or south into San Diego.

It has hosted what was initially known as the San Diego Open since 1968. The event was first played in 1952 and had six different homes before it settled at Torrey Pines. By then it was known as the Andy Williams–San Diego Invitational. In those days, the tour frequently asked celebrities to lend their name to tournaments to add glamour to them. Bing Crosby created the first celebrity tournament in 1937, and Bob Hope added his name to the Palm Springs Golf Classic in 1965.

That opened the celebrity floodgates. Over the next few years, Jackie Gleason, Sammy Davis Jr., Glen Campbell, Danny Thomas, Ed McMahon, and Williams all lent their names to PGA Tour events. With the corporate takeover of the tour, only Hope's name survives on a tournament masthead, and his event is now known as the Bob Hope Chrysler Classic. Recently, Justin Timberlake added his name to the tournament in Las Vegas, bucking the trend of the past thirty years.

San Diego has been through four corporate title sponsors since 1981 and has been known as the Buick Invitational since 1992. Four corporate sponsors in twenty-eight years is not at all atypical in this day and age. The event now known as the BMW Classic has had seven different title sponsors since 1987.

Torrey Pines is a municipal facility, owned by San Diego County. It has two golf courses — north and south — but it is the south that has always been its signature. Both golf courses are used during the Buick Invitational. Players play one round on the south and one round on the north before playing the weekend rounds on the south after the cut has been made. In 1968, Torrey Pines South played at 7,021 yards from the back tees. Forty years later, by the time Tiger Woods won the Buick Invitational for the sixth time in January of 2008, it had been lengthened to 7,568 yards. Its official length for the Open would be 7,643 yards — 379 yards longer than any previous Open course.

Woods, who grew up outside Los Angeles, played Torrey Pines frequently as a kid and played in a number of important amateur events there as a teenager. His familiarity with the golf course and the deal he had with Buick, which paid him about $7 million a year until the troubled car manufacturer canceled it in 2009, were the reasons he always played the Buick Invitational.

It wasn't until 2001 that the idea that Torrey Pines could host a U.S. Open first became a serious notion in anyone's mind. After the USGA had awarded the 2002 Open to Bethpage Black, making it the first municipally owned golf course to host an Open, members of the Century Club, which operates Torrey Pines, began to wonder if they could do the same thing.

"They came to us and said they were going to have Rees [Jones] do a redesign, and they wanted to know if we would

consider awarding them an Open," said USGA executive director David Fay, who had spearheaded the move to play the Open
at Bethpage. "We told them we would of course consider it, but
we didn't make any guarantees. To their credit, they were willing
to go out and spend the money without being promised anything
in return."

Rees Jones, the son of famed golf course designer Robert
Trent Jones, has become known in recent years as "the Open
Doctor." If a golf course wants to apply to host an Open, or if it
wants to prepare for an Open after being awarded one, Jones is
the architect usually brought in to do the work. Torrey Pines was
the eighth redesign he did with an Open in mind. His first redesign for an Open course was at the Country Club in Brookline,
Massachusetts, in 1988. Fay had asked Jones to do the redesign
at Bethpage Black as part of his plan to bring the Open there.

"Bethpage Black was a different situation, though," Fay said.
"The deal we made with the State of New York was different
than anything we'd ever done before. Bethpage was a great golf
course in poor condition. We agreed to pay to both redesign it
and get it into great shape again as the rental fee for 2002. Rees
did the redesign of Bethpage for nothing because I told him it
was the right thing to do and because he knew he'd get a lot of
positive publicity out of it. In San Diego, they paid Rees to do
the work before we committed to anything."

What was working in Torrey Pines's favor was the well-known
fact that Fay very much wanted to continue the new trend of
awarding the Open to municipal golf courses. The fact that there
was a second golf course on the property that could be used for
things like corporate tents and parking and the USGA's massive
souvenir tent also factored in Torrey Pines's favor.

Working against it was the fact that it already hosted a PGA Tour event. Generally, in picking golf courses, neither the USGA nor the PGA likes to go to golf courses that have an annual tour event. "But there was precedent because of Pebble Beach," Fay said. "We'd played at Pebble four times in the past after the tour event there. It also helped that the conditions in June would be very different than in January."

And so it was that Torrey Pines was awarded the '08 Open late in 2002. The announcement was greeted with mixed enthusiasm in the golf world. Everyone understood the idea of going to another municipal course. But Torrey Pines didn't have the same cachet as Bethpage Black.

"Most of us had never played Bethpage when it was awarded," said longtime tour player Paul Goydos, who had grown up playing on a municipal course in Long Beach, California. "But we knew *of* it. We knew its reputation, and when we got there it more than lived up to that reputation. Torrey Pines is an okay golf course, but I don't think anyone would put it in the same category as Bethpage."

The USGA was well aware of that fact. "We all knew that Torrey Pines didn't appear on any list of the top hundred golf courses in the country," said Mike Davis, who would be responsible for setting up the golf course before the championship began. "But we also thought it had a lot of things going for it: We need more West Coast venues — among other things it is great for TV because we can finish so much later. It's very scenic, with all the water that is around it. And we thought with the Rees redesign and some time to put our stamp on it, we could make it a golf course the players would enjoy playing an Open on. At least we hoped so. I'd be lying if I told you any of us thought it was a slam dunk."

The Jones redesign lengthened the golf course by about four hundred yards and added a number of wrinkles to it. Most players liked the changes, although some thought the course had been stretched out too much—as is frequently the case these days with Open layouts.

One person who had never been crazy about Torrey Pines was Rocco. "I had just never played well there," he said. "I'm not even sure I can tell you why, but I hadn't. I was hoping that it would play harder and faster in June than in January and that the USGA's setup would benefit me. Their emphasis is always on making guys keep the ball in the fairway, and that usually works well for me."

In truth, the USGA's demand that players keep the ball in the fairway had changed somewhat. Davis had taken over most of the course setup responsibilities from Tom Meeks in 2005. Meeks, with the approval of Fay and the USGA board, had always taken the approach that a hazard was a hazard, and that included both the rough and the bunkers.

At most PGA Tour events, if a player barely misses a fairway, he will more often than not have a lie that allows him to get his club solidly on the ball and, often as not, put spin on it when it lands on the green. At a lot of tour courses, the bunkers are so smooth and so perfect that players barely notice that they're dealing with sand at all.

That's never been so at the Open. Some bunkers provide relatively simple shots; others can be close to impossible. When Tim Morgahan was the USGA's agronomist, his answer when players complained to him about the quality of the bunkers was simple: "If you don't hit your ball in there, you won't have a problem. They *are* supposed to be hazards, aren't they?"

The same is true of the rough. Under Meeks, a player could hit a ball a few yards off line and be lucky to find it. Most rough at a U.S. Open was what is called "pitch-out rough." In other words, find the rough and very often your only shot was a pitch-out back to the fairway.

After players went ballistic over the setup at Shinnecock in 2004 — which had as much to do with the speed of the greens on Sunday as anything else — the USGA decided to make some changes beginning in 2005.

One change was to "graduate" the rough. If a ball was a yard or two off the fairway, a player was likely to have a shot at the green. If he was in the middle of the rough, it was tougher, and if he was way off line he probably would find himself pitching out.

"I think it took us until this year [2008] to actually get it right," Davis said. "The first few years we weren't as consistent as I'd have liked us to be. Some holes were just right, others weren't. I thought this year was as close to getting it right as we've come."

Davis was also more likely to water greens that looked like they might be baking out than had traditionally been the case in the past. That had been the major cause of all the trouble at Shinnecock. The greens had been very fast on Saturday and with dry, windy weather predicted for Sunday, watering made sense.

"The golf course was right on the edge today," Nick Price said after the third round. "If they don't get water on it tonight, it's going to go over the edge."

They didn't get water on it. That led to the embarrassing sight of holes being watered during the final round, an order that came down from on high after several players in early groups putted balls off the seventh green.

"We blew it," Fay said later. "We always like to have our courses right on the edge, but the danger in that is that if you go over the edge, there's no turning back. We went over that edge and there wasn't time to fix the problem. You can't have that during the last round of the U.S. Open."

Even though the winning scores in 2006 (six over par) and 2007 (five over par) at Winged Foot and Oakmont respectively were very high, there were few complaints about the setups. "They were just very hard golf courses," said Jim Furyk, who finished one shot behind the winner both years. "They weren't unfair, they were just very, very hard."

That was what the USGA was hoping for at Torrey Pines — hard but fair. USGA officials like to claim they really don't care what the winning score is at the Open, but the fact is they protect par like the Secret Service protects the president. When Tiger Woods shot 12 under par at Pebble Beach in 2000, there was near-panic at USGA headquarters in Far Hills, New Jersey. The only thing that kept everyone semi-sane was the fact that no other player in the field came close to breaking par. Ernie Els finished second — 15 shots behind Woods at three over par.

"I think the feeling was that we'd simply witnessed one of the great performances in golf history," Davis said. "The golf course held up fine. If ten other players had been under par, it might have been different."

Even though the players routinely complain about how tough the golf courses are, they too have come to expect Open courses to be difficult. In 2003, when Furyk and Vijay Singh were the 36-hole leaders at Olympia Fields at seven under par and a total of eighteen players were in red numbers at that stage, there was much whining from the players about the fact that the course was playing like a regular PGA Tour venue. "Doesn't feel like an Open," was the oft-heard complaint.

The USGA agreed. The golf course was much tougher on Saturday, and with the hole locations in the hardest possible spots on Sunday, the entire field went backward. By the time it was all over, only four players—Furyk, Stephen Leaney, Mike Weir, and Kenny Perry—were under par. Even so, the consensus was that Olympia Fields really didn't have what it took to be an Open venue.

"The key is finding just the right spot between hard [and] impossible," Fay said. "A lot always depends on the weather conditions and how you adapt the golf course to suit them. I think we're getting a little better each year. At the very least I would make the claim that we've learned from our mistakes."

Most players arriving at Torrey Pines prior to the 2008 Open were very happy with what they found. Some thought the new tee on the par-four sixth hole, which made the hole play 515 yards, was too far back—Phil Mickelson called it "ridiculous." Others wondered about the wisdom of finishing an Open on a par-five. Most often, the Open ends on a long par-four where making a par to win can be difficult.

That had never been more evident than at Winged Foot in 2006, when Colin Montgomerie and Mickelson each stood on the 18th tee needing a par to do no worse than playoff (Montgomerie) or win (Mickelson), and both made double bogeys.

The USGA had swerved away from this tradition once in

recent years, in 1997, when the 18th hole at Congressional Country Club was a par-three. In the past when tournaments had been played at Congressional, the par-four 17th had been played as the 18th hole, but Fay thought a par-three with water might make for a dramatic finish. He was wrong. Players in contention simply played an easy middle-iron to the center of the green and happily took a par. The tournament was decided on the 17th hole, when Tom Lehman found the water and Montgomerie (poor guy) made a bogey, allowing Ernie Els to beat them.

"We thought a risk-reward par-five could make for an exciting finish," Davis said. "You get guys standing on the tee with a chance to make anything from three to six, and it should add to the suspense. It was a reachable par-five but only if you hit a good drive."

ROCCO HAD GONE HOME to Florida for a few days after qualifying for the Open, and he flew to San Diego on Saturday morning. His plane landed around lunchtime, and he went straight to the golf course to meet Matt Achatz.

"I wasn't at all tired," he said. "I was very pumped up to be there. I didn't want to hit balls or anything. I just wanted to change my shoes and go play a few holes. I was walking down the path from the locker room to the first tee and I ran into Mike Davis. We talked for a couple minutes, he congratulated me on making it in, and I kept going. I decided it was some kind of omen running into him, that I was going to like the golf course."

If he was looking for omens, the next one wasn't nearly as good. When he walked onto the first tee and pulled his driver out of the bag, the head came off it. "Something must have happened on the plane," he said. "I freaked out completely. I had driven the ball so well at Memorial and the thought of having to find a new driver the week of the U.S. Open just about made me crazy."

At most tournaments, the equipment reps and their trailers don't arrive until Monday morning. For a major, they get to town earlier. Rocco found a Callaway rep and asked him if he could build a couple of new drivers for him to try out. "I didn't know what to think," he said. "I was hoping they could come up with something that would feel similar to the driver I'd been using."

Once he got back on the golf course, Rocco didn't stay very long. "It was just so windy," he said. "The chances were good, at least I hoped, that it wasn't going to play that way once the tournament began. I gave up after seven holes. I was tired from the trip, I knew I needed to get on the range and figure out what to do about my driver, and the wind made playing pretty worthless in terms of getting a feel for the golf course. I decided I'd be better off getting out of there, getting a good dinner and some rest, and then coming back in the morning."

He checked into the players' hotel, a Hilton located a few hundred yards from the golf course. He called Lee Janzen, who was in the field because 2008 was the tenth year of the ten-year exemption he had earned by winning the Open in 1998 at the Olympic Club. They decided to get out early the next day and try to play 18 holes.

Rocco was at the golf course early on Sunday morning. The Callaway people had taken the shaft from his old driver and built a new driver from it. "I hit it on the range for a little while, and it felt almost exactly like the old one," he said. "It was a huge relief. By the time Lee and I teed it up, I felt pretty good about things."

They played the entire course in a twosome, which is unusual for a practice day at the Open. Often as not, players will join up with one another on the golf course. But on Sunday, there still weren't that many players on the grounds, and Janzen and Mediate had most of the course to themselves.

"It was spectacular," Rocco said. "The weather was gorgeous and the course was almost empty. I think we might have seen five spectators the whole day out there. [The USGA doesn't let spectators onto the course until Monday, so anyone on the golf course on Sunday was a tournament volunteer or a USGA staffer.] It was great to play with Lee, since we hadn't seen each other for a while. It was a good day all around. I felt good."

Janzen noticed. "He was hitting the ball well, which never surprises me," he said. "Rocco hitting the ball well isn't news. When he isn't hitting the ball well, you wonder if something is wrong, because as long as I've known him he's been able to fall out of bed and hit the ball well.

"The question is always his putting. That day he was rolling the ball very well. He made a bunch of putts but, more important—after all, we can all make putts in practice—he looked very comfortable to me with the short putter. I don't think I'd seen that for a while."

Rocco was just as aware of how he was putting and hitting the ball. Given a chance to play the golf course in less than gale-force winds, he felt comfortable almost from the start. "I just felt like Mike [Davis] had really nailed it with the setup," he said. "It definitely felt a lot different than it did in January. Everything was faster—the fairways, the greens. They had the ability to make 14 play as a driveable par-four if they wanted, which I'd never seen at an Open before except for the 17th at Oakmont, where they had no choice but to play it that way.

"The new driver felt good and that was a huge relief. I'd been really concerned about it on Saturday. And I was putting the ball well. I liked the greens right away, although I said to Lee, 'You can bet these things will be faster by Thursday than they are now.'"

Green speed is always an issue, especially at the Open and at the Masters. The greens at Augusta National are so notorious that their speeds are considered a state secret. The speed of a green is measured by a very simple instrument called a Stimpmeter. For all intents and purposes, it is an angled piece of wood from which a ball is rolled. How far the ball rolls on the green is how fast the green is considered to be running. If the ball rolls five feet, the green is a five. If it rolls ten feet, it is a ten. And so on.

At most PGA Tour events the green speed is usually—again, depending on weather—somewhere between 11 and 12. Anything slower is considered too easy and anything over 12 too fast. There are players who insist that the greens at Augusta National are consistently kept at 14, perhaps even higher.

"I've seen them 15, maybe even 16, at Augusta," said Brad Faxon, generally regarded these days as the tour's best putter not named Tiger Woods. "Honestly, there are times when you roll a putt and you know you have no chance of the ball stopping unless it hits the hole square in the middle. It can be frightening."

The USGA doesn't go that far, but it does like fast greens. "Generally speaking, we don't want to get to 14, but we're okay at 13," Mike Davis said. "It's a balancing act all week. We do keep them a little bit slower for the practice rounds, not because we're trying to fool the players but because we know if we get them too fast too early in the week they might get away from us on the weekend. The players know that a green isn't likely to putt on Thursday or Friday the way it did on Monday or Tuesday. We try to move the speed up gradually so it isn't a shock to anyone when the championship starts."

Rocco was fully aware of the fact that making putts on Sunday was going to mean very little on Thursday. But he felt good—very good—after he had finished his round with Janzen.

"It just all felt as if it was coming together exactly the way I would have hoped it would leading into an Open," he said. "I liked the golf course, I was hitting the ball well, and I felt comfortable rolling the ball on the greens. I had played well at Memorial and in the qualifier. The back felt good. I really felt like I had a chance."

After he and Janzen finished, they had lunch in the club-house and then Rocco decided to go to the putting green to hit some putts before calling it a day. While he was there, his phone rang. It was Paul Azinger—a longtime friend and, perhaps more important, the U.S. Ryder Cup captain for 2008.

"Hey, just calling to see what's up," Azinger said. "I forgot to check. Did you make the Open?"

"I'm standing on the putting green at Torrey Pines right now you——," Rocco said, laughing because in truth there was no reason for Azinger to know he'd gotten in.

"It's not like I was a serious candidate to make his team at that moment," Rocco said. "I'd had one pretty good tournament all year. At the start of the year, having played okay in '07, I said to myself, 'This is your year to make the Ryder Cup team.' I think I'd been close to either making it on points or getting chosen a couple times in the past, but I was thinking with Zinger as captain, knowing he might need some older leadership with what was looking like a young team, I might have a chance if I played well.

"The way I'd played the first half of the year, I'd almost stopped thinking about it because it seemed pointless. I guess he had too."

Azinger asked how things were going, how Cindi was feeling, how he thought his game was.

"I must have sort of gushed about everything," Rocco said. "I told him I was hitting the ball great, that I loved the greens, my back was wonderful, and I was driving up to L.A. to see Cindi that night. I think I said something like 'Life is pretty close to perfect right now.'"

Azinger listened to his friend and, even knowing how enthusiastic he could be, was impressed. "You sound like you think you can win the tournament," he said.

Rocco thought about that for a minute. "You know what," he said. "You're right. I do think I can win."

It was the first time he had actually thought in those terms. He liked the way it felt.

As PLANNED, HE DROVE TO LOS ANGELES that night to see Cindi, to get her to work on his back, and to spend a couple of days relaxing before heading back to San Diego. It was not exactly the approach most players take to a major.

"First of all, I think practice rounds are overrated," Rocco said. "Especially if you know the golf course. Even with the changes and the different conditions, I knew Torrey Pines. People don't understand that when you play 18 holes in a practice round, it's almost like playing two or three practice rounds. You hit two or three shots off the tee, you play the ball from different spots on the fairway, you putt to places where you think they might put the pins once the tournament starts. It isn't like you're just playing one ball and trying to post a score; you're not. You're trying to get to know your way around the golf course.

"After playing a few holes on Saturday and 18 holes on Sunday, I felt I had the feel for the golf course. Lee and I got lucky on Sunday because we were out early and a lot of guys weren't there yet or were just arriving. Plus, there were almost no spectators, so it was easy to get around.

"By Monday, when everyone's in town and they let the fans in, playing a practice round is a lot tougher. It can take forever because guys are hitting two and three balls, so pace of play can be brutally slow—especially at an Open, where you have a lot of nontour players in the field who really want to try to get to know everything they possibly can about the golf course.

"The other thing was I wanted to be absolutely sure I was rested and ready to go on Thursday morning. I wanted my back to feel strong and I wanted to feel fresh. You can overpractice. You can even overthink. If you're at the golf course for three or four straight days before a major, you can obsess about it. You start thinking about what to hit off certain tees, where you want the ball on certain greens. You can walk onto the first tee on Thursday and already be mentally exhausted. I wanted to avoid that."

He spent two relaxed days in Los Angeles, playing a little hit-and-giggle golf with his friends Brad and Tom Shaw, all the while having Cindi work on his back to make sure he would be physically ready to go when he got back to Torrey Pines. On Tuesday night, he and Cindi drove to San Diego.

Wednesday morning he was back on the golf course. By now, everything had changed since Sunday. There were people everywhere—the Open, like the Masters, sells at least as many tickets for practice rounds as it does for the four days of play. There were fans wall-to-wall. The locker room was packed. So was the golf course.

After warming up, Rocco walked to the first tee, where Adam Scott, the young Australian who was ranked number three in the world, was getting ready to tee off. Butch Harmon, swing coach to the stars (his pupils in the past have included Tiger Woods and Greg Norman; currently he works with Scott and Phil Mickelson, among others), was also on the tee, preparing to walk a few holes with Scott. Rocco and Matt joined Scott, Harmon, and Tony Navarro, Scott's caddy, whom Rocco had known for as long as he had been on tour.

"It was actually kind of fun to hook up with them," Rocco said. "I don't know Adam that well, but he's a good guy, and Butch and Tony are old friends. You walk on the first tee to play a practice round at a major, it's almost like a crapshoot. You might find someone there you don't really like or a complete stranger. Either way, it isn't going to be ideal because you can't say, 'I don't want to play with you'—it's rude. I was very happy to be with those guys."

Rocco actually felt sorry for Scott. The USGA had taken the unprecedented step of pairing the top twelve players in the world with one another for the first two rounds. Although the USGA doesn't do its pairings by computer or have a specific system, it has traditionally kept the bigger stars far away from one another in terms of tee times for a couple of reasons.

One reason is traffic flow on the golf course. It is less than ideal to have Woods and Mickelson on the same nine at the same time because it is likely that more than half the fans on the grounds will be following those two groups. Other name players—like Sergio Garcia, Ernie Els, Vijay Singh, and Jim Furyk—will also draw large audiences, so they are usually spread out too.

The other reason—of course—is television. The Open is televised by NBC and ESPN. All the weekend play is on NBC and most of the Thursday–Friday play is on ESPN. Naturally, the networks would rather have Woods in one wave of players, Mickelson in the other wave, and the other stars spread around them. Most tournaments—including the Open, even the Masters—routinely cooperate to keep the TV people happy.

It was Mike Davis who had first thought about doing the pairings based on world rankings. "Things are a little bit different with a West Coast start because people start watching TV later in the day in the east and the Midwest," he said. "I thought if we put the Tiger-Phil group a little bit early one day and a little bit late the other, it could work out. We were still going to have to deal with a huge amount of people trying to follow one group, but to be honest, it couldn't be that much bigger than what Tiger normally gets. There simply wouldn't be room."

Davis floated the idea with Fay, who liked it. And so, when the pairings were announced, there were the top three players in the world, Woods, Mickelson, and Scott, playing together.

Under the best of circumstances, that was going to make it a difficult two days for Scott. He is a very popular young player, especially overseas, and is especially popular with young female golf fans — it doesn't hurt that he's rich, handsome, and single. Playing with Woods and Mickelson, though, he was going to be the invisible man. He was going to have to put up with multiple security people — none of whom would have much interest in protecting him — walking every step of the way with his group for 36 holes.

Worst of all, that wasn't Scott's biggest problem. A week before the Open, as he was preparing to get into a car, a friend had accidentally slammed the door on his right hand and broken it. He was trying to play with a bandage on his hand, and his discomfort swinging the club was obvious.

"He was struggling," Rocco said. "I mean, he was managing. He could grip the club just enough to get it back and get through the ball, but he didn't have any of his usual power. I could tell he was going to have a rough time of it. I felt for him. Normally he could have just gone off and played and only a few people would have been around watching him try to play at 50 or 60 percent. Now he was going to have the whole world — not to mention Tiger and Phil — watching him try to play at 50 or 60 percent."

At that moment, on Wednesday afternoon, less than twenty-four hours before Tiger, Phil, and Adam were scheduled to tee it up, no one was 100 percent sure if Tiger was going to make it to the first tee.

"I think we all thought he would play," Rocco said. "But there was certainly plenty of talk about what kind of shape he'd be in. He hadn't played at all since the Masters. He wasn't playing a full practice round — which wasn't that big a deal, since he knew the course so well, but how ready could he possibly be?

"If it was anyone else in the world, you'd say, 'No way, he has no chance.' But when it's Tiger, you never say that. Still, I'm not sure anyone — maybe even including him — knew what kind of shape he'd be in when he got to the first tee."

Woods, Mickelson, and Scott were scheduled to tee off at 8:06 A.M. Pacific daylight time. Rocco had a 7:33 A.M. tee time. Chances were pretty good that a few more people would be watching the Woods-Mickelson-Scott group than his. That was fine with him. He was ready to play.

11

A Good Beginning...

THURSDAY MORNING, JUNE 12, dawned clear and breezy in La Jolla, something of a relief to USGA officials.

"Our only weather concern was what they call the 'June gloom' out there," David Fay said. "We'd had some problems in the past getting started at Pebble Beach because of fog issues in the morning, but we were told this wasn't usually as bad. Still, when you've got 156 players to get around the golf course, you really don't want to start the day with any kind of delay."

There was no delay. The first groups off the first and tenth tees at 7 A.M.—D. A. Points, Patrick Sheehan, and David Hearn off number one and Robert Garrigus, Peter Tomasulo, and Craig Barlow off number 10—were on the golf course right on schedule, and Torrey Pines buzzed with activity as 42,500 people poured onto the grounds for day one of serious play. Most of the buzz was about one player: Eldrick Tiger Woods. Would he play? And, if he did play, *how* would he play, fifty-eight days after knee surgery, having not walked an 18-hole round of golf during that time?

"To be honest, I think we were all concerned with how Tiger would play," Mike Davis said. "Part of it was that you always want the best player in the world to be in contention because it's good for the event. But I was also a little worried that if he came out and played poorly on a golf course where he'd won six times—where he'd once shot 22 under for 72 holes and had been 18 under six months earlier—people would blame it on our setup. I knew it was more likely if it happened it would be because of the knee and rustiness, but I also thought we might get some heat if he somehow missed the cut."

Woods was in his twelfth year as a professional. The Open was his forty-sixth consecutive appearance in a major championship. He had won thirteen times, been second five times—including to Trevor Immelman at the Masters in April—and had missed one cut. That had come at the 2006 Open at Winged Foot. He had played there six weeks after the death of his father, his first tournament since Earl Woods's death on May 3 and his first event since that year's Masters.

He had clearly not been all there emotionally, reacting almost calmly to poor shots and off-line putts. He had missed the cut comfortably—by four shots. If nothing else, his inability to come storming back so soon after losing his dad proved him human. Of course he had then gone on to win both the British Open and the PGA Championship, quieting anyone who had wondered if he would somehow lose some of his fire with his father no longer around.

This was very different. Woods wasn't battling his emotions, he was fighting a frailty in his body. The April surgery had been the second one on his left knee. What the public didn't know as the Open began was that he also had a stress fracture in his leg and had been told by his doctors that he was going to need more surgery soon. He had decided to play the Open, knowing he probably would not be able to play either the British Open or the PGA, because it was the Open—the major in which he'd had the least success (he'd won it "only" once)—and because it was on a golf course he loved.

"I think every single player in the field was aware of what was going on with Tiger and had thought about it," Rocco said. "How could you not? Any time he's in a golf tournament, it feels different than when he's not. And if he's on the leader board, even if he's five or six shots back of the leader, you're crazy if you're not aware of his presence. You can't not be. Any time he does anything, if you're on the golf course you hear the reaction and you know it's him. No roar in golf sounds like a Tiger roar. I'm guessing it was that way for Arnie once upon a time and for Jack, but now it's that way for Tiger and Tiger only."

Mike Davis had made a point of letting both Woods and Mickelson know in advance that they were going to play together. He knew they would be asked questions about it and wanted to give them some time to prepare. Woods and Mickelson have never exactly been pals—to put it mildly—and Davis wasn't sure how they would respond to being paired together on the first two days of a major.

Both had come to Torrey Pines in the week prior to the Open to get a look at the golf course when no one was around. That was when Davis had told them what he was planning.

"I was pleasantly surprised," Davis said. "They both seemed up for it. In fact, the first thing Phil said to me was 'It's about time.' Tiger said it was fine with him, which actually didn't surprise me that much because in all the years we've dealt with him, I don't think he's ever complained about anything. You just tell him what's going on and he deals with it."

Davis's trepidation about the pairing was understandable given the history between the two players. It wasn't all that surprising that they rarely spoke to each other when paired in a tournament. Neither is terribly chatty on the golf course to begin with. In fact, Woods has been known—especially on Sundays and even more so on Sundays at a major—to shake hands on the first tee and not say another word to anyone but his caddy, Steve Williams, until the handshake on the 18th green.

"I don't think he's being mean or unfriendly when he does that," Lee Janzen said. "I think he just feels like he has a job to do and he's not going to start chatting about family or ball games until the job is done."

Most players tend not to talk that much on the golf course. Thursdays and Fridays at a regular PGA Tour event you may hear some chatter, especially in groups where the players know one another well. It is quieter on Saturdays, and rarely do you hear much more than "Nice shot" on Sundays—especially in the later groups, where big money or a tournament title is on the line.

"We have a tendency to go into a zone," said Davis Love III, who has won twenty times on tour. "I know people would like to see us talk more and smile more, but that's just not where your focus is. There are exceptions. Trevino loved to talk, Arnold always interacted with the crowd, and Rocco never stops. That's his way of letting off steam. Most of us aren't that way, though. He's an exception to the general rule."

Woods and Mickelson didn't only fail to talk when competing against each other. In 2004, American Ryder Cup captain Hal Sutton decided to pair his best two players on the first day of the competition at Oakland Hills, hoping to get his team off to a fast start and set a tone. Woods and Mickelson did indeed set a tone. They lost both their matches and never uttered a word to each other during eight hours on the golf course as a "team." Europe jumped to a huge lead and won that weekend going away.

No American captain since then has even thought about pairing Woods and Mickelson in either Ryder Cup or Presidents Cup play.

"I don't think they hate one another," Rocco said. "They're just very different guys."

That's certainly true. Woods has actually grown far more comfortable through the years around his fellow pros. He enjoys "busting balls," as the players put it, and is good at being given a hard time in return. He calls almost everyone by some kind of nickname—not necessarily clever ones, but adding a Y to people's names or, in Rocco's case, calling him Rocc, as many people do.

Woods has loosened up a little when it comes to talking about his personal life since the birth in June 2007 of his daughter, Sam. (Her name is Sam, not Samantha, because Earl Woods called Tiger Sam as a boy.) He will talk occasionally—though generically—about the joys of fatherhood. But Elin, his wife, stays in the background almost all the time, and Woods doesn't like anyone in his entourage—caddy, agent, swing coach, clothing rep—talking about much of anything other than golf. He's fired a caddy, an agent, and a swing coach at least in part because they were too forthcoming with the public and the media.

Mickelson has had the same caddy and the same agent since he turned pro in 1992. When he changed swing coaches in 2007, going from Rick Smith to Butch Harmon, he agonized over it and has made a point of staying friends with Smith since he made the change. When Woods fires someone, that is usually the last time he speaks to him except perhaps in passing.

Mickelson is the father of three and loves nothing more than talking about how important his wife, Amy, is to his success. Any time he wins a tournament there is usually a four-person stampede in his direction as he comes off the 18th green — Amy and the three children. The day Elin Woods races onto a green to hug her husband after a winning final putt will be the same day Bill Clinton or Barack Obama is voted most popular politician on the PGA Tour.

Woods is image-conscious in the sense that he tries not to say anything controversial and tends to steer clear of political issues. He is one of the few players on tour who is not a registered Republican — he's a registered Independent.

Mickelson is so image-conscious that other players call him Eddie Haskell. To his credit, he is the most accommodating player on tour when it comes to signing autographs (Woods hates signing autographs), usually blocking at least forty-five minutes after every round to sign. He also does things like referring to Ryder Cup or Presidents Cup captains as "Captain Nicklaus" or "Captain Azinger," when everyone else calls the captains simply by name — as in Jack or Paul (or Zinger).

To be fair, though, a lot of the animus through the years is simply the result of both being fierce competitors and the fact that Woods's presence on tour during Mickelson's career has probably prevented Mickelson from going down as one of the great players of all time. Mickelson had won three majors and thirty-four tournaments in all at the end of 2008 — Hall of Fame numbers by a wide margin — but probably would have at least doubled his wins in majors if Woods had gone to law school instead of playing golf.

In one of his most candid moments, Mickelson revealed what he honestly thinks about having to compete with Woods coming down the stretch in majors. Tied for the lead after 54 holes at the 2004 Masters, he was asked if it helped to have Woods nine shots back and (for once) not in contention. Instead of giving the standard "I just play the golf course and worry about my own game" answer, Mickelson smiled and said, "It doesn't suck."

Now, as the 2008 Open began, Woods and Mickelson—along with the wounded Adam Scott—were on the golf course at 8:06 A.M. surrounded by so many people it appeared as if most of San Diego County was following their group. For golf fans, the feeling about the two of them being paired together at the start of the U.S. Open was pretty much the same as Mickelson's feeling in Augusta four years earlier: It didn't suck.

Rocco's tee time on Thursday morning was 7:33. His pairing was a young-old one: One of the other players was twenty-two-year-old Michael Thompson, who had gotten into the Open by finishing second in the U.S. Amateur Championship the previous summer. The other player was fifty-two-year-old Brad Bryant, who had gained an exemption by beating Rocco's hero Tom Watson down the stretch in the 2007 U.S. Senior Open. Rocco was the only player in the group who had made it to the Open through qualifying.

He was up at 4:30 that morning after a restless night. "It was one of those deals where you're trying so hard to relax and stay calm that you can't," he said. "I was keyed up because I really thought I had a chance to do something, to play well. I finally got up because I couldn't sleep anymore. I wanted to get to the golf course and get started as soon as possible. If they had put up lights for us to tee off, I'd have been ready to go."

He and Cindi went through their preround routine: forty-five minutes on the table as soon as they woke up to get him loose, then a search for bagels and coffee. That turned out to be easy: There was a Bruegger's bagel shop near the hotel with a Starbucks next door. After his bagels, Rocco bought a four-shot espresso before they headed to the golf course. "That'll get you going early in the morning," he said, laughing.

He was in the clubhouse by 6:30, meeting Matt on the range to go through the warm-up ritual. He was teeing off on the 10th tee, so he needed to give himself a few extra minutes, since players going off the back nine had been instructed to be ready to be transported out to the 10th tee at least fifteen minutes prior to their tee time. Torrey Pines is not a golf course that comes back to the clubhouse after nine holes, so players teeing off on number 10 had to be driven to the 10th tee.

The Open has only used two tees on Thursday and Friday since 2002. Until then, everyone went off the first tee, with tee times as early as 6:30 A.M. and as late as 4:30 P.M. With the pace of play in golf slowing with each passing year, it became almost impossible—even on two of the longest days of the year—to get all 156 players around 18 holes by sundown. The two tee start provided a lot more flexibility, with the latest tee time at Torrey Pines being 2:42 in the afternoon. That meant even if the late groups needed six hours—not uncommon at the Open on a difficult golf course with fast greens—they would be able to beat darkness.

Of course, getting players to the 10th tee can be an issue. In

2002, at Bethpage Black, the easiest route for transporting play-ers went through a Superfund cleanup zone, and the Department of Environmental Protection was willing to allow the vans to go through the area only if everyone in every van stopped to sign a waiver sheet each day. The USGA opted for a different route.

Each player at Torrey Pines was allowed to bring two people with him in the van when being driven to the 10th tee: his caddy and one other person. In Rocco's case it was Cindi, who was almost as nervous as he was as they made the drive out. Rocco was wound up but ready. "If you don't have some butterflies on the first day of a major, something is wrong," he said. "I'd have been worried if I didn't have them."

This was also the first major for Matt, since Rocco hadn't played in the Masters. He was also keyed up, but he looked okay to Rocco. "I was actually amazed at how calm he was," Rocco said later. "I've seen caddies freak out in pressure situations. Matt did great, not only that morning but the entire week."

They arrived on the tee just as the group of K. J. Choi, Steve Stricker, and Jim Furyk was walking down the fairway. They went through the usual pre-tee-time rituals: handshakes with everyone within a mile of the tee, the other players and caddies, the starter, the rules official who would walk with the group, the standard-bearer who would carry the board showing their score for 18 holes, and the scorekeeper.

"You can have a sore hand before you tee off if you aren't careful," Rocco joked.

At precisely 7:33, starter Jim Farrell began introducing the players as each stepped to the tee. At a lot of tournaments, the starter will mention everything a player has ever done in his life back to and including what role he had in his high school play. At the Open the introductions are simple. If someone has won the Open, he will be introduced as an Open champion: "From Windermere, Florida, the 2000 and 2002 U.S. Open champion, Tiger Woods."

Right after Thompson had hit his tee shot, Rocco heard McCarthy say simply, "From Naples, Florida, Rocco Mediate."

It was time to play.

THE 10TH HOLE AT TORREY PINES is probably one of the easier par-fours on the golf course—a much easier starting hole than number one. Starting there, as opposed to number one, on the first day with Open nerves rumbling and the weather still cool—in the 50s—was an advantage for Rocco.

"All I wanted to do was get the ball in the fairway and not do something goofy to start the tournament," he said. "When I saw the ball come off the club and I knew it was going to be in the fairway, I breathed a deep sigh of relief. My thought was 'Okay, that's over. Now let's see what we can do out here.'"

He hit a six-iron into the middle of the green just as he had planned in his mind's eye the night before and two-putted from 25 feet for a routine par. Everyone on earth would love to start an Open with a birdie. No one on earth is unhappy with a par.

"All I wanted to do was get through the first few holes without any trouble," Rocco said. "Once you get out on the golf course, you almost forget for a while where you are. It's just a round of golf. But you need a little time to settle yourself down. That's why the first few holes are so crucial. I probably talked the ears off poor Brad and the kid [Thompson] the first hour. That's how I relax myself."

He got off to exactly the sort of start one wants at an Open. He parred the difficult par-three 11th hole, parred the 12th, and then birdied the first par-five he played, the 13th. That was the first time he noticed his name on a leader board. At one under par, with only a couple dozen players on the golf course, he was tied with a handful of players who had also gotten off to solid starts.

Thirty-three minutes after Rocco's group teed off, the Woods-Mickelson-Scott group went off number one. Just the fact that Woods had gotten onto the golf course and to the first tee was a source of great relief to the USGA, to NBC, and to ESPN.

That said, Woods got off to a less than auspicious start. His opening tee shot on the 448-yard first hole sailed left into deep rough. By the time he had hacked the ball out and gotten it onto the green, he had taken four swings. Two putts later he walked off the green talking to himself after a double-bogey six.

Though some people instantly began murmuring about the knee, Woods's being wild off the tee — especially early in a major — was hardly a new phenomenon. If he's had anything approaching an Achilles' heel during his career it has been his driving. One of the reasons he so often pulls off spectacular recovery shots is because he puts himself in position to need spectacular recovery shots. At the 2003 British Open, he had started the tournament by actually losing a golf ball in the deep rough off the first tee at Royal St. George's. So a poor drive and a lousy opening hole were not new items on the Woods résumé.

As if to prove that this wasn't going to be a Winged Foot redux, Woods proceeded to make three birdies on the front nine — at the difficult par-four fourth hole and then back to back at the par-three eighth and the par-five ninth. Thus, he made the turn at one under par, looking very much like the real Tiger Woods.

Rocco also made the turn at one under. He had bogeyed the 14th after his birdie at 13. The 14th was arguably the most interesting hole on the golf course. It could play as long as 435 yards and as short as 269 yards, the USGA having agreed to Jones's idea to have a tee that appeared to be almost on top of the green to create the possibility of a drivable par four. The hole was being played from the back tee on Thursday, though, and Rocco missed his first fairway, leading to the bogey. He bounced back at the par-five 18th, laying up with his second shot and then pitching the ball to five feet. From there, he made the putt to turn in 35 — one under par.

There had been some debate within the USGA about how to play the 18th hole. During the San Diego tournament it had always played as a relatively short par-five, reachable in two as long as a player hit his drive in the fairway and made sure to clear the pond that fronted the left side of the green.

"Traditionally we would have turned the hole into a long par-four for two reasons," David Fay said. "The first is, we usually like to play the Open on a par-70 golf course. [Pebble Beach, normally a par-72, had played to a par-71 in 2000 after the USGA turned the par-five second hole into a par-four.] Second, we normally end the tournament with a long, difficult par-four, which is what the hole would have become if we had converted it.

"Initially that was the plan. But the more we thought about it, the more we all liked the idea of creating a true risk-reward finishing hole. If a player needed a birdie at 18, he would have a decision to make on his second shot if he found the fairway. And, even though the green was reachable, with the pond and the length of the hole, it wasn't one of those par-fives where a good drive means you're hitting six-iron on your second shot."

The hole played at 573 yards, which by today's standards isn't that long. In fact, it was the shortest of the three par-fives on the golf course: The 9th was 612 yards long and the 13th was 614. Once upon a time, a 600-yard hole was an anomaly and considered completely unreachable in two shots. That had changed as equipment—clubs and golf balls—improved through the years. In 1997, when the Open had been played at Congressional Country Club, no player in the field had attempted to reach the 602-yard ninth hole in two. Eight years later, when the Booz-Allen Classic was played at Congressional, players were using irons for their second shots to the hole.

Rocco has never been one of the longer players on tour. When he was younger he would rank somewhere between 80th and 100th in driving distance on the tour. Nowadays, he is never in the top 100—even though he hits the ball about 25 to 30 yards farther off the tee now than when he first came on tour.

"When I was first out here I probably averaged 260 to 265 off the tee, and I was pretty average in length, usually in the top 100. Now I hit it about 285 typically, and I'm nowhere close to the top 100. [In 2008, his average drive was 278.6 yards, which ranked 170th on the tour.] If I was still hitting it the same length as I hit it when I first came out, I wouldn't be in the top 100 on the *ladies* tour. That's how much it's changed."

Rocco's strength is in his accuracy off the tee. In '08, even though he didn't play especially well in the fall, he finished 86th in driving accuracy. A year earlier, he was 38th. In 2003, before he hurt his back again, he had finished 21st on the tour in driving accuracy.

The 18th was anything but an automatic two-shot hole for him. "Only if I hit a perfect drive," he said. "Even then, it was a three-wood for me and there was some risk in the shot."

As it turned out, the 18th was the one hole on the golf course where Rocco's inability to bomb the ball like some others — Woods included — would turn out to be critical. For the week, Woods would average just over 320 yards per drive — 40 yards more than Rocco. But on Thursday, Rocco wasn't concerned with that. He was more than happy to lay up at 18, hit his wedge close, and make his birdie. Having turned in 35 — one under, thanks to the USGA's decision to make 18 a par-five — he was feeling very comfortable with his game and with the way his first round was going.

Unlike Woods, he found the fairway at number one and parred the hole. After a par at number two, he walked onto the tee at the third hole and was stunned by what he saw. The hole is 195 yards long, but since it is close to the water, how it plays depends on the direction of the wind.

"When Lee and I played it on Sunday, I hit a three-iron to get on the green," Rocco said. "They had moved the tee up a little bit, but the wind was with us. Matt and I had to decide between six and seven-iron."

They finally decided on the six, and that turned out to be the right decision. "For a second I thought I'd holed it," Rocco said. "It rolled just past the hole." That shot led to a tap-in birdie. He then birdied the fourth, and as he walked off the green, it struck him that he was — at that moment — leading the championship.

"It wasn't yet noon on the first day," he said. "Half the guys weren't even on the golf course. Still, it was kind of a cool feeling. It's the kind of thing you'd sort of like to take a picture of.

I mean, how often can you say you're leading the U.S. Open? I certainly don't think I'd ever done it before — even for a hole."

He only had one hiccup over the last five holes. At number seven, a hole he would struggle with all week, his drive found a bunker down the left-hand side of the fairway. "The hole really sets up best if you cut the ball around the dogleg," he said. "I can play a cut sometimes. At the fifth I cut the ball off the tee all week. But I really thought if I started the ball out right with my draw, I could keep it on the fairway. Problem was, instead of hitting a draw, I kept hitting hooks. That's what got me into trouble."

He had to lay up out of the bunker and missed a 10-footer for par. That dropped him to two-under. He parred the eighth and the ninth — there was no chance to go for the green at nine — and was very happy to sign for a two-under-par 69.

He was also exhausted. "Whether you're playing well or not, 18 holes of Open golf is draining," he said. "There's pressure on every shot, not just because it's the Open but because there's so little margin for error. Sometimes you don't realize how hard you're grinding until the round is over and you feel like you want to just go curl up somewhere and sleep for about ten hours."

Of course he couldn't do that. It was early in the day, and the USGA was planning on bringing all of the Big Three into the massive interview room once they finished, so they didn't want to back up traffic in there. Players who play well on Thursday and Friday but aren't considered interview room–worthy are taken to what is known as the "flash area," behind the 18th green. There is a small podium, and TV cameras can be comfortably set up a few yards from the player. Most players would much rather go to the flash area than the interview room, which is usually far enough from the clubhouse that one needs to be taken there in a cart. What's more, with a large media contingent in the interview room, there are more questions and the sessions last longer.

At Torrey Pines the media tent was next to the second fairway of the north course, which meant a cart ride for those asked to go there to talk. Even so, Rocco would have been fine going to the interview room. He's one of those rare players who enjoys the give-and-take with the media. "I know they like me because I tend to tell them the truth," he said. "And I like talking, so why wouldn't I enjoy it?"

He was perfectly happy to go to the flash area, especially since he was tired. Someone asked if he liked being under the radar. "I've been under the radar my whole career," he answered, laughing.

He was asked a total of seven questions — the last one, naturally, was about Woods and how tough it might be to come back after such a long layoff.

"I've been injured over the years and come back, but not obviously so that everyone knew or made it a big deal. Everyone is watching him, everything he does is news, and he is the best player that ever walked on grass.

"So yeah, it's got to be really hard, but he's — look, everyone has asked me and my friends, Is he still the favorite? Absolutely he's still the favorite. No disrespect to anyone else, but he's still the favorite. He's the best player in the world. He has some rust going maybe, but if he shoots around par, even par, one-under, one-over, he'll be very happy."

At that moment, Woods was playing the 17th hole and he wasn't especially happy. He had hit another wild drive, this one at the 14th hole, and it had led to his second double bogey of the day. That put him back to one over par for the tournament. When he three-putted the 18th for par, he finished the round at one over par, shooting 72. By then, though, he was far more sanguine than he had been walking off the 14th green.

"In all, I'm happy with where I am," Woods said. "I felt okay out there, and even though I made a couple mistakes, I'm still in a good place, just a few shots back. I can't imagine anyone is going to go very low on this golf course."

That analysis would prove correct. At the end of the day, the leaders — as is often the case at the Open — were a couple of unknowns. One was Justin Hicks, who had been the only other player to make birdie on the first playoff hole along with Rocco ten days earlier in Columbus. He had shot 68. Hicks was thirty-three, a player who had conditional status on the Nationwide Tour and had made a little more than $8,000 coming into the Open. The other leader was Kevin Streelman, a twenty-nine-year-old PGA Tour rookie who had played solidly the first half of the year and would go on to a superb second half, making more than $1 million for the year, finishing 74th on the money list.

No one thought that either Hicks or Streelman was going to be a serious threat to win the Open. In fact, you probably could have gotten better odds that night on one or both missing the cut than on either of them winning the championship. A first-day leader missing a cut is rare in majors but not unheard of: In 1993, Joey Sindelar led the Open at Baltusrol on Thursday and didn't play the weekend. Six years later at the British Open, Rod Pampling did the same thing.

The list of players people thought might be in contention late on Sunday began with the four players at 69: Geoff Ogilvy, the 2006 Open champion; Stuart Appleby, an accomplished player who had come close to winning majors in the past; Eric Axley, a past winner on tour but still considered a long shot; and Rocco—also considered a long shot but someone the media was hoping to see continue to play well because he was, they all agreed, a good story and a great talker.

There were five players at 70—most notably two-time Open champion Ernie Els and Lee Westwood, one of Europe's best Ryder Cup players, who had flirted with winning major championships in the past. That made eleven players under par, just about right for the first round as far as the USGA was concerned.

Seven players were at even par 71, among them Mickelson and Vijay Singh. Woods was in a group of twelve players at 72, and Adam Scott had shot 73. It was exactly the kind of bunched-up leader board one would expect at the Open.

Woods had accomplished two goals on Thursday: He'd gotten through the round without falling or doing any more damage to his knee (as far as anyone knew), and he had done what all great players try to do on Thursday at a major: not lose the tournament. One of golf's oldest sayings is that you can't win a tournament on Thursday but you can certainly lose it. Sitting just four shots behind the leaders—three behind those he would have considered serious threats—Woods had every reason to sleep well on Thursday night, especially since he didn't have to be on the first tee the next afternoon until 1:36. This was the USGA's dream: Woods and Mickelson teeing off together late afternoon on the East Coast, their round stretching well into prime time—it would be well after nine o'clock in the east before they finished—with both still in contention

Rocco's round was also scheduled to start relatively late—at

1:03 Pacific time. He felt great about the way he had played on the first day but knew from experience that a good first round, even a great first round, was a long way from being in contention on Sunday afternoon.

"I slept much better that night," he said. "What the first day told me was that I hadn't been fooling myself when I thought I could play well on the golf course. I didn't want to get too excited—it was much too soon for that. I told myself, 'Keep having fun and you'll be fine.'"

He smiled. "Of course, that's a lot easier said than done—especially at the Open."

12

Tiger Shows Up

THE JUNE GLOOM THE USGA had been concerned about made an appearance on Friday morning. It wasn't a heavy fog, the kind that made it impossible to play, but it was enough to make the morning temperatures a little warmer and the wind a little less brisk.

"I had thought playing in the afternoon Friday we'd get some wind and a very fast-running golf course," Rocco said. "But the fog coming in made everything softer. You don't really expect relatively soft greens playing in the afternoon on Friday at the Open, but that's what we got."

Players will always tell you they prefer playing in the morning than in the afternoon. Most golfers are by nature morning people, accustomed to getting out of bed early to get to the golf course either to beat summer heat or the crowds or to play and then get on to whatever else is on their calendar for a given day. And there is usually less wind and the greens are more pristine—fewer spike marks, since many players on tour still wear metal spikes—earlier in the day than later.

"More important than that, when you play in the morning

you have less time to think," Rocco said. "That's a bigger factor on a weekend when you're in contention, but it's true on Thursday and Friday too."

On tour, everyone plays early one day and late one day during the first 36 holes of a tournament. The same is true at an Open, only more so because the USGA stretches the tee times out a little more than other tournaments do to take into account the difficulty of the golf course. Most PGA Tour events have a nine-minute gap between threesomes, occasionally going to ten. The USGA separates each Open group by eleven minutes—meaning the last tee time of the day is about an hour later than at most events.

That's why Rocco, even though he and Thompson and Bryant were in the fourth group of the afternoon wave of players, didn't tee off until 1:03 P.M. This time they played the front nine first. Once again, Rocco was very happy to find the fairway with his opening drive and perfectly satisfied when his five-iron landed 30 feet from the hole on the putting surface.

But he got a little jumpy on his birdie putt and watched helplessly as his ball ran a good 12 feet past the cup. "I forgot that when you're putting toward the water, which I was, you have to figure the ball is going to pick up speed even if it's not straight downhill," he said. "I just kind of mind-blocked for a second."

He took his time with the par putt and managed to sneak into the right side of the hole for a deep-sigh-of-relief par.

"When you've played well the first day, the last thing you want is to start the second day badly," he said. "That's not an easy opening hole—ask Tiger. But after hitting the green, there would have really been no excuse for making bogey. You know you're going to make them out there; you just don't want to make one right out of the chute. That par putt was a big deal for me."

It became a little bit bigger when he birdied the second hole. "I didn't feel comfortable on that tee all week," he said. "I decided to hit three-wood because it took the left bunker out of play—I couldn't reach it. That made me feel better standing on the tee box."

He made a 25-footer for birdie there, meaning he had made two long putts to start the round. Given his history—always a good driver, not always a good putter—that was both an encouraging start and a positive harbinger for the day.

"Those two putts and those two holes got the butterflies out quickly," he said. "You never tee it up in a major—unless it's Sunday and you're in the first group and have absolutely no chance—without feeling some butterflies. Making those two putts gave me a real shot of confidence and made me feel like it was going to be a good day again."

At three under par, he was back on top of the leader board. Streelman had teed off early that morning and had shot 77 to drop back, and Hicks, playing a couple of groups in front of Rocco's, was in full reverse on his way to an 80. He would make the cut—by one shot.

Rocco's play on the front nine was virtually flawless. He birdied the fourth hole—making another long putt, this time from closer to 30 feet—for the second straight day, playing his natural draw on the hole by starting the ball out well right and letting it drift back to the fairway. "Those four holes [three through six] were a key part of my playing well," he said. "I played those holes well all four days, and especially on the three days I started on number one, that section of the course helped get me into a good mind-set for the rest of the day."

In all, he would play those four holes in one under par and the other 14 holes in one over par. That doesn't sound like much of a difference, but on a golf course that wasn't giving up many birdies, on a difficult stretch of holes without a par-five involved, that was very solid golf.

He had to lay up again at the ninth and settled for par, but as he walked to the 10th tee he was four under par for the championship and in the lead. "Twenty-seven holes is way too soon to start thinking about anything serious," he said. "But I was certainly feeling good at that point."

Not long after Rocco's group teed off at the 10th, the group of Woods, Mickelson, and Scott walked from the 18th green to the first tee. There wasn't a smile to be found anywhere near the world's three top-ranked players.

Woods had again started poorly, bogeying the 10th and 12th holes to fall to three over par. He had then bounced back in typical Tiger fashion, reaching the 13th green in two and draining a 25-foot putt for eagle. That got him his first real Tiger roar of the week and jumped him back to even par for the day and one over for the championship. But he bogeyed both 16 and 17 to go back to three over, meaning he trailed the leader (Rocco) by seven and was only four shots inside what would be the cut line at the end of the day.

"I really didn't feel as if I was playing that badly," Woods said later. "I felt comfortable out there; I just made three mistakes in a row—bogeying 16 and 17 and then making a par at 18 with the tees way up. When we went to the back [actually front] nine, I was thinking if I could get back to even par for the tournament by the end of the day, I'd be okay."

Things weren't going any better for Mickelson—the one player in the group who didn't have an injury excuse to fall back on—or for Scott. Mickelson had been tied with Woods on the first nine holes of the day and was at two over par after 27 holes. Scott was one shot back of Mickelson.

As the group made the turn, there was considerable concern among the USGA and NBC honchos. David Fay, sitting in the NBC booth as he always did when the network was on the air in case a rules explanation was needed, wasn't seriously worried that Woods would miss the cut. But he was worried about how much longer he was going to be able to continue playing.

"You could see right from the beginning that there were certain swings where he was in a lot of pain," Fay said. "He wasn't playing well, and I honestly wondered if he might make a swing that would put him on the ground and that would be it.

"After the first day [Woods's agent Mark] Steinberg had been very honest with our guys. He'd said that Tiger was hurting. Of course we could all see it, but that confirmed it. I didn't think he would miss the cut. But I wasn't entirely convinced he would finish 72 holes."

For NBC, Woods making the cut wasn't really enough. The network didn't need him teeing off with the rabbit groups on Saturday morning; it needed him in contention. Even with Mickelson in contention until the final hole at Winged Foot, even with a wild and crazy finish there, the ratings without Woods had dropped noticeably from 2005, when he had finished second at Pinehurst. They had gone up again in 2007, when he was in the last group on Sunday at Oakmont.

So while Rocco was making his way around the back nine that afternoon having the time of his life, there was a good deal of attention surrounding the group that went off the first tee shortly after four o'clock Pacific time.

As he had done on Thursday, Woods drove the ball wildly on number one. This time, though, he caught a break—one that might have changed the tone of the entire week for everyone involved in the championship. Instead of burying in the rough or going behind a tree where he would have no shot, Woods's ball came to rest just to the left of a tree trunk on some hardpan dirt, where his lie was decent and he had a difficult but hardly impossible shot to the green.

"Give him an opening and he'll make something happen with it," Rocco would say later in the week.

This was no exception to that rule. "It was a lucky break," Woods said. "I had about 157 yards [to the] hole and a pretty clear shot, plus I could control the ball off the lie I had. I was able to get at it with an eight-iron."

The only real issue on the shot was that Woods had to stand on a cart path to take his swing. By rule, he was entitled to a drop because of that, but he opted to play the ball from where it was. "If I had dropped, I would have had to drop behind a tree," he explained.

These days, many pros have taken to wearing golf shoes with soft spikes in them, because they are lighter and more comfortable to wear than metal spikes. Woods still wears metal spikes, meaning he had to be careful not to slip while standing on the cart path. He didn't.

The ball ended up on the green, 18 feet from the hole. When Woods holed the putt for birdie, he shook his fist—not the exaggerated Tiger fist-pump that is so often imitated, just a little 'Okay, let's get going' type of fist-pump. Instead of making another bogey after a bad drive, he had made birdie. Suddenly, he felt he was back in the game.

When Woods starts to feel confident, particularly with his putter, he can get on the kind of roll that no other player in the world can get on. This turned out to be one of those afternoons. He drained a 20-foot putt for birdie at the second hole, made another 18-footer at the fourth, and then swished a 25-footer at the fifth. That made four birdies in five holes and sent him from three over par to one under par. He went from a tie for 55th as he made the turn, seven shots back, to a tie for fourth, just one shot back of the coleaders at that moment, Stuart Appleby and Rocco, who had bogeyed the 10th hole and the 12th hole to fall back to two under par.

More than that, it changed the mind-set of everyone on the grounds. Woods went from shuffling around, head down, wondering if he really should be on the golf course given the condition of his knee, to pumped up, full of confidence, knowing he could win the championship. The only player Woods believes can stop Woods is Woods. He certainly didn't look at the leader board and worry about Stuart Appleby or Rocco Mediate or anyone else up there. The only name that mattered to him, now in a red number as opposed to a black one, was his own.

Around the golf course, in the clubhouse, on the driving range (where a large TV screen had been set up), and around the country—it was now prime time on the East Coast—people watched the Woods birdie binge. Most thought the same thing: Here comes Tiger; his knee is just fine.

They were half right. The knee wasn't fine. Tiger was coming anyway.

———

Rocco, a couple of holes deeper into his round than Woods because he'd started thirty-three minutes earlier, certainly noticed when Woods's name appeared on the leader board. Unlike some players who claim not to look at leader boards—sometimes to the point of actually doing stupid things as a result—Rocco looks at them all the time. He wants to have an awareness, regardless of how early or late it is in a tournament, of where he stands, how the golf course is playing (the best scores tell him that), and whom he might be competing with should he get into contention.

"Tiger on the board is like no one else on the board," he said. "He's Tiger. Tiger at his very best you aren't going to beat. Tiger playing okay you're still going to have to work to beat. When he popped up on there after not being there for a while, I thought, 'Okay, he's here now; he isn't likely to go away any time soon.'"

Rocco had bogeyed the 10th hole, disappointing because it was not one of the tougher holes on the golf course, but not too upsetting because it was his first bogey of the day. "You're going to make bogeys at the Open," he said. "There wasn't a hole out there where you could fall asleep and not get into trouble. I hooked my drive left of the bunkers and had no chance to get on the green. There's never a hole at the Open where you can make a mistake like that and expect to get away with it. This isn't like a regular PGA Tour event where guys can go out almost any day and make six birdies, an eagle, and no bogeys. You hope to make birdies at the Open, but you almost never walk off a hole after a par feeling anything but good."

The wind was coming up a little bit by now, and the greens

were beginning to speed up. The USGA had wanted them at about 13, but they had been a bit slower in the morning because of the June gloom. By late afternoon, they were probably in the 13 range.

"Fact is, I missed a couple of shots on the back nine," Rocco said. "On the 12th, I simply can't afford to miss the fairway, because it's a 500-yard par-four [actually 504 on the scorecard], and even from the fairway I'm going to need a long club to get to the green. I don't mind that; I'm very comfortable hitting long clubs, and I can hit them high enough that the ball will stop on the green. But there's no margin for error on that hole."

He missed the fairway left at 12, his drive starting down that side and drawing into the rough—again beyond the bunker—instead of starting down the right and drawing into the fairway. From there, he found a green-side bunker, blasted out to ten feet, and missed the putt for his second bogey of the day.

He had to lay up at the par-five 13th, so he settled for par there, and then he missed another fairway at the 17th, leading to his third bogey in eight holes. By then, for the first time all week, he was a little frustrated.

"I wasn't mad and I wasn't down," he said. "I just wasn't happy with myself for missing three fairways out of six [11 and 16 are par-threes], because that's not me, especially when I'm playing well. I mean, there are times, when I'm home and out playing with guys and there's no pressure, where I might go a week without missing a fairway. I'm not exaggerating. Now, this is different. There's pressure and you're talking fairways as wide as my hotel room. [The Open fairways ranged from 24 yards to 33 yards wide, far narrower than those of just about any other tournament in the world. At Augusta National, the fairways are generally about 50 yards wide.] So I don't expect to hit every fairway. But three out of six sucks."

Standing on the 18th tee, now one under par for the championship, Rocco wanted badly to finish the day with a birdie. "The only way for me to have a chance to go at the green is to really blast a drive," he said. "I had to hit my draw and get it out there in the fairway to have any chance. If I miss, it isn't that big a disaster; it just means I have to lay up. I went after that drive a little bit."

He hit it perfectly—not well, perfectly.

"One of the best drives of my life," he said. "I really drilled it. Even so, I still had 248 to the front and 266 to the hole, and I had to stand there in the fairway and think for a moment if I wanted to take a shot at it. The last thing I wanted to do was miss the shot a little bit, end up in the water, make six, and shoot 40 on the back nine. That would not have been good. But I really thought I could get the three-wood there and I could aim it a little bit right to stay away from the water, so I decided to go for it."

The gamble paid off when he bounced the ball onto the green, leaving himself a 35-foot eagle putt. He hit a good first putt, leaving himself about two feet—his shortest birdie putt of the first two days. He knocked that one in to finish the day at even-par 71: two-under-par 33 on the front nine, two-over 38 on the back. There had been three birdies (2, 4, and 18) and three bogeys (10, 12, and 17).

"If I had parred the 18th, it still would have been a pretty good round, and I certainly would still have been in contention," Rocco said. "But finishing with a birdie always feels good, especially when you've bogey-trained it for a while before that. I was very happy with where I was walking off that green."

He was not the only one of the three players in his group who would play the weekend. As is often the case for the Senior Open champion, the golf course was just too long for Brad Bryant. He shot 77–79 to miss the cut by seven shots. Michael Thompson, though, had no trouble with the length of the golf course and managed his game surprisingly well for an inexperienced twenty-two-year-old. He followed his opening day 74 with a 73 that put him comfortably inside the cut line.

Rocco was extremely impressed with the youngster, who had just finished his senior year at the University of Alabama.

"As we were going up the 18th fairway, I called him over and I said, 'Let me tell you what I want you to change before you turn pro: nothing.' I liked his golf swing; I liked his demeanor. I think he's got great potential."

Thompson proved Rocco right on the weekend, adding a 73 and a 72 to finish tied for 29th place, making him the low amateur among the three who made the cut.

At the moment that he finished his round, Rocco was tied for the lead with Appleby, who still had two holes to play, at two under par. Even though the Woods-Mickelson-Scott group was only about forty minutes from finishing, it was a no-brainer to bring the Open coleader after 36 holes into the interview room. Along with Cindi, Rocco jumped into a cart to make the trip to the media tent. They were both fired up. He was halfway through the Open, and no one in the 156-man field was ahead of him.

"On the one hand, I'd played enough golf tournaments to know halfway through is only halfway through," he said. "On the other hand, it had only been a couple weeks since I shot a million on the front nine in the third round of the Memorial and thought I had no chance to make the Open, much less be in contention. So right then I was feeling pretty good."

His session in the media room was lengthy—eighteen questions in all, meaning he stayed about twenty-five minutes—and his answers were predictable Rocco stuff: He was excited to be in contention in his favorite tournament, he loved the setup, his back felt good, he was comfortable with the conventional putter.

Naturally, he was asked the inevitable Tiger question. His answer surprised most of the people in the room. He said all the things you are supposed to say about Woods, but then he added a thought most players would not have added.

"You want him in this event," Rocco said. "You don't want him seven over par or something. If you're going to win this tournament, it would be great to go up against him and maybe somehow, you never know... But to go up against the best, whether you win or lose, it's just—you get to go up against the best. That's what I like.

"I don't have many more shots at this or playing golf with him. If I do this weekend, I don't know how the pairings will go, but that's what you want as a player, is to see what you've got against the man. And then you've got the golf course too, that you have to deal with, which is as hard as they get.

"That's what I always relish—the opportunity to play with the best player in the world. And I don't know why you wouldn't. You just never know sometimes."

Most players, though they might not admit it, hardly relished the notion of going head-to-head with Woods ever, much less at a major championship on the weekend. The tone for Playing with Tiger in a Major had been set in 1997, when Colin Montgomerie trailed Woods by three shots going into the third round at the Masters. On Friday afternoon, Montgomerie had expressed confidence that his experience would pay dividends when paired with the kid playing in his first major.

Twenty-four hours later, Montgomerie was singing a different tune after Woods beat him by nine shots—65 to 74. At that point, Woods led the field by eight shots. A year earlier, Greg Norman had led the Masters by six shots after three rounds only to collapse in the final round while Nick Faldo went past him to win by five shots. Someone asked Montgomerie if a similar rally by Constantino Rocca, who was second to Woods, was possible.

Montgomerie might still have been shell-shocked from his afternoon with Woods, but he hadn't lost his biting sense of humor. "There is no way that's going to happen," he said. "With all due respect, Rocca is not Nick Faldo, and this young man [Woods] is by no means Greg Norman."

Those words echoed through the years as one player after another faded when paired with Woods late in a major. Mike Weir, who would win the Masters in 2003, was paired with Woods in the final group of the final round during the 1999 PGA. He shot 80 that day.

"It's just not something you can prepare yourself for," Weir said. "It's a little bit of everything: the pressure of contending in a major, the crowds, just the presence Tiger has. It's not like anything else you experience in golf."

Two players had managed to hold their own paired with Woods on the last day of a major, and neither was a star: Bob May had shot 66 at the 2000 PGA before losing in a three-hole playoff, and Chris DiMarco, who had actually caught Woods from behind on the last two holes at the Masters in 2005, only to lose when Woods birdied the first sudden-death playoff hole.

"Most guys, if they're being honest, will tell you they'd rather play a group or two in front of him or, maybe even better, behind him," said Davis Love III, who had also experienced the Tiger Effect. "He's not an easy guy to stare down."

And yet here was Rocco, saying he would relish the chance. Most people listening thought it was a nice little speech. Few believed he would do much better than anyone else had if he actually did get the chance to go head-to-head with Tiger.

As it turned out, he would not have that chance on Saturday. Appleby made a 70-foot putt for birdie on the 18th hole to add a one-under-par 70 to his opening-round 69. That put him at three under for the championship and in the lead by himself. Rocco was one shot back and, since he had been the first person to post a two-under-par score, he would play in the final group with Appleby. When players are tied after two or three rounds, the first player to finish is the last player out when pairings are done for the third or fourth round.

After his birdie binge, Woods parred six, seven, and eight. He actually had reasonably good chances to make birdie at the seventh and the eighth but, proving he is occasionally human, missed. Then he hit a huge second shot at the ninth hole, which led to his fifth birdie of the back nine. That meant he had shot 30 on the front nine for a round of 68, matching the low round of the championship over the first two days. It put him in a tie for second place, one shot back of Appleby, along with Rocco and Robert Karlsson of Sweden. One shot further back were four players: Spanish Ryder Cupper Miguel A. Jiminez; Great Britain's Lee Westwood, also a past Ryder Cup star; D. J. Trahan, an up-and-coming American player; and Davis Love, the 1997 PGA champion who had been battling injuries and, like Rocco, had been forced to go through qualifying to get into the tournament. Among the five players one shot behind them at even par were past Open champions Ernie Els and Geoff Ogilvy.

The pairings for Saturday would be Rocco and Appleby in the final group and Woods and Karlsson right in front of them.

The front nine on Friday afternoon had not gone nearly as well for the other two players in Woods's threesome. (Many people refer to players paired together as "playing partners," which is a misnomer. They are competing against one another and, thus, can't be partners. "Fellow competitor" is more accurate).

Scott, although insisting that his hand really wasn't an issue, was clearly struggling, He managed to shoot 73 again, which left him at four-over-par 146, seven shots behind Appleby. Mickelson was also at 146 after shooting 75 on Friday. Given his relationship with Woods, watching him post the 30 while he was adding a 37 to his back nine 38 had to be painful. The two men had been tied after 27 holes, then Woods had blown Mickelson away—by seven shots—during their final nine together.

Like any great player, Mickelson almost never sees himself as being out of contention. During a brief appearance in the flash area after the round, he admitted he was disappointed but said he still believed if he could get back to even par on Saturday—which would mean shooting 67, a round no one had posted yet—he would have a chance to win on Sunday. Doggedly, he insisted that the pairing had been "really fun."

That wasn't exactly the way it appeared to others after the group finished on the ninth green. Lee Janzen was playing in a threesome directly behind the Big Three and was waiting in the fairway while they putted out.

"To be honest, I was so wrapped up in trying to get something going with my own game [he missed the cut by four shots] that I spent most of two days almost unaware of what those guys were doing. But on Friday afternoon, when Tiger got on that roll, you couldn't help but hear the roars. I mean, they practically engulfed the entire golf course.

"Watching them on nine, I noticed when they finished that Tiger and Adam had a nice handshake [even though Scott had to use his left hand] and kind of chatted for a minute. Tiger and Phil were practically running when they shook hands. I have to think, especially in his hometown, that was tough for Phil."

Because they had been in the same group and shot the same score, Mickelson and Scott would be paired together again on Saturday. They would be the 21st of 40 twosomes to tee off that day. Eighty players had made the cut thanks to the fact that the USGA still uses the "10-shot rule," meaning anyone within 10 shots of the leader after two rounds plays the weekend. Most golf tournaments cut to 70 players and ties. The USGA takes either 60 and ties or all those within 10 of the lead, which often makes for an unwieldy weekend. The only other tournament in the world that still employs the 10-shot rule is the Masters, but the field there is rarely more than 90 players at the start of the week. The British Open abandoned the 10-shot rule after the 1995 championship, when 103 players made the cut. The Royal and Ancient, which administers the Open, decided that risking that many players on the golf course for the weekend—not to mention paying them all post-cut money—wasn't worth the trouble.

Among the 76 players who missed the Torrey Pines cut was 2007 champion Angel Cabrera, who shot 79 the first day to knock himself out of any chance to defend his title. Cabrera might have been done in by the laws of San Diego County. All municipally owned venues in San Diego County are smoke-free—no smoking allowed at all. That includes Torrey Pines.

Cabrera had been a smoker for years. After winning at Oakmont, he had been asked about his smoking. "Some guys have swing coaches and psychologists," he answered. "I smoke." Knowing he would not be able to smoke on the golf course at Torrey Pines, Cabrera had quit smoking earlier in the year. He had not been the same player since. Coincidence? Perhaps.

Because there were so many players inside the cut line, the first tee time would be at 8:30 A.M Pacific time on Saturday—even with the round scheduled to end at 7 P.M., 10 P.M. on the East Coast. Mickelson and Scott had an 11:50 tee time. That was three hours before Woods and Karlsson, who would tee off at 2:50. Ten minutes later, the final group, Appleby and Rocco, would tee it up.

That meant NBC would get its wish: Woods playing more than half his round in prime time on a Saturday night in the east. You could bet that America would have the chance to watch Woods from the moment he got out of his car until his last putt went in the hole. Rocco would also get some TV time. But the focus, 36 holes into the Open, was clearly on the man with the sore knee.

"If I was at home watching, that's who I'd want to see too," Rocco said.

He would not be home watching. His view of Woods would be similar to Janzen's on Friday. He would be right behind him — on the golf course, trying to win the U.S. Open.

13

Serious Stuff

Rocco, Cindi, and Rocco's college roommate Steve Puertas, who had driven down from his home in Los Angeles to spend the weekend, had a quiet dinner in the hotel on Friday night. Puertas—known to one and all as Sticky—volunteered to drive to Fleming's, a nearby steak house, and bring food back so that Rocco and Cindi wouldn't have to deal with the crowds in the restaurant. Rocco happily took him up on the offer. After dinner, the three of them stayed up later than usual for the simple reason that Rocco didn't want to wake up too early.

"The less time you sit around thinking about things," he said, "the better off you are."

Players understand that part of the job on the weekends if you are in contention is killing time before you go to the golf course. This is especially true at the majors, in part because the pressure is so much greater, but also because tee times are usually an hour or so later than at regular PGA Tour stops. On tour, the finishing time most weeks is six o'clock eastern time—occasionally it slides to seven when the tour is on the West Coast—but the last tee time often as not is between 1:30 and 2 P.M. eastern time.

Normally, on the West Coast, tee times are squeezed to get

everyone on the golf course by ten o'clock local time. Instead of playing in twosomes and having everyone tee off on number one, as is the norm on weekends, the players go out in threesomes and half the field tees off on number 10. It is the only way to finish when TV wants tournaments to finish.

Two-tee starts on the weekend in majors are strictly verboten, unless weather creates havoc with the event, and TV usually pushes the finish times on majors as late as possible. In fact, CBS intentionally schedules the final round of the Masters to run past seven o'clock on the East Coast so that the final minutes will pick up extra viewers tuning in to watch *60 Minutes.* The golf telecast benefits from that, and *60 Minutes* benefits from golf fans who stick around to watch the newsmagazine show. Frequently that night's *60 Minutes* will include a sports story to entice the golf fans to watch.

Because the last putt almost never goes into the hole until after seven o'clock, there isn't all that much daylight left on an April evening when a Masters playoff occurs. Remarkably, no Masters playoff—since the 18-hole Monday playoff was abandoned for sudden death in 1979—has gone past the second hole.

"I'm waiting for the year when they finally get nailed," David Fay said. "Tiger and Phil will be going to the third playoff hole and they'll both say, 'It's too dark; let's come back in the morning.'"

Fay acts as if the Masters is the only tournament that times its finish to accommodate TV. If anything, the USGA is *more* accommodating. In 2002, NBC asked for a 3:40 tee time for the final group of Woods and Sergio Garcia, which meant a finish at about 7:45 local time. That would leave about forty-five minutes of daylight if all went well. In spite of the fact that there were thunderstorms in the forecast, the USGA didn't move the starting times up. It rained, there was a forty-seven-minute delay, and Woods and Garcia finished in virtual darkness while Fay and other USGA officials cowered behind the 18th green, terrified that the two players would say it was too dark to finish.

"We blew that one," Fay said. "We were lucky Tiger had a three-shot lead or he might have insisted on coming back Monday morning. I told the NBC people after that one that we weren't going to schedule any finishes after seven o'clock local time. We need that extra time in case of weather."

The weather forecast for San Diego on the weekend was identical to what it had been all week: a little bit of June gloom early, but perfect sunshine and cool, comfortable temperatures by the time the leaders teed off.

Rocco had contended in majors in the past, but he had never been in the last group on a Saturday or a Sunday. That certainly upped the ante a little bit. Even though he would have loved to be paired with Woods, Appleby was, he thought, a good pairing for him.

"Stuey is one of the good guys on tour," Rocco said. "Plus, he's been in situations like this before, so he's going to be relatively calm about it. I just hope I don't jump out of my skin before we tee off."

He was fine, going through his morning ritual much later than usual: Bruegger's, Starbucks, and then the short drive to the golf course. He walked to the range with Cindi and Matt and went through his usual warm-up, although he couldn't help but notice there were only a few players on the practice tee, since most of the field was on the golf course by the time he arrived. He walked onto the tee seconds after Woods and Karlsson had departed. "Funny thing about the week was I never laid eyes on Tiger except on a television set, until Saturday after we finished playing. Our paths just never crossed."

As he had done on Thursday and Friday, Rocco got off to a solid start. His tee shot on number one just bounced into the first cut of rough, but he had a good lie and was able to get the ball on the green for a routine two-putt par. "Deep breath after that one," he said. "That's a hard enough opening hole that, especially with nerves in play, you can easily make bogey—or worse."

Woods had started with a double bogey on Thursday and had been saved by a lucky bounce on Friday. On Saturday he hadn't been as lucky. His third straight wild drive on the first hole led to another double bogey. Appleby also bogeyed the hole and, just that quickly, Rocco, Appleby, and Karlsson were tied for the lead, with Woods two shots back.

"You can't get caught up in that stuff on Saturday," Rocco said. "You're always aware of the scoreboard, but in a way it's exactly like the first two days. You just work your way around the golf course trying to make pars, throw in a birdie if you get a chance, and most of all avoid big numbers. You know if you can do that, at the end of the day, you're going to be in position to win on Sunday. Which is ultimately what you want."

Still uncomfortable on the second tee, Rocco again hit three-wood and again positioned the ball perfectly. Just as he had done on Friday, he hit a solid second shot and drained a putt—this time a 12-footer—for birdie to get to three under for the tournament and take the lead.

The third hole was playing remarkably short with a front hole location, so short that Rocco hit a pitching wedge. "Remember, this is a hole I hit a three-iron on during a practice round," he said. "I'd hit six-iron and seven-iron the first two days."

His shot landed squarely in the middle of the green, but he ran his first putt six feet past the hole and missed coming back. It was his first three-putt of the week. "Disappointing," he said. "But it was bound to happen on U.S. Open greens. Still, I hated giving the shot back that quickly."

He rebounded two holes later, again hitting a perfect cut off the tee — "People don't think I can hit a cut, but I can when I really need to," he said — that led to a 10-foot birdie putt. The rest of the front nine was relatively routine. He missed the green at the par-three eighth but pitched the ball to four feet and made the putt for par. His drive found the rough on number nine, so he had to lay up.

"Even if I hit the fairway on that hole, I'm probably laying up," he said. "The par-fives were really the only holes where my lack of distance came into play. I think I hit one of them [the 18th, on Friday] in two. The longer guys, Tiger included, of course, almost always had a shot to go for the green in two."

Most players considered the front nine at Torrey Pines more difficult than the back nine — Rocco included. "The back has two par-fives and a couple of short fours," he said. "It should be the easier nine."

After three days, Rocco had played the front nine in four under par. He had played the back nine through two days in one over par. It was a pattern that would continue.

While Rocco was piecing together a steady front nine, players were going in all different directions around the golf course. Woods had continued to struggle on the nine that he had annihilated the day before. He bogeyed the fourth hole before making his first birdie of the day at the seventh. A three-putt par at the ninth frustrated him greatly and meant he made the turn at two over par for the day and even par for the championship. At that moment, with Rocco a hole behind, Woods trailed by three.

Up ahead, Lee Westwood was putting together an excellent round and had moved into second place, three shots behind Rocco. The other contenders were falling back. The USGA had made certain the greens were stimping at 13 at the start of the day, and the hole locations were a little bit tougher than they had been on the first two days. What's more, Open nerves were now very much in play.

The most surprising collapse of the day was Appleby's. He was not a player who hadn't been in the crucible of a major before. Appleby was thirty-seven and had won eight times on tour. He had been part of a four-man playoff (won by Ernie Els) at the British Open in 2002 and had played in the last group on Sunday at the Masters with Woods in 2007. He hadn't fared well that day—finishing in a tie for seventh—but that hardly made him abnormal. Playing with Rocco, the loose and easy motormouth, should have been a far better pairing for him than playing with Woods.

But the day started poorly for Appleby, with a three-putt at the second and a four-putt at the fifth, and went downhill from there. As focused as he was on his own play, Rocco couldn't help but feel compassion for Appleby. "You know we all have days like that," he said. "It's especially baffling when it happens after you've played well for two or three rounds and that much more frustrating because it isn't as if you can't play. The day before, you *could* play. That's the game, though; that's why it's the hardest game in the world.

"Here's the thing about golf: If you go onto the golf course without confidence and without your best swing, you aren't going to play well. If you go onto the golf course with confidence and with your best swing, you might play well, but there's no guarantee."

Appleby ended up shooting 79, which eliminated him from contention. After 36 holes in a golf tournament, a player who is 10 shots back or less still has a fighting chance to win (especially if his name is Woods), because two low rounds can get you close to the leaders. After 54 holes, that number is usually cut in half. Once in a blue moon a player six shots back (see Nick Faldo, Masters 1996) going into Sunday may win, but most of the time that involves a collapse by the leader (e.g., Greg Norman) combined with few players ahead of him on the leader board. If someone is five or six shots back going into Sunday and there are ten or twelve players ahead of him, he has virtually no chance to rally. After his 79, Appleby was eight shots behind the leader and in a tie for 19th place. Game over.

The game was still very much on for Rocco, Woods, and Westwood. By the end of the day, they had created some separation between themselves and the rest of the field.

For a brief moment, it appeared that Rocco might actually separate himself from everybody. He birdied the 10th hole to get to four under par and at that moment led Westwood by three shots and Woods by four. Even then, he wasn't focused on the margin—too soon—but on trying to keep what was now a very good round—he was two under par for the day—rolling in the right direction.

"Part of you is thinking, 'Hey, just keep this going and if you can get it into the house at four under or if you somehow can get it to five with two par-fives still to play, you're going to be in great shape,'" he said. "But there's this little tiny voice in there that reminds you this is the Open and Tiger's still out there and it isn't going to be that easy. That's just not the way golf is."

Sure enough, it was a par-five that tripped him up and put his round into reverse. His drive at the 13th hole found the rough, not a big deal in itself, since he was probably going to lay up anyway. He laid up well enough, but his wedge wasn't especially good, leaving him with a downhill 25-foot putt.

"It was one of those you aren't trying to make, you're just trying to get it close: have a tap-in par and get out of there," Rocco said. "But it was one of those putts where if I just breathed on it, I wasn't going to be able to stop it."

The putt rolled five feet past the hole and the par putt slid just low for an ugly bogey. There are few things golfers hate more than a six on their scorecard. Rocco had avoided making one for 48 holes.

"It's annoying, but you know it's going to happen," he said. "I mean, Tiger started his tournament with a six on a par-four and he was still doing okay. I needed to shake it off. Unfortunately, I didn't."

He parred the 14th hole, but then came the par-four 478-yard 15th. "I hit two bad shots and got two bad lies there," he said later. "To be honest, I probably made a pretty good six."

Though there really is no such thing as a pretty good six, this was something close to it. His drive went left into a hole in the rough and he had to gouge the ball out. Still in deep rough, he came up short of the green with his third shot. From there, he spun a pretty good wedge to about 15 feet and two-putted.

That made two sixes in three holes after none in 48. In three holes and 30 minutes, Rocco had gone from leading the championship by three shots to trailing Lee Westwood, who had just finished with a one-under-par 70 to post 211—two under par—for 54 holes.

Rocco was tied with Woods, who, as he so often does, had turned what looked like an awful day into a good one with one spectacular hole. It was the 13th, the same hole that had started the trouble for Rocco. It wasn't surprising to see Woods turn his day around on a par five, because par-fives are one of his greatest strengths. There aren't very many that he can't reach in two, and when he doesn't get on the green he is almost always somewhere around the green, where his superb short game frequently leads to an up-and-down birdie.

Until that point, his play on the par-fives for the week had been ordinary, actually below ordinary for him. As he walked onto the 13th tee on Saturday afternoon, he had played seven par-fives in the tournament and was four under par, pretty good by most standards, not so hot for Woods. By comparison, after his bogey on 13 a few minutes after Woods played the hole, Rocco would be two under par on the par-fives. Given that he had only had one chance to even think about going for a green in two, this was a small margin.

It all changed for Woods beginning on the 13th, a hole he had eagled on Friday to turn his round in the right direction after bogeying two of his first three holes. He was three over par for the day and one over for the championship when he reached 13, and he needed to make something happen.

Naturally, he did.

Just as naturally, he did it in a way only he could possibly even think about. His drive on 13 was way right, another off-line tee shot in a day that was full of them.

"When I was warming up, I didn't hit anything that was particularly crisp or clean," he said later. "Even warming up, I had a two-way miss going that I was trying to clean up where at least I just had a one-way miss, you know, miss it one way, left or right. I went on the golf course and had a little bit of a two-way miss, but not as bad as on the range."

This miss was well to the right, but as often happens with Woods, he caught a break. The ball landed behind a concession stand. Since a concession stand is an immovable object but not a natural hazard like a tree, he was entitled to a drop. After looking over his options left or right of the concession stand, he opted to drop on the left.

"My tee shot was a terrible shot," he said, laughing. "When I looked to the right of the concession stand [which he didn't know was a concession stand until told later in the interview room], the grass wasn't all that great. On top of that, I would have had to try and carry that barranca on the right-hand side. If I didn't get a good enough lie, I didn't know if I could carry that.

"So I went left. And if I happened to draw a poor lie there, at least I know I could wedge out to the fairway, bottom of the hill, and try and make par and move on. If I happened to catch a good lie, then I could probably get to the green and maybe steal a four out of there."

He caught a good lie. The rest became part of Open lore soon after. "I had 210 [to the] front and I hit a five-iron," he said. "I was actually aiming at the back bunker because I did not want to leave the ball short of that pin. It landed on the top of the green, and I was surprised that it stopped. It somehow landed soft enough where it stopped."

The ball actually hit on the front of the green, rolled all the way through the green, and stopped just on the fringe about a foot from rolling into the back bunker.

Only Woods could hit a drive that far off-line and somehow end up looking at a putt for eagle. Granted, the putt was about 65 feet long, but at least, he thought, a two-putt would be good enough for birdie and get him turned around in the right direction.

"Robert's [Karlsson] ball, his mark, was off to the right-hand side and Stevie [Williams] and I read it and we were saying, well, if you hit it just above there, if you die it on the high side of that, that should be about right. And I said, well, if I just get the speed right, I should get inside three feet.

"And it went in."

Ho-hum, a 65-foot eagle putt he was just hoping to get to within three feet after hitting an almost impossible shot to get on the green. What's more, it wasn't a fluke putt by any stretch, one that happened to hit the hole going very fast. The ball was never going anywhere but the middle of the cup. A perfect putt.

The roar that accompanied the putt dropping could be heard all over Torrey Pines and most of San Diego County. Woods, who had been relatively unemotional for most of the week (perhaps not wanting to make any sudden movement that could jar his knee) did one of his Tiger fist-pumps, a triple pump, in fact. "It's all spontaneous," he said later. "On that one, I went nuts."

Back on the tee, Rocco certainly heard the roar. "I knew he'd made an eagle," he said. "That definitely wasn't a birdie roar; it was an eagle roar."

And so the 13th hole proved to be a turning point in the tournament for both Rocco and Tiger. It halted Rocco's momentum and it got Woods going. Rocco went 6-4-6 on the 13th, 14th, and 15th. Woods went 3-5-4, bogeying the 14th. That still represented a four-shot swing. By the time Rocco reached the 16th tee, Woods had parred the 16th and was even par after 52 holes of play. Rocco, who had been four under and five shots ahead of Woods a little more than an hour earlier, was now one shot ahead of him and a shot behind Westwood, who was in the interview room at that moment, talking about what it would mean to him to win a major championship.

For two days, Rocco had been doing one of two things off most tees: hitting a draw that found the fairway or the first cut of rough or, on occasion, turning his draw into a hook and ending up in trouble on the left side. Standing on the 16th tee, he felt a little bit frazzled for the first time all week. Two sixes will do that. So will leading by three one minute then looking up the next and finding yourself in second place, with the third-place guy, who happens to be named Woods, just one shot behind.

"It wasn't like I was freaking out or anything," Rocco said later. "But I didn't have that sense of calm I'd had all week. For the first time, I was a little upset with myself. I knew I had three holes to play and that I just needed to stay calm and not do anything stupid the rest of the way and I'd be fine. Lee wasn't going to win the golf tournament on Saturday. Neither was Tiger, and for that matter, neither was I. I just needed to get a good tee shot, get the ball on the green, and get going in the right direction again."

He didn't get what he needed. The 16th is a 225-yard parthree. It is long enough that Woods, during his warm-up, had practiced hitting some cut five-woods, thinking that might be the club he would need later in the day at the 16th. There wasn't quite as much wind when he got there, and he had hit a four-iron. Rocco tried to hit a three-iron, but just as he had been doing with his driver of late, he lost the ball left, landing in a green-side bunker. When you're on a roll, you're on a roll. He drew a difficult lie and was fortunate to get his shot from the bunker to about 15 feet. From there he two-putted for another bogey, meaning he had played his last four holes in four over par.

He was now tied with Woods at even par for the championship. Westwood had a two-shot lead. When Woods hit another horrific drive at 17, it looked as if Westwood would be the 54-hole leader. No one else had made any kind of move as the golf course got tougher and tougher in the late afternoon and early evening. Geoff Ogilvy had managed to shoot 72 and was at one over par through 54 holes. D. J. Trahan had shot 73 and was also at one over. Hunter Mahan, who had shot 69, the low score of the day among the leaders, led a group of six who were at two over par.

Westwood was the only player in red numbers at that moment, with Woods, in trouble deep in the right rough on 17, and Rocco, fuming as he walked off the 16th green, both at even par.

Woods hit an ordinary second shot, a seven-iron. The ball headed left, coming to a halt on a tongue of one of the bunkers in relatively deep rough. He wasn't that far from the hole, about 30 feet, he calculated later, but the ball was likely to come out of the rough "hot"—moving fast—so he faced a difficult task to get the ball up and down for par. The ball was on an uphill lie, and he had to stand awkwardly to keep from falling backward into the bunker. A tricky shot, to say the least.

"I hit it too hard," Woods said. "It came out hot. And then one hop and it went in."

Yup, went in. Even when he's bad, Tiger Woods is good. If the ball hadn't hit the flagstick it would have been at least — according to Woods — eight feet past the hole. It might have been more. But it hit the flagstick dead-on and dropped straight into the hole for a miraculous birdie. The roar was even louder than when the putt had dropped at 13, in part because the ball's going in was such a shock to everyone watching.

"When he makes a putt like the one he did at thirteen, it's amazing, but you can see the ball rolling in the direction of the hole, you know it's a good putt, and then you start to think, 'Hey, that might go in,'" Rocco said. "When he chips in, you're thinking, 'Whoa, that's moving fast; *oh my God, it went in.* Even for him, that was an amazing shot."

Somehow, Rocco managed not to become unhinged by the roar echoing back at him and by the awful four holes he had just played. He hit arguably his best drive of the day, and after Woods and Karlsson had left the green, he floated an eight-iron to about 10 feet. "I thought, 'Wow, a makeable birdie putt; I remember what those look like,'" he said. "I also thought it would be really nice to make one."

He did just that, the ball dropping in the side of the hole, the speed close to perfect. His birdie wasn't as dramatic as Woods's had been, but it was at least as important because it stopped the bleeding. He walked to the 18th tee one shot behind Westwood and tied with Woods, who had found the fairway with a pretty cut shot off the tee.

When Woods reached his ball and checked his distance to the green and the hole, he almost smiled. Always meticulous in his preround preparations, he had hit a number of five-wood shots during his warm-up, thinking he might need to hit a five-wood off the tee at the 16th. The wind change had made the hole play shorter, but now he found himself 227 yards from the hole—pretty close to the exact distance he thought he would hit his five-wood.

"I hit the same shot I had been practicing," Woods said. "It carried to the middle of the green."

The flagstick was up middle-left behind the water, so there was almost no chance to get close to it with a wood. Woods's shot landed on the front of the green and rolled hole high, about 30 feet to the right of the pin.

As he and Karlsson walked onto the green to a screaming ovation from the crowd, Westwood was leaving the interview tent figuring that he would be tied for the lead with Woods at two under par or perhaps there would be three leaders if Rocco could also birdie the 18th.

Naturally, Woods had other ideas. After he had looked the putt over from about fifteen different angles—no one in golf takes longer looking over a putt than Woods, but the results often make the wait worthwhile—he gently rolled the putt across the green. As the ball approached the cup and picked up some speed, it was apparent that it was going to be dead center. The only question was whether the speed was right.

It was exactly right. The ball disappeared into the cup as the crowd noise got so loud that Rocco and Appleby, waiting in the fairway, were practically knocked backward.

"I almost started laughing," Rocco said later. "I mean, the guy is just ridiculous sometimes. He makes eagle from off the planet on 13, chips it in at 17, and then makes another eagle at 18? Come on. That's a joke."

Woods's reaction to the putt going in was different from his normal reaction to a monster putt. There was no fist-pumping, just a big smile and a fist in the air for an instant. "I can't tell you why," he said. "At 13, I went nuts. At 18, I just thought, 'Sweet.'"

It was very sweet, because it jumped him over Westwood into the lead, the first time in three days he had been the outright leader in the championship. It also put him in a place he had been thirteen times before — leading a major after 54 holes. His record in those situations was decent: thirteen leads, thirteen titles. Everyone in golf was fully aware of that stat.

Back in the fairway, Rocco knew that Woods had the lead after his putt went in. He was a little more than 100 yards from the flag, having laid up to comfortable wedge distance, hoping for a birdie-birdie finish. While Appleby was playing his third shot, Rocco walked over to Mark Rolfing, who had been walking with the group all day for NBC, and asked him if a birdie would put him in the final group Sunday with Woods.

"No," Rolfing answered. "Westwood's at two [under] already. Since he finished first, he goes last."

"Damn," Rocco said, disappointed.

Somewhat surprised, Rolfing reported Rocco's reaction to Dan Hicks and Johnny Miller in the tower. None of them was accustomed to someone actually wanting to play with Woods on the last day of a major.

As it turned out, it was a moot point. Rocco had to make sure he didn't leave his wedge short and bring the water into play, so his shot went about 15 feet past the flag. His putt slid to the right, and he tapped in for par and a one-over-par 72. Given that only three players had broken 70 that day—led by Brandt Snedeker, who had made the cut on the number and had shot 68 to move into a tie for 15th place—and only six others (Woods included) had shot 70, that was a solid round starting the day in the last group, especially when compared with the scores of some other players who had started the day in serious contention.

In addition to Appleby's 78, Karlsson had shot 75, Davis Love had come in with a 76, and Ernie Els had produced a 74. Any hopes of a miracle rally by Phil Mickelson had gone aglimmering when he made a nine on the 13th hole after being 80 yards from the flag in two.

"I've made nine on that hole before," Mickelson said afterward. "I was eight years old at the time, but I have made a nine there."

He limped home with a 76, leaving him at nine over par (12 shots behind Woods) in a tie for 47th place. He was behind— among many others—Rocco's amateur playing companion of the first two days, Michael Thompson, who had shot a very respectable 73 to finish the day at seven over par for the championship, tied for 35th place. Mickelson would be on the tee Sunday morning at 9:20, meaning he would be finishing his round right around 1:30 —the last tee time of the championship—and exiting the golf course just as Woods entered it. There was some sort of symmetry in that, though no one was exactly certain what that symmetry was.

The pairings for the final day were now complete: Woods and Westwood would be the final group, with Rocco and Geoff

Ogilvy—who trailed Woods by four shots—right in front of them. D. J. Trahan and Hunter Mahan would go right before them, with Robert Allenby and the rapidly rising youngster Camilo Villegas, both at two over, directly in front of them. Those who still had an outside chance if they could somehow go low, very low, were Ernie Els, Mike Weir, and Sergio Garcia, who were all at three over par.

"Catching Tiger from six shots back," Els mused later when the subject came up. "Not something I would count on."

Catching Woods at all on a Sunday at a major had never been done, so Els's analysis, though simple, was almost certainly going to be accurate.

AS SOON AS HE SIGNED his scorecard, Rocco headed for the flash area. On the last two days of the Open, the USGA asks the leaders to go through two interviews: a relatively brief one in the flash area that is for TV crews who just want a quick sound-bite or two about the round and for deadline-rushed writers. On a Saturday night (early deadlines), with the round ending after ten o'clock in the east, quite a few people were in that situation.

Woods was just finishing his session in the flash area when Rocco walked in and saw him departing the podium.

"Excuse me, Mr. Woods, can I ask you a question?" he said, acting as if he were a reporter. Seeing Rocco, Woods smiled. "Are you out of your mind with what you're doing out there? Are you sick or something? I mean, come on!"

Woods laughed and high-fived Rocco as he departed. It was the first time the two men had been face-to-face all week.

Rocco was now very much in the spotlight. Woods had played

the last six holes in four under par to take the lead and he had hit extraordinary shots at 13, 17, and 18. His limp was becoming more pronounced with each passing day, and he admitted that it was getting worse. He was clearly everyone's lead story. Most of America's columnists would be waxing eloquent about the greatness of Tiger in the Sunday-morning papers.

But Rocco was a big part of the story too, arguably the lead supporting actor. People wanted to know where in the heck he had come from after playing so poorly all year prior to the Memorial, to know how his back felt, to hear his story about the qualifier and laugh at his one-liners. While Woods was amazing America, Rocco was charming America.

"I just can't begin to tell you guys how much fun I'm having out there," he kept saying. "This has been an amazing experience. I can't wait for tomorrow."

He was being honest. He was keenly aware of Woods's record when leading going into the final day of a major. When someone brought that up in the interview room, Rocco didn't even wait for the question to be finished.

"When Tiger has a lead going into the final round, as you know..."

"He's never lost."

"Right."

"Yeah, I know about all that."

"How difficult..."

"It's going to take a ridiculous round by one of us to beat him. If we can go out and shoot four or five under par, one of us, you never know... But you can't ever count on anything. It's just you can't really predict what is going to happen.

"But it's not over yet. And I'm sure he'll tell you the same thing. Because this is a U.S. Open course, and you just don't know what the heck is happening sometimes.

"But it will take a pretty spectacular round, it will take a perfect day, a perfectly clean day for me, with making five or six birdies and no bogeys, to win this golf tournament. And that still might not do it. You never know. But it will take something crazy."

He also said—again—that he was disappointed not to play with Woods. "How many chances do you get to do that?" he said. "Because he was in front of us, it was just exciting all day, it was just cool to be part of that." He smiled. "Maybe he'll get to see me do something good tomorrow. You never know."

Many in the media were skeptical about the notion that someone would actually want to play with Tiger in the final round. Rocco was asked repeatedly to explain why he felt that way.

"Look, it's the most, it's the most difficult pairing, because there is so much going on," he said. "He's the best in the game, so everybody is watching him and pulling for him.

"But I don't understand why—I feel like he either brings out the worst in you, when he's against you, or the best. And I've loved playing with him, like I said, a handful of times over however long he's been out here, ten, eleven years. And I've played some of my best golf with him. And I love that fact. And nine times out of ten, yeah, he's probably going to kick my butt, but that one time is what you're looking for. Because if you can, he's one of those guys where you can say to, you know, I can say to my boys, like when I beat him in Phoenix in '99, when he was a couple years out, I can always tell my kids, 'I beat the best player in the world this week, guys.' It doesn't happen very often."

He paused. "Actually, that's the only time I can tell them that so far. I just want another chance to try to compete against him. You want to see what you have. I don't want to lose before I tee off. I know it's easy to do that. But if I get beat, I want to get beat going down there and fighting, just like he does. That's what you want to do. You always want to be around the best players. I haven't been there that many times, but I loved it when I have been."

Though not in the same twosome, he would get the chance to compete with Woods, the next day, with a U.S. Open at stake. That, he thought, was a pretty good deal.

When Rand Jerris, the USGA press conference moderator, wrapped up the thirty-minute session, Rocco said the exact same thing that he had said as he departed on Friday. "Thanks. Hopefully I'll see you guys back here tomorrow."

14

One Inch Away

IT WAS WELL AFTER EIGHT O'CLOCK by the time Rocco finished in the interview room. Often, when players are in contention in a major on Saturday evening, they will try to spend time on the range, hoping to find something that will make them a little better on Sunday and perhaps be the difference between winning and losing.

Woods will frequently do this, even when he's leading, sometimes staying on the range by himself until nightfall in his never-ending search for perfection.

But none of the leaders went to the Torrey Pines range after finishing up on Saturday. Woods needed to get treatment for his knee. Rocco — and everyone else — was exhausted, and the late finish hadn't left very much daylight anyway.

Rocco, Cindi, and Steve Puertas headed straight back to the hotel room. The group had grown since the start of the week. Michael, Cindi's son, had driven down from Los Angeles, and a friend of Steve's, Gary Dylewski, was also there, as was Vince Monteparte, a boyhood friend of Rocco's who lived in San Diego. Steve and Gary went back to Fleming's to perform what had become the nightly pickup ritual.

They all sat around eating and watching replays of the day. Once again they stayed up late so that sleeping in wouldn't be so difficult. The tee times were earlier the next day—NBC didn't want as late a finish on a Sunday as on a Saturday—but there would still be plenty of time to kill in the morning.

Even though his back nine had been shaky—two bogeys, a double bogey, and two birdies for a 38—Rocco felt good about the way he had played, buoyed in large part by the birdie at 17. "If I hadn't gotten that late birdie after what happened at 13 and 15, I might have been a little down," he said. "But I'd been able to bounce back and I was still right there. I knew how tough Tiger was going to be to beat, but I also knew he was hurting and it was the U.S. Open. I had a chance. That was all I could possibly ask for."

He had arranged through a friend to get Cindi a media badge for the next day so she would be able to walk inside the ropes. It hadn't been that tough to follow his group the first two days, but on Saturday, as the crowds swelled, it had become more difficult for her to get a clear view of what was going on. This would allow her to move around more easily and see what was happening.

"I wanted to look like a reporter," she said. "So I got a pen and carried it with me. The only problem, if anyone was looking closely, was that I didn't have anything to write on."

Rocco slept well—better, actually, than he had thought he would. Perhaps not being in the lead helped. Even though he was no longer under the radar, he still wasn't the focus of most people's attention—Woods was. No one really expected him to win the next day with the exception of a handful of friends and family—and, increasingly, Rocco himself.

Sunday was one of those perfect San Diego days. Rocco and Cindi went back to Bruegger's for a fourth straight day and then on to Starbucks again. By the time they made the short drive to the golf course, the sun was shining brilliantly and there was just the hint of a breeze. The cool weather would make for a fast golf course, but that was okay. The only real concern was the greens. Poa annua greens, which grow best on the West Coast, tend to get bumpy after a lot of play on them. After a week of practice rounds and three days of play without a hint of rain, they would be bumpy.

"It could come down to someone getting a lucky bounce or an unlucky bounce," Rocco said to Cindi as he warmed up on the range. As always, Cindi was standing on the range with him just in case he needed to have his back loosened up one more time before he walked to the tee. As it turned out, there was no need. The back felt fine.

There are few places quieter than the range on the last day of a major, especially once the early groups have teed off and their spots have been taken by the players who are in contention. In all there were thirteen players within six shots of Woods. But while the most important thing at stake was the title, there were other things to play for too: The top 15 finishers automatically qualified for the 2009 Open; the top eight qualified for the 2009 Masters. There was also a good deal of money on the table, a total of $7.5 million in prize money.

Walk onto a range on a Thursday or a Friday at most tour stops, especially in the afternoon, and you might think you've blundered into Cheers. In fact, Jeff Sluman, the 1988 PGA champion who is now on the Champions Tour, has been known to his friends as Norm for years because when he walks onto a range everyone yells, "Slu!" in anticipation of him telling stories for the next hour. "He's the only man in golf who needs two hours to hit one bucket of balls," his friend Jay Haas has often said of Sluman.

Rocco can be that way too. But not on Sunday, June 15—Father's Day to most of the country, U.S. Open Sunday to the golf world. Like everyone else, he was quiet warming up, knowing he had a long day and a big job ahead of him. He was paired with Geoff Ogilvy, like Appleby an Australian and someone whose Open pedigree was strong—he had won the championship two years earlier, after Phil Mickelson's epic 18th-hole collapse at Winged Foot.

"Loved the pairing," Rocco said. "Geoff's a good guy and a really good player. It was great."

Understand, if Rocco had been paired with Ebenezer Scrooge (before his Christmas Eve dream), he would love the pairing. Rocco can play with just about anyone, which is one reason why players enjoy being paired with him.

"He's going to talk all day, but guys don't mind," Lee Janzen said. "They know that's Rocco and they know he isn't doing it to get inside their heads or anything. He's just being Rocco when he does it."

Janzen was at the golf course early that day too. He had missed the cut but had stayed for the weekend. He was flying to Hartford on the charter plane the tournament was sending the next day. He went out to the range early to work on some things before the players still in contention got there. Once he finished his work, he left to spend some time with his fourteen-year-old son, Connor, and a friend of Connor's.

"I knew I was going to be too nervous to sit there and watch for the entire afternoon," Janzen said. "So I made plans to do stuff with the boys during the early part of the afternoon, and then I figured I would go back to the hotel and see how Rocco was doing."

By now, all of those who knew Rocco were completely caught up in what was happening outside San Diego. Tony and Donna, who had moved into a new one-story house to make it easier for Donna to get around, didn't invite anyone over to watch with them that day.

"It would have been too nerve-racking," Donna said. "Tony can never sit still when Rocco's playing well. He has to get up and walk around and talk as if Rocco can somehow hear him. 'Come on, you need this putt,' or 'Make sure this one's in the fairway.' He feels inhibited when people are there and it makes him more nervous."

Frank Zoracki had planned a golf outing with friends in Michigan long before Rocco had even qualified for the Open. On Saturday night he called Rocco to remind him about the dream he'd had in which Rocco had been holding a trophy. "Maybe both our dreams are about to come true," he said.

All of Rocco's old golf buddies from boyhood and from Florida Southern had gathered in different places to watch the last day. Logic told them that if their old pal finished in the top five, it would be a great week. But something else told them that winning wasn't out of the question. "That's always been the thing with Rocc," said Dave Lucas, his friend dating back to when the two of them would be dropped at the golf course and not play golf. "When you think there's no way he can do something, he somehow finds a way to do it."

Jim Ferree, watching with friends in Hilton Head, had that same feeling. "When Rocco was on the leader board on Thursday, people were saying to me, 'So your old student can still play a little, that's nice,'" he said. "I told them not to be surprised if he was still in contention on Sunday. I was looking at his golf swing. It certainly wasn't the same swing I'd taught him, but it had a lot of the basics. He's had to adjust it through the years because of his back, but it's still a very good golf swing."

In Naples, Rocco's sons had invited friends over to watch their dad play that afternoon, his tee time not coming until 4:20 on the East Coast. Linda Mediate watched as her sons and their friends cheered her husband on and couldn't help but feel bittersweet about it all.

"I couldn't help it," she said. "A big part of me was thrilled because I knew he had dreamed of being in this situation — especially at the Open — his whole life. We had talked about it for years. I was nervous the whole day because I wanted him to do well. But I couldn't help but feel sad that none of us was there with him — on Father's Day. That part was tough."

When Rocco had walked onto the 10th tee early on Thursday morning, there weren't more than a couple of hundred people watching. Now, as he and Ogilvy walked onto the first tee, every inch of available space was packed with people. Many had been there for a while, jockeying for position to see Woods and Westwood, and would stay right there once Rocco and Ogilvy left the tee. But many others wanted to see the kid from Greensburg.

"I think it was one of those deals where a lot of people were going to stay with me as long as I still had a chance," Rocco said. "That turned out to be quite a while."

Nerves jangling, Rocco again managed to find the fairway on

number one. It was the fourth straight day—the third with his stomach in a knot at the start of the round—that he had found the fairway on his first hole.

In fact, his start was almost identical to Saturday's. He hit the green with a six-iron at the first and made a routine par—except that nothing was routine now. Then he hit a perfect three-wood once again at the second and an almost perfect seven-iron to 10 feet. When the putt rolled in, it occurred to him that this was not going to be a day of simply trying to hang on to make a good check. He had a chance to win.

"It wasn't as if I didn't think it before the round began," he said. "But the good start and then seeing Tiger's double bogey on number one go up...I remember thinking, 'Wow, the game is really on.'"

Rocco was on the third tee when he saw that Woods had somehow double-bogeyed the first hole for the third time in four days. What he didn't know was that Woods had actually gotten up and down to make six. "Made a nice little two-footer," Woods joked later.

His drive had again gone straight right—"a snipe," as Woods called it—and he had to play his second shot from the trees well right of the fairway. "The second shot wasn't actually that hard," he said. "I had a funky lie. I didn't know how it was going to come out, and it squirted left. I didn't envision that happening. I didn't think that the lie would turn my club that much. I had the face open to make sure if it turned it would turn into the left bunker, no big deal, easy pitch. But it turned straight into the tree."

Still in the trees lying two, Woods popped his third shot into another tree. "I came down too steep and hit it right into the tree," he said.

From there, he chopped the ball out of the rough to a spot just in front of the green. "I hit a good little pitch from there to get to two feet," he said.

Having made a weekend hacker's double bogey at the first hole, Woods made an ordinary bogey at the second, missing the fairway by a mile again, laying up to where he could pitch onto the green and two-putt for a five. Thirty minutes after he teed off trailing Woods by two shots, Rocco walked off the third green — having just made par — leading him by two. At that moment, he was two under par for the championship, Westwood was at one under after a bogey on the first hole, and Woods was back to even, his late-Saturday heroics wiped out in two holes.

Later, Woods would be asked if his horrific starts all four days — he played his first hole each day in a total of seven over par — had something to do with his knee perhaps not being loosened up when he started playing.

"No," he said firmly. "The three double bogeys at number one were the result of terrible, terrible golf shots. The bogey at number ten on Friday was just a three-putt."

One of Woods's more admirable qualities is that he never makes excuses. He may occasionally behave badly on the golf course — throwing clubs, looking as if the world is out to get him when he misses a putt, spraying profanities — but when all is said and done, he always places blame for his failures squarely on himself. In fact, he is so self-critical that there are times when he doesn't give enough credit to that rare player who happens to beat him.

Even though Woods's start wasn't all that different from the other three days, there were murmurs around the golf course that he might not finish the round. David Fay wondered in the NBC TV booth, especially after Woods hobbled off the second tee using his driver as a cane to support himself. Many in the media who were walking with Woods and Westwood thought he might quit at any moment.

According to Woods, that was never going to happen. "I was going to finish," he said. Then he added with a smile, "I might have been on the clock [being timed for slow play], but I was going to finish."

He settled down after the double bogey–bogey start and began grinding out pars, which, in the end, is always the best way to play on an Open Sunday. He parred the next six holes, grimacing at missed birdie chances but knowing that every par he made kept him very much in contention.

Rocco backed up his birdie at the second hole with pars at number three and number four, but caught a bad break at the fifth when his tee shot took a big hop off a hard fairway and instead of landing in the first cut of rough, ended up in the second cut or, as he put it, "the gunk."

"I actually thought I'd hit a beautiful shot there," he said. "I caught the ball smack in the middle of the club face, but it probably started out two yards farther left than I wanted it to. Once I got down there and saw the lie, it was pretty much take your medicine, make bogey, and get out of there. I hadn't planned on playing a bogey-free round, but that one hurt because I felt as if I got burned for a mistake when I really didn't make a mistake."

On the sixth hole he made another bogey. "Probably the toughest hole on the golf course," he said. "I could play that hole pretty well and still make a bogey. On Saturday, I had to hit a perfect rescue club from the fairway to get it on the green. The hole is 515 yards. That's a long par-four for me. I didn't hit a bad tee shot; I just didn't hit it well enough that I could get my second shot on the green."

The back-to-back bogeys dropped him out of the lead. Westwood was now in front at one under, with Rocco and Woods one shot back. No one was making any kind of move from behind. In fact, all the players who had been chasing at the start of the day from within six shots of the lead were going backward. None would break par, none would make any kind of serious move on the leaders.

It was now clearly a three-man tournament: Rocco, playing with Ogilvy—who would shoot 74 and finish in a five-way tie for ninth—and Woods and Westwood behind him.

After his opening bogey, Westwood had gotten into a par groove, making seven in a row. From the third hole on, Woods did the same, making six straight pars. They were proving definitively Rocco's theory that there's no such thing as a bad par on the last day of the Open. By the time the three men had finished the eighth hole, the standings were the same: Westwood leading by one over Woods and Rocco. Rocco had parred the seventh and eighth holes.

Once again, Rocco had to lay up at the ninth, leading to a par. Westwood and Woods were both able to go for the green and both made birdie—the first one of the day for either man.

The par-fives would prove critical to the final outcome. Over the four days of the championship, Rocco, laying up almost every time, played the 12 par-fives in two under par. He made four pars at the ninth; a birdie, two pars, and a bogey at the 13th; and two birdies and two pars at the 18th. Woods played the 12 par-fives in nine under par. He made three birdies and a par at the ninth; two eagles, a par, and a bogey at the 13th; and an eagle, a birdie, and two pars at the 18th. The seven-stroke margin on those three holes was critical.

With their birdies at nine, Westwood and Woods made the turn in first and second place, Westwood one shot clear of Woods and two ahead of Rocco.

Rocco understood the situation but didn't think there was any reason to panic. "Tiger had clearly gotten his act together," he said. "But I still felt good about the way I was playing. My shots were still coming off the club the way I wanted them to. There are birdie holes on the back nine. I knew they had moved the tee way up at fourteen to make it driveable and that was going to give me another chance. A two-shot margin at the Open can go away in the blink of an eye."

Most of the people on the grounds were now following the last two groups. The crowds around each tee and each green were massive. In the media tent, fighting terrible deadlines because of the nine- and ten-hour time difference, writers from Europe were sending hole-by-hole updates to their papers. In Great Britain, where it was midnight when the players made the turn, people sat up watching to see if Westwood could become the first player from Great Britain—from all of Europe, in fact—to win the U.S. Open since Tony Jacklin in 1970.

Westwood wasn't getting carried away with the fact that he had taken the lead. As he pointed out later, a one-shot margin with nine holes left—especially when the person one shot back is named Woods—is not exactly a good reason to start planning a victory celebration.

Woods may have had the best reason to feel confident. He had recovered from his brutal start, he had finally made a birdie, and in spite of the double bogey–bogey beginning, he was only one shot behind with a back nine on which he had produced two eagles and a birdie the day before still to play.

The 10th hole produced yet another momentum swing. Westwood's tee shot found a fairway bunker and he skulled his second shot over the green, leading to a bogey. Woods made a routine par, but Rocco, after a perfect drive, hit his second shot to 10 feet and made the putt for a birdie. Suddenly, with eight holes to play, the three men were tied for first at one under par. Everyone else had fallen by the wayside.

The next two hours were a roller coaster. Woods took the lead again when he hit his tee shot to three feet and made a birdie at the 11th, but he and Westwood stunned everyone—including themselves— by making bogey sixes at the 13th. Both went for the green in two, both hit the ball left into the ravine that fronts the green, and both had to take a penalty drop as a result. Westwood had also bogeyed the 12th. That meant he had bogeyed three holes out of four, and four during the round, after making five bogeys the first three days. Pressure? What pressure?

Rocco parred the 13th—a disappointment until he saw what had happened to Woods and Westwood. After Woods and Westwood made their bogeys at 13, Rocco and Woods were again tied for the lead. Westwood was two shots back at one over par and seemingly ready to fade out of the picture.

The USGA had decided to play the 14th hole from the way-up tee on Sunday, shortening it from 435 yards to 267 yards. "We thought it would be interesting to force the players to make a decision on whether or not to try for the green under the gun on a Sunday at the Open," Mike Davis said. "I thought it worked out really well."

It certainly worked out well for Rocco, who didn't hesitate before pulling out his three-wood and swinging for the green. He left the shot out just a little bit to the left and found the left bunker. But he hit a gorgeous bunker shot from there to about 18 inches and tapped the putt in for birdie. That put him at two under par and back in the lead.

Then came a critical moment that involved none of the three players in contention. One group ahead of Rocco and Ogilvy, Hunter Mahan had found trouble on the 15th hole. He had to search for his ball for a good long while, and when he found it he needed a ruling on where he was allowed to drop.

Under any circumstances, Rocco likes to play fast. He is not someone who spends a lot of time deciding what club to hit or looking over a putt from fifteen different angles. He makes a decision on what shot he wants to hit or how he thinks a putt will break, gets over the ball, and plays.

He walked onto the 15th tee pumped up after making birdie at 14. He did not know at that moment what was going on back at the 13th hole with Woods and Westwood, but he knew he was two under par and, at worst, he was probably tied for the lead with Woods.

"I was ready to go," he said. "Take the driver out and smack it."

Only he couldn't, because officials on the tee told him that there was a delay in the group ahead of him. Rocco and Ogilvy sat down, figuring the delay wouldn't be more than a couple of minutes. Five minutes passed, then ten. Rocco couldn't sit still. He got up and began pacing around the tee. Every few minutes he asked Jeff Hall and Jim Bunch, the two rules officials assigned to the group, what was going on.

They could only shrug helplessly. "They're trying to get a ruling" was the best answer they could come up with.

"It takes this long to get a ruling?" Rocco said. "This is unbelievable."

It was actually more than just a simple ruling that was causing the delay. Mahan had hit his ball into an immovable obstruction and was entitled to relief. But when he picked up his ball and went searching for the nearest point of relief, it turned out to be a water hazard. That was clearly no good. He and the walking officials with his group searched for a spot where he could drop that was no closer to the hole, not in a hazard, and still a legal spot.

Finally, another opinion was sought.

During major championships, there are two kinds of rules officials present. One group consists of those who walk with the players—each group is assigned an official who can make a ruling on the spot when needed. The late groups on Saturday and Sunday are also assigned an "observer"—a backup rules official—in case there is any kind of problem or controversy.

In Mahan's case, neither the rules official nor the observer was able to come up with an acceptable solution. So a call went out for one of the roving officials to come and help. The rovers are just what they sound like—officials who patrol different areas of the golf course to intervene if needed in a situation like this. The walking rules officials are often men and women who are not full-time rules officials—the players call them amateurs, even though they have to pass the same rules tests as the full-time officials—but people who volunteer their time during majors. The rovers are full-time officials from golf tours around the world.

The rover in the area was John Paramour, chief rules official of the European Tour. Paramour is generally considered to be as good as anyone in the world at what he does. He is a man who takes his job very seriously by day and then spends his nights cracking his colleagues up with his storytelling.

Now he rode to the rescue and, after being apprised of the situation, found a spot for Mahan to drop and continue play.

By the time Mahan got his ruling and the players were told they could continue playing, twenty-five minutes had passed. "I don't like to make excuses," Rocco said. "But that really bothered me. It shouldn't happen that way under any circumstances, much less during the last round of the U.S. Open."

Woods and Westwood were unaffected by the delay. To begin with, both are slow players and they had already dropped a hole behind Rocco and Ogilvy (also a fast player) even before they got to 13. Then, when both found the ravine at 13 and had to get their own rulings on drops, they fell even further behind. In fact, if the Mahan ruling hadn't occurred, they probably would have been a solid two holes behind Rocco and Ogilvy. By the time they reached the 15th tee, Rocco and Ogilvy were down the fairway.

Westwood had finally ended his slide at the 14th hole by driving the green and making a two-putt birdie to get back to even par. Woods had actually been hurt on the 14th by his length off the tee.

Rocco and Westwood had each hit a three-wood to try to reach the green; Woods was actually between clubs. As he explained at great length later—Woods loves to go into detail when describing clubbing decisions—he wasn't sure whether a three-wood or a five-wood was the correct shot.

"I couldn't have had a worse number [yardage]," Woods said. "It was a five-wood front number for me, but it was into the wind. I can't get a five-wood there. Now, if I lean on a five-wood, which means it brings the left bunker into play, I don't know if I can get it all the way to that left bunker. If I bail right, I have absolutely no pitch. If I hit a cut three-wood, I have a choke-down three-wood and hit a cut. That's not exactly an easy shot. If I overcut, I'm in the right bunker with virtually no shot. If that tee would have been on the back part of the tee, I could have hit a three-wood with no problem. But it was on the front part, and I was perfectly caught between clubs. I said all right, no big deal, I can still make three laying up. I laid up to a good number, had a little wedge, and hit it a little hard and ended up making par."

For those scoring at home, that's 179 words to describe one decision on one shot. The only thing that took longer was the conversation between Woods and Williams before deciding to lay up.

Contrast that with the exchange when the condition of his knee (a fairly important issue) was brought up:

Q: You've been pretty forthcoming about the knee thing. So let me throw this one at you: Is what you are experiencing right now residual soreness from the surgery or is this the way it is going to be forever and ever?

A: It's different.

Of course that's Woods. He will go into chapter and verse about anything relating directly to his golf game. Stray from that even a little, and you will either get a two-word answer or a lengthy answer that means nothing. He is not only a master on the golf course, he is a master of the sound-bite non-answer.

As Woods and Westwood stood on the 15th tee, Rocco again

had the lead. Woods trailed by one, Westwood by two. But now it was Rocco's turn to be in trouble. After the interminable wait, he had hooked his tee shot on 15 into deep rough on the left. From there, he couldn't reach the green, and his pitch went 10 feet past the hole. A two-putt bogey dropped him back into a tie with Woods and left him just a little bit angry as he headed for the 16th tee.

"I don't like to make excuses," he said. "But that wait definitely hurt me."

Interestingly, in the "official annual" that the USGA puts out after each year's Open, there is absolutely no mention of Mahan's problem or Rocco's wait. It simply reports that he hooked his drive at the 15th, leading to a bogey.

Woods didn't have to wait on the 15th, but his tee shot wasn't much better than Rocco's. He was also in the rough, and his second shot was still in the rough. He hit a reasonably good pitch to 10 feet but missed the putt.

"At that point," Woods said later, "it looked like I was shooting myself out of the tournament."

He was far from out of it, but he was out of the lead with three holes to play. Rocco, having just parred 16, led by one over both Woods and Westwood. Woods and Westwood also parred 16. Rocco's lead was one, with two holes to play.

Back in Greensburg, Tony Mediate simply couldn't sit still. He paced in and out of the family room while Donna sat patiently and watched every shot. "He kept up a running commentary," she said later. "It was 'Oh, no, that's too long a putt,' or 'I hope he puts this one in the fairway.'"

"I wasn't exactly Johnny Miller," Tony said, laughing.

It was with Rocco on 17 that Miller got himself into trouble.

Rocco hit an almost perfect drive that almost split the fairway in half. He then hit a gorgeous floating seven-iron that checked up about 10 feet behind the hole, giving him a solid look at a birdie putt that would give him a two-shot lead. With 18 being a par-five that Woods and Westwood could reach in two (Rocco, not so much), a two-shot cushion would be almost immeasurably important.

It was after seeing Rocco's second shot that Miller blurted out his soon to be infamous line about Rocco looking more like Tiger's pool boy than a U.S. Open champion.

Miller is so famous for saying things that get him into trouble that the Golf Channel actually put together a thirty-minute show dedicated to his ten most outrageous comments. In truth, this one was pretty innocent. He was simply expressing amazement that on the 71st hole of the U.S. Open, the 158th-ranked player in the world, a forty-five-year-old with a perpetually sore back, was standing toe-to-toe with Woods and clearly not cracking under the pressure.

"That's exactly the way I took it," Rocco said later. "When I heard him say it on the tape, I laughed. I know he didn't mean anything by it other than expressing amazement that I was playing so well. Hell, I was pretty amazed by it myself."

Rocco looked over the birdie putt at 17 with a little more care than usual. He read it as having a slight left-to-right break, a putt that if he got it rolling with any speed at all in the direction of the hole would feed down into the cup.

"I hit that putt exactly the way I wanted to hit it," he said. "It could not have felt better coming off the putter. When it was halfway there—I'll never forget this—the thought flashed through my head, 'I'm going to win the U.S. Open.' I thought it was going in and I was going to win."

Somehow, the putt didn't take the final turn to the right that Rocco had been certain it would take. It stayed just above the hole and went five feet past. Rocco had to take a deep breath, regroup, and make sure he hit a solid putt for par. It went straight in, and he walked to the 18th tee still leading by one but knowing the chance—perhaps of a lifetime—had just come and gone.

Westwood and Woods both made par at the hole, Woods having to make a five-footer but, steely as always, rolling the putt in.

One hole to play. If Rocco could make birdie, he would force Woods and Westwood to have to go for the green in two and make eagle. "I was thinking I needed birdie to win," he said. "I was fairly certain at least one of them would make a birdie."

He aimed his tee shot down the middle and watched it drift a little farther left than he wanted it to. It found the left rough, in decent enough shape, but the lie took away any chance he might have had to go for the green in two.

"To be honest, if I'd been in the fairway, I'm not sure I would have gone for it anyway," he said. "I just over-hit my drive and it went a little left. I did that a few times down the stretch. I had 247 to the front and that's a long shot for me. I might have gone for it and aimed the ball right to stay away from the water, but I'm not sure. Being in the rough eliminated any doubt. I had to hit a good layup and try to make birdie from there."

He laid up to 106 yards, a perfect wedge shot. "Maybe I was just a little more excited than I thought," he said. "I wasn't scared of the water or anything; I wasn't worried I was going to spin the ball back into the water. I just hit the ball about six or seven yards farther than I wanted to hit it."

The pin was up front on the right side of the green, and Rocco's wedge landed behind it, took a hard hop, and rolled to a stop 35 feet away. As Rocco and Matt approached the green, Ogilvy dropped back so that Rocco could walk onto the green alone. The ovation was almost overwhelming.

"I'd never heard anything quite like it in my life," he said. "I mean, the crowds had been loud all day. But at 18, it was amazing."

He gathered himself for the long birdie putt. "I wanted to give it a chance," he said. "I didn't want to leave it short."

He didn't leave it short, but it was moving to the right of the hole several feet before it got there. He tapped in for an even-par 71, which meant he had finished 72 holes at 283—one under par for the championship. Now came what would be the hardest part of his day: the wait.

LEE JANZEN HAD GOTTEN BACK to the hotel while the leaders were playing the 15th hole. When he saw what the situation was, he left Connor and his friend to watch on TV while he headed to the golf course.

"It was such a zoo I actually had trouble getting back," he said. "Even with my player badge I had trouble talking my way through all the crowds to get where I wanted to go—which was behind the 18th green. I wanted to be there when Rocco finished."

He made it and actually saw Cindi first. She had managed to get Steve inside the ropes, and the two of them were standing in the tunnel behind the green that led to the scoring area while Rocco finished. Janzen hugged Cindi, who was hanging on to her emotions for dear life at that point.

After Rocco tapped in for his final par and shook hands with Ogilvy, the first person he saw when he reached the tunnel was Janzen. "Rocco had been the first person there when I won in '93," Janzen said. "I wanted to do the same for him. I would have loved to have said, 'My God, you won the Open.' Instead, I just said, 'No matter how it turns out, I couldn't be more proud of you.' I wanted him to know that was the way I felt."

After Rocco signed his card, he sat in a small room next to the scoring area and watched Woods and Westwood play the final hole. Cindi, Steve, and Janzen were all there. So was Jon Miller, executive vice president of NBC Sports. His job was to make sure Rocco didn't somehow disappear if he became the U.S. Open champion.

"We lost Jim Furyk in 2003," Miller said. "He signed his card and instead of going to do his postmatch interview with us, he went into the flash area and was talking to some of the print guys. We need to get the winner right away, before the awards ceremony, before he talks to anyone else. My job since 2004 has been to make sure the minute we know who the winner is, we get him on the air."

Woods and Westwood could still win if one of them made eagle on the 18th hole. But that chance virtually evaporated the moment each teed off. Woods's drive was left, finding a fairway bunker. Westwood also found a bunker — on the right side.

Westwood had no chance to go for the green and laid his second shot up. Woods caught such a good lie that he actually thought for a moment about taking a shot at the green.

"If it had been a practice round, I would have gone for it," he said. "Any other day I would have given it some serious thought. But not now. Too risky. I had to figure I had a good chance to make four if I laid up."

He took a nine-iron and produced one of the worst under-pressure swings of his career. The ball flew almost straight right and landed in deep rough to the right of the fairway. Furious with himself, Woods let out a couple of profanities and slammed his club on top of his bag. He knew he would now need an up-and-down that was, to say the least, difficult in order to force a playoff.

Rocco was stunned when he saw Woods mis-hit his second shot. "It's just not like him," he said. "At that moment, just for a second, I let myself think that I might win."

Westwood was actually now in better position to make birdie than Woods, since he had found the fairway with his second shot. But almost no one watching was even thinking about him.

"To be honest, I completely forgot that he could birdie to force a playoff," Lee Janzen said. "I was totally focused on Tiger. I'm not completely sure I even knew Westwood was just one shot back."

At Oakland Hills, Rick Smith had been joined in the upstairs locker room by several friends. But the place was completely quiet as Woods and Westwood approached their third shots. "My mouth was completely dry and my hands were sweating," Smith said. "I couldn't have talked if I wanted to talk. I knew Tiger had a really tough third shot. I also knew if anyone could pull it off, it was Tiger."

Westwood played first and, like Rocco a few minutes before, he allowed his adrenaline to take over. He hit a shot similar to

Rocco's, landing it well behind the flag and watching it roll 30 feet past the pin. He still had a chance, but it was a slim one.

Woods took a long time deciding what to do with his third shot. As he would say later in another lengthy explanation, he was again between clubs. "I had 95 [to the] front and 101 [to the] hole," he said. "It was just a perfect number for my 56, but I didn't think I could stop a 56 — if I hit a 56, I had to hit it short of the green, bounce it in, and that wasn't going to be the shot. We decided to go with 60, hit it hard, make sure you play to the right, just in case it doesn't get there."

The number references are to the loft on wedges. Once upon a time, a golfer carried two wedges: a pitching wedge and a sand wedge. Now there are players who will carry as many as five wedges. The higher the loft, the higher the ball flies coming off the club and the more likely it is to spin and stop quickly. Woods was afraid that his 56-wedge wouldn't put enough spin on the ball to stop it near the hole. Instead, he opted to try to hit his 60 hard, knowing if he got the ball on the green, he would be more likely to be able to get it to spin to a stop.

He had also caught a lucky break — the kind that only he seems to ever catch. Rocco noticed it right away. Few others did.

"He was in a divot," Rocco said. "Normally that's the worst break you can catch. But in this case it helped him because it made the ball spin more than it would have if he had just been in the deep rough over there. He actually had a better chance to get the club on the ball the way he needed to because of the divot."

After his lengthy conversation over club selection with Steve Williams, Woods finally got over the ball and hit a spectacular shot. The ball flew just the way he wanted it to, checked up, and then rolled back toward the hole, stopping 12 feet away. It was a near-miraculous shot.

"People talk about the putt," Rocco said. "The shot that saved him was the wedge. I'm not sure anyone else in the world could get the ball that close from where he was. In fact, I'm pretty sure no one else could."

Rocco had now gone from thinking he had a good chance to win to thinking a playoff was likely. "Again, anyone else, the odds are he isn't going to make it," he said. "It's a 12-foot putt on a bumpy Poa annua green where the ball is bound to bounce before it gets to the hole. But it's Tiger. That makes it all different."

Westwood had to putt first. Amazingly, with a chance to play off for the U.S. Open at stake, he left the putt short. It never had a chance, rolling to the right and checking up two feet from the hole. Westwood would talk later about how upset he was not to get into the playoff, but then add that if someone had told him on Thursday he would finish third, one shot out of a playoff, he would have been quite happy.

Which probably explains why he has won all sorts of tournaments around the world but never a major.

With Westwood finished, the stage was now cleared for Woods. He stalked the putt from every side while millions watching held their breath. Most people thought he would make the putt for the simple reason that, historically, he always makes putts that he absolutely has to make.

"I'm thinking, 'This is not an easy putt,'" Mike Davis said. "But I'm also thinking, 'Yeah, but it's Tiger. He's going to make it.'"

In the NBC TV booth, David Fay wasn't so much thinking Woods would make the putt as wanting him to make it. "Normally, the last thing we want is a Monday playoff," he said. "This was different. If it had been Westwood, I'd have been praying for a miss. But since it was Tiger creating a Monday playoff, I wanted him to make it."

Rocco expected Woods to make the putt. But he would not have been shocked if he had missed it.

"I knew the moment wouldn't get to him," he said. "He lives for moments like that. I knew he would read it right, I knew his hands wouldn't shake, I knew he would put a good stroke on it, and I sure as hell knew he wasn't going to leave it short.

"But I also knew at that moment on that green he could do all those things and he still might miss. He could hit a perfect putt, and if it hit a bump at the wrong moment it could swerve an inch outside the hole."

Woods was thinking almost the same thing.

"The putt was probably about two and a half balls outside right," he said. "The green wasn't very smooth. I kept telling myself, Make a pure stroke. If it bounces in or out, so be it, at least I can hold my head up high and say I hit a pure stroke. I hit it exactly where I wanted to and it went in."

It *just* went in, catching the right corner of the hole, spinning around, and, at the last possible moment, dropping in. It could have, as Woods put it, "plinkoed in or plinkoed out." It plinkoed in.

Woods, famous for his reactions to making crucial putts, went completely nuts—shaking his fists, screaming with joy—as the crowd went crazy.

Even though he wasn't surprised, Rocco's heart sank when the putt went in. He had been one inch—almost literally—from winning the U.S. Open. Now he had to go home, try to sleep, and come back the next morning to go 18 holes against the best player in history.

Mark Rolfing was right there with an NBC camera seconds after the putt went into the hole.

"Unbelievable. I knew he'd make it," Rocco said bravely. "That's what he does. It was an amazing day out there, and I can't wait for tomorrow."

Later, in the interview room, he said almost the same thing. He liked the 18-hole playoff format, going head-to-head with Tiger was a dream come true, he had incredible respect for him but wasn't afraid of him. As he got ready to leave, he had one last thought: "I think we'll give you guys a good show tomorrow. It's going to be a blast."

15

A Great Fight

As Rocco was leaving the interview room, he encountered Woods, who was on his way in to give his version of what had just taken place.

"I guess we have a game tomorrow," Woods said.

Rocco laughed. "You better be ready, big guy," he answered. "I'm going to be ready for you."

He had laughed and joked his way through his session with the media. He had never had a day like this one on the golf course, he was living his dream, he was "toast," but he would be ready by the time he and Woods teed it up at nine o'clock (Pacific) the next morning.

He meant everything he said. He wasn't afraid of Woods, because he knew there were only a handful of people in the world who thought he had any chance to win. "Which meant," he said, "that I had nothing to lose."

The group eating Fleming's steaks out of plastic containers in room 1422 at the Hilton was the same as the night before: Rocco and Cindi, Sticky, Gary, Michael, and Vince. Everyone ate dinner and watched replay after replay of what had just taken place.

All of which made Cindi nervous.

"He was getting a lot of love from the commentators, from everywhere," she said. "But it had been *so* close, and it hadn't happened. I thought it was actually energy sapping to sit there and watch it over and over. Plus, it was starting to get late and, unlike the last three days, he had a morning tee time, which meant we had to be up early. I knew he wasn't going to sleep much, but I wanted him to at least have a few hours to lie down and close his eyes."

Cindi finally got everyone to leave at about 11:30. Rocco still wanted to watch TV. The Golf Channel was showing the last few holes and the post-round interviews and commentaries over and over.

"I probably would have stayed up all night watching if she hadn't stopped me," he said. "I was mesmerized by everything that had happened."

He slept better than he thought he would, no doubt completely exhausted by the events of the day. When he woke up, shortly after 6 A.M., Cindi did her usual morning work on his back and then he showered and went to get dressed.

"I only had one clean shirt left," he said. "It was red."

Woods has made the red shirt his Sunday trademark. Rocco wondered if he would wear red for a Monday playoff or if the color was reserved strictly for Sundays. Either way, he had no choice. "My options were a red shirt, a dirty shirt, or no shirt," he said. "I went with red."

The hotel lobby felt empty early in the morning, since most of the players had already flown home. He and Cindi got in the car and drove to Bruegger's. As soon as they got out of the car, Cindi cringed. "It was closed," she said. "They were tearing it apart. The sign said, 'Closed for renovations.' I guess they had stayed open through Open Sunday and then started the work first thing Monday morning."

Rocco shrugged it off, but Cindi was not happy. "Bad harbinger," she said. "He'd had this perfect routine going for four days: Bruegger's, Starbucks, golf course. Now it was broken."

They still went to Starbucks for Rocco's quadruple shot of espresso, but Cindi was already feeling queasy when they pulled into the virtually empty players' parking lot at eight o'clock. She couldn't help but notice that the range was completely empty, which made sense, since there were only two players left competing for the championship.

"I like to go out on the range with him when he warms up," she said. "I feel comfortable because I know everyone now and they know me. Plus, if he needs that last stretch before he goes to the tee, I can do it right there and it literally takes a few seconds. But with no one out there and so much media around, I felt like I'd stand out. I couldn't blend in the way I normally do. So I decided not to go."

Cindi was already nervous about media attention. A number of people who regularly covered golf knew her and knew she had been traveling with Rocco regularly. He had confided to a few friends in the media that he and Linda were getting a divorce. Rich Lerner from Golf Channel had walked nine holes with Cindi on Saturday, and Jeff Babineau from *Golfweek* had secured her media armband to get her inside the ropes on Sunday and Monday.

Now, though, with Rocco suddenly in the spotlight, a lot of people who didn't cover golf as often were wondering who she was. The simplest answer was that she was his physical therapist, the person who had helped him overcome his back problems. That in itself made her a story. Cindi knew a number of members of the national media wanted to talk to her in more detail about her relationship with Rocco. She wanted none of that.

"I just wanted it to be about him," she said. "If I talked to them at all, it became at least in part about me, and I didn't think that was right."

She made herself scarce, hiding out in the player-family dining area while Rocco warmed up. He was the first one on the range. Woods arrived a couple of minutes later and walked over to say hello. Only he didn't say hello.

Dressed in his Sunday red for a Monday, Woods walked over to Rocco, hand extended, and said, "Nice fucking shirt!"

Rocco cracked up. Instead of explaining that this was his only clean shirt, he said, "I thought you only wore red on Sundays!"

That set the tone for the day.

"I know how he is, especially when he's got a major on the line," Rocco said. "But I wasn't going to change who I was. I was going to talk because that's what I do. I was going to have fun because that's what I do. That doesn't mean I wasn't trying to kill him and he wasn't trying to kill me, but it just wasn't going to get tense like I know it does sometimes with him and some other players."

The only U.S. Open playoff that may have been comparable to this one in terms of contrasting personalities had taken place at Merion in 1971 between Lee Trevino and Jack Nicklaus. Trevino, a nonstop talker like Rocco, had tossed a fake snake at the ever-serious Nicklaus on the first tee to loosen things up. Whether that played a role or not, Trevino won the playoff by three shots. Rocco wasn't going to throw any snakes, but he also wasn't going to let Woods go into one of his no-talking trances for 18 holes.

"I wasn't trying to psyche him out by talking," he said. "In fact, I think it probably loosened him up a little. But I had to go out there and play and act the way I would play and act on any other day on the golf course."

THE USGA IS GOLF'S LAST GOVERNING BODY that still clings to the 18-hole playoff format. The Masters has played sudden death since 1979, and the British Open and the PGA Championship both conduct four-hole playoffs.

Eighteen-hole playoffs are anachronistic, almost always boring and anticlimactic, and are a logistical nightmare for almost everyone involved.

People count on a Sunday finish for golf tournaments. Players are accustomed to going back out on the golf course on Sunday to play off when tied for first place. TV has to juggle schedules if a tournament bleeds over into Monday. Volunteers, who are critical to any golf tournament, most often are scheduled to go home or back to work (or both) on Monday. Airplane flights have to be changed. And yet, the USGA won't let the 18-hole playoff go.

"I hear all the arguments, and they make sense," David Fay said. "And I'll admit we've had our share of clunkers. But I still think eighteen holes is the fairest test; there are no fluke winners. And I like the fact that we're the only ones still doing it. It makes us different."

True enough. But the USGA has abandoned 18-hole playoffs in its other championships, so the implication is that the

U.S. Open is more important than the U.S. Women's Open or the Senior Open. Which, to be fair, it probably is—except to the people playing in the other Opens.

The USGA didn't actually settle on the 18-hole format until 1950, when Ben Hogan beat Lloyd Mangrum by four shots at Merion Golf Club outside Philadelphia to climax his miraculous comeback less than a year after he almost died in a car accident. There were actually people trying to compare Woods's playing on a bad knee to Hogan's comeback, which, as Woods himself pointed out, was patently ridiculous.

Prior to 1950, there had been 18-hole playoffs, 36-hole playoffs, and, in 1931, a 72-hole playoff, Billy Burke beating George Von Elm 296 to 297 at Inverness after they had tied at 292 at the conclusion of the first 72 holes. Woods versus Rocco would be the fourteenth 18-hole playoff since the 18-hole format had taken root. The last one had been in 2001: Retief Goosen beating Mark Brooks by two shots at Southern Hills in one of Fay's "clunkers." That had been the Open in which Rocco finished fourth, his best previous finish in a major.

By now, Cindi and Rocco had developed a pre-tee-off routine, stopping several yards from the first tee, around a corner where they were just outside the view of the grounds and the TV cameras. "This is exactly what I've waited for my entire life," he told her, his voice very soft. "I know," she said. "Go get it done."

Cindi headed back inside the ropes, carrying her trusty pen. When the two players arrived at the first tee, the mass of humanity they found there was remarkable. The USGA would report later that 25,000 people were "scanned" coming through the gates that morning. That was fewer than the 42,500 who showed up each day of the tournament, but it was a huge throng for a Monday playoff, especially when one considered that every one of them was following the only twosome on the golf course.

"It just shocked me when I walked on the tee," Rocco said. "You expect it to be crowded, because even if the overall crowd isn't that big, we're the only ones playing. But it was just unbelievable. Everywhere you looked, all you could see were people."

Woods was in his third playoff in a major championship. He had beaten Bob May in a four-hole playoff at the 2000 PGA and Chris DiMarco in sudden death at the 2005 Masters. Overall, he had been in eleven playoffs as a pro, winning ten of them. His only loss had been to Billy Mayfair in Los Angeles in 1998. Rocco was 2–0 in playoffs, having beaten Curtis Strange for his first tour victory at Doral in 1991 and Steve Elkington — on the fourth hole — at Greensboro in 1993.

Woods had the honor on the first hole, and for the first time in five tries, his drive found the fairway. He was so happy to be in the short grass that he threw his arms into the air in (semi) mock celebration. Rocco may have felt a bit tight starting out, but he split the fairway with his drive. From there, he missed the green with a slightly nervous five-iron and ended up making a two-putt bogey. Woods found the center of the green and made a routine par. On the hole that had been his Achilles' heel all week, Woods had quickly taken a one-shot lead.

"Not the start you want, but it's just that — a start," Rocco said. "At that moment I was awfully glad we weren't playing sudden death. I'd have been down the road in a hurry."

He settled down on number two, making a par. Even that was a little bit disappointing, since he had birdied the hole three days out of four, but this was all different and new. The par gave him a chance to catch his breath. Woods, off to a much steadier start than on Sunday, made another routine par.

The third hole was playing fairly short, but not as short as it had on the weekend. Rocco hit a six-iron that he thought for an instant might go into the hole. It landed just in front of the pin and rolled right past it before settling 18 inches from the cup. Woods missed the green, hit a poor chip, and two-putted for bogey. When Rocco's tap-in birdie putt went in, he had suddenly gone from a one-shot deficit to a one-shot lead.

"At that point I knew I was okay, that I had come to play," he said. "I thought before the round that would be the case, but when I started with the bogey, it shook me just a little. The birdie brought me back to where I wanted to be. The nerves were almost completely gone after that. I was playing golf."

Rocco may have been calm, but Cindi was not. "I was trying so hard to keep myself together," she said. "I just couldn't do it. It was so tense inside the ropes, so many people. We got to the third hole and I just started to lose it. I went outside the ropes and found Sticky [Puertas] and said, 'I'm losing it.' I was crying, couldn't stop myself. He said, 'My God, Cindi, it's the third hole. You can't start breaking down on the third hole.' I said I'd try. But it was really, really hard."

The rest of the front nine didn't make Cindi feel any better. Both players parred the fourth hole, then Rocco bogeyed the fifth after missing the green and hitting a mediocre bunker shot. Woods made par and they were all even. Woods had not yet made a birdie. That changed on the sixth hole, when he rolled in a 15-foot birdie putt. He followed that with another birdie at the seventh, and just like that he had a two-shot lead.

"For some reason I wasn't panicked," Rocco said. "Look, it's

Tiger Woods. He isn't going to go 18 holes and not make some birdies. But the way the weekend had gone, I had to figure he wasn't going to play a perfect round either. His knee was hurting; I could see that. I didn't expect him to fall over or anything like that, but I thought there was still a lot of golf left to be played if I could just get something going on my side of it."

Woods did make a mistake on the eighth, finding the rough off the tee and making his second bogey of the day from there. Rocco's par brought him to within one again.

But then it was Rocco's turn to make a mistake. On the ninth, his third-shot wedge went 18 feet past the hole, leaving him with a longer birdie putt than he wanted. Trying too hard to make it, he watched it roll five feet past the hole. Then he missed coming back. Woods made a par, and they turned with Rocco two shots behind.

Around the country, as NBC took over the telecast from ESPN at two o'clock eastern time, most people who hadn't been paying attention until the network telecast began shook their heads knowingly when the nine-hole scores went up: Woods — 35; Mediate — 37. Rocco certainly wasn't embarrassing himself, but Tiger — as usual — appeared to be firmly in control.

As the players made their way to the 10th tee, Cindi was receiving almost constant text messages from friends around the country. They all said basically the same thing: "Tell him to slow down!"

"When I get my adrenaline pumping, I can get too fast at times," Rocco said. "I'm too fast getting ready to hit the ball, too fast with my swing — everything. I'd done a very good job for four days not letting that happen, even under the gun on Sunday. I was very calm, going at a very good pace for me the entire time.

I guess for a while there on Monday, I got a little too wound up after he made those two birdies and got a little bit fast."

With the text messages flying at her, Cindi knew she needed to find a moment to get close enough to Rocco to look him in the eye and remind him to slow down. The problem was she had gone back outside the ropes, in part because crouching and kneeling and lying down on her stomach to stay out of the way of the fans screaming, 'Get down!' at all those inside the ropes was starting to wear her out, and in part to calm herself down again.

"I knew I needed to get someplace where he would see me," she said. "The problem was the crowds were so huge I couldn't get back inside the ropes on 10."

In fact, at one point she got trapped when security decided to hold the portion of the crowd she was in to try to spread people out a little bit. "I was waving my media credential, saying, 'I'm with the media,'" she said, laughing later. "To say that no one cared is putting it mildly."

She finally managed to wedge her way back inside as the players reached the 10th green. By then, Rocco was in more trouble, having missed yet another green. Woods made par, but Rocco couldn't get up and down for par. He had made back-to-back bogeys on two of the easier holes on the golf course and hadn't made a birdie since the third. Woods led by three strokes with eight holes to play.

"Now or never," Cindi thought.

As the players walked onto the 11th tee, she got Rocco's attention and waved him over close to her. "Slow down!" she hissed.

"What?" he said, initially unsure of what she was saying.

"I said, slow the f—— down!" she said emphatically.

This time Rocco got it. "Okay," he said, returning to the tee as Woods went through his pre-shot routine.

If there was ever a moment when TVs around the country were going to be turned off, this was it. Tiger Woods with a three-shot lead on the back nine is about as close to a lock as anything on earth short of the sun rising in the east or the New York Jets collapsing in December.

In Greensburg, Tony Mediate paced around and told his wife, "He's in trouble."

"Calm down," Donna said. "I think he's going to be okay. It's not even close to over."

A few miles away, Dave Lucas, Rocco's childhood buddy, felt the same way as Donna, even though he knew there was no logic to it. "It's just always been Rocco's way that when he gets to a point where his back is against the wall and there's absolutely no reason to believe he can succeed, he figures something out," he said. "It gets back to the self-confidence he always had that always seemed so misplaced. Put him in a spot where he has no chance, and he's really dangerous. What could be more of a no-chance than three down to Tiger?"

Rocco's family and close friends often saw him as Han Solo in the famous *Star Wars* scene in which Solo is trying to maneuver his spaceship through an asteroid field. "Sir," shrieks C-3PO, "the odds of successfully navigating an asteroid field are 3,720 to 1!"

To which Solo replies, "Never tell me the odds."

Rocco never wanted to know the odds. They simply didn't matter as far as he was concerned.

With Cindi's "slow down" mantra echoing in his head, Rocco watched Woods miss the 11th green. The hole was playing

221 yards, so he needed a three-iron. Taking his time, Rocco put a perfect swing on the ball and found the green. When Woods couldn't get up and down, and Rocco two-putted for par, the margin was back to two.

"Two shots is nothing," Rocco said. "You can make up two shots on one hole on a golf course like that. I realized I still had a great chance to win the thing. A thousand things could happen over seven holes."

What happened next was that Woods bogeyed the 12th. He would talk later about how the Monday round was a microcosm of his week. "A little of everything. I made eagles, birdies, hit great shots, hit terrible shots. I'd birdie two in a row, then bogey two in a row. I never knew exactly what was going to happen next."

Neither did anyone else.

On 13, Woods missed the fairway to the right. Rocco was down the middle, but had to lay up.

Woods found the green—again—from the rough, missed the eagle putt but tapped in for birdie. He didn't gain any ground on Rocco, though, because he had hit his third-shot wedge—after laying up—to five feet and made his putt for birdie. The margin stayed at one with only one par five left to play.

The tee was up again at 14, the USGA having decided that playing the hole short on Sunday had added a lot of suspense and decision making to the round. The hole was playing a little bit longer than Sunday, though, because the teeing area was on the back portion of the tee rather than on the front of it, and the players had a little bit of a wind in their faces.

That made the clubbing decision easy for both: driver for Rocco, three-wood for Woods.

"Playing it longer helped me," Woods said later. "I wasn't between clubs the way I was on Sunday. I actually hit the ball in a good spot and had what should have been an easy pitch. But the lie was just a little bit funky."

Both players barely missed the green, Rocco's ball ending up right in front, Woods's a little to the right, just in the rough. For once, Woods got a bit of a bad break: There was a small tuft of grass under his ball, which made it harder for him to spin the ball the way he normally would. His pitch ended up about 15 feet from the hole. From there, his birdie putt slid just past the cup. Rocco, with nothing impeding him, hit a pretty shot to about two feet and holed the putt for a birdie.

Tie ball game. Both players were now one over par for the day.

"I got to playing some military golf right there," Woods said. "You know, 'left-right, right-left.' I was putting so well I kept thinking if I could just get the ball on the green on each hole, I'd have a chance. I knew three shots up on this golf course the lead could go away quickly." He smiled. "I guess I was right."

There were four holes to play, and they were dead even. By now, most of the country was riveted. Since NBC.com was streaming live, a lot of people sitting at desks in their offices were watching on their computers. During the last two hours of the playoff, trading volume on Wall Street plummeted.

Curtis Strange, who had worked the first two rounds of the tournament for ESPN, was back home, unable to move from his TV. "I got a call from my son Thomas, who lives in Charlotte," he said later. "He was in a restaurant watching with some friends and he said people were just going nuts on every shot."

Arnold Palmer had watched Sunday's round at home, surrounded by friends. On Monday, he sat in his office with his friend and confidant Doc Giffin. "If I'd had people around, it would have been too much," Palmer said. "I was nervous and proud at the same time. There were moments when I wanted to say to Rocco on the screen, 'I *told* you for years that you could do this.'"

Rick Smith had completed his outing-related duties in the morning and was back in the locker room at Oakland Hills. "I almost couldn't breathe by the time they got to 15," he said.

Cindi, having done her job by telling Rocco to slow down, was now a complete mess. "The last few holes, no matter how hard I tried, I couldn't stop crying," she said. "At one point, Sticky had come inside the ropes, and I was about to say to him, 'Help me calm down here; I need to stop crying.' Then I looked at him and *he* was crying."

The calmest person in the storm was Rocco. He hit another perfect drive at 15. Woods, still in the military mode, missed the fairway dead right. "I was in a zone then," Rocco said. "I'd hit the ball, look at it in the air, and say, 'Yup,' and then move on to the next shot. If I hit a shot that wasn't exactly what I wanted, I was surprised."

Woods would later describe his drive at 15 as a "pitch out." "Catcher called pitch out, and I hit it over there to the right," he said.

He was so far to the right that on the one hole on the golf course that didn't have a bunker, he had found one—on the adjoining ninth hole.

He had a difficult lie but a reasonable angle to the green and was 170 yards away—a seven-iron shot for him. "I had to start the ball at the middle of the right bunker and just rope it in there," he said. "I hit it so flush it was probably the best shot I hit all week, feeling-wise. And it hit up right behind the hole."

"We were so far away we really couldn't see what Tiger was doing over there on the other side," Rocco said. "When he finally got over the ball and hit it, Matt said to me, 'Where'd it go?' I said, 'Just watch the flag.' Sure enough the ball came from out of nowhere, landed on the green, and stopped ten feet away."

It was a superb shot, one of those one-in-a-million shots Woods pulls off. Even though Rocco's drive had found the fairway, he had still been away and hit a solid second shot that had stopped 18 feet above the hole. Woods's shot rolled inside Rocco's, finally stopping no more than 10 feet from the hole.

"Ridiculous," Rocco said. "I run out of words to use when he hits a shot like that. Think about it: I hit a good second shot, and he's inside me hitting his second shot from Pluto."

Woods was likely to make his putt, so Rocco hit his birdie putt hard, figuring he had to make it to stay even. "When he hit it," Woods said, "I thought it was going at least 10 or 12 feet by the hole."

So did Rocco—until just before the ball got to the hole, when he realized his line was perfect and the ball was headed straight for the middle of the cup. As the ball got close to the hole, Rocco sensed something special was about to happen. "Oh, wow," he said. "Oh, wow. Oh, wow…" The ball hit the hole and almost popped up into the air, but since it had hit the back of the cup dead center, it stayed in. The roar was, to put it mildly, deafening.

Which was good, because Rocco was so stunned, he let loose with "Oh, my f—— God" after dropping his head in disbelief when the putt went in.

As tense as the situation had just become for him, even Woods couldn't suppress a small smile. "I couldn't believe it when it went in," he said. "Neither could he. I can't repeat here what he said when he realized he'd made it."

Now, suddenly, Woods had to make his putt to stay even. He went for it just as Rocco had, but it veered inches wide of the hole and didn't stop until it had rolled a good four feet past the hole. Shockingly, Woods had to make a true "throw-up zone" putt (as in, when a player sees he has that much left he wants to throw up) or he would be two shots down with three holes to play.

"I looked at it and said, 'Well, here's the tournament. If I miss this putt, the tournament is over. I make this putt, I can still win in regulation. Here we go. Get it done.'"

And, as he always seems to do when there's no choice in the matter, Woods made the putt. Even so, Rocco led by one. He had birdied three holes in a row under the most incredible pressure imaginable. He had gone from three strokes down on the 11th tee to one up on the 16th tee.

Even Woods, who has done just about everything that can be done on a golf course, said, "That hat trick [the three birdies] was one of the more impressive things I've ever seen on a golf course. For all of his talking, Rocc gets himself into a nice little zone when it's time to get over the ball. He talks and talks and then he goes into that zone, hits his shot, and then it's blah-blah blah all over again. It's actually kind of cool to see." Or, as Paul Azinger had said in a text to Cindi earlier in the day, "The world is about to learn our little secret; the boy can play!"

The tension was now officially unbearable. The crowd had been riding along, perfectly happy to see Woods win, but when

Rocco turned things around so emphatically and so quickly, they began to sense that they were witnessing one of the great golf duels — and perhaps one of the great golf upsets — in history.

"You could tell," Cindi said later. "It wasn't that anyone was rooting against Tiger. It was that Rocco had won them over."

That was exactly right. The great TV director Frank Chirkinian, who produced Masters telecasts for CBS for almost forty years, once made the point that golf may be the only sport on earth where neutral fans root for the stars and against the underdogs.

"They don't mind seeing the little guy compete with their heroes," he said. "But in the end, they want their hero to win."

That had almost always been the case with Woods. Most fans liked to see him win, liked to see him pull off unthinkable shots and comebacks. Now, though, it was Rocco who was trying to pull off the unthinkable, and many, if not most, who were watching wanted to see it happen. Early in the day the roars had been equally loud for both players. By the time they walked to the 16th tee, the Rocco roars were almost drowning out the Tiger roars.

Both players made par on the par-three 16th. For a split second it looked as if Woods's 30-foot birdie putt was going to go in, but it stopped a couple of rolls short of the hole. "Thought I'd made it," he said.

Rocco was now two holes from winning the U.S. Open. In the back of his mind was the memory of Sunday, especially knowing that Woods would have the advantage again on the par-five 18th. "I had almost birdied seventeen on Sunday," he said. "The thought occurred to me that if I could birdie it now, it would be almost impossible for him to beat me."

That thought occurred to Woods too. He hit a solid second shot to inside 20 feet, and after Rocco's 35-footer had gone wide, he again hit a near-perfect putt. But it came up just short. Both players tapped in for par.

They were now exactly where they had been a day earlier: one hole to play, Rocco leading by one. The only difference was that they were playing together rather than one group apart.

In Rocco's mind, he needed a birdie to win the championship. He knew that if Woods found the fairway with his drive, he would probably have an iron in his hands for his second shot. Rocco had been able to go for the green only once all week—on Friday—and that had been with a three-wood after he had crushed his drive. For the week, Woods was driving the ball almost exactly 40 yards past him on the holes where the USGA measured for length off the tee.

"I knew, just like on the other days, I was going to have to really rip one to get it out there where I could go for the green," Rocco said. "So I went for it, swung hard. I hit the ball right on the center of the club, caught it just about perfect. But I hit it a few yards left of where I was aiming. I was trying to start it out down the right side and have it drift back to the middle and bounce to the left side of the fairway. I started it out right in the middle; it drifted to the left side and bounced into the bunker. That eliminated any questions about going for the green."

Woods, knowing he probably couldn't afford to miss the fairway the way he had on Sunday, crushed his drive. "I was actually thinking eagle to win," he said. "But I wanted to make sure I at least made four, because after Rocco's drive I knew there was a good chance that would at least keep me alive."

The drive was Woods's best of the day, one of his best of

the-week. It flew 320 yards and left him with 217 yards to the hole—a four-iron shot for him.

Rocco hit a good second shot, laying up to almost exactly 100 yards. The flag was deeper on the green than it had been Sunday, 19 yards from the front edge and six feet from the right edge. That meant he had a little more room to work with.

Woods's second shot was a dart that landed in the middle of the green and rolled to a stop 35 feet from the hole. Rocco was now certain he had to make birdie to have a chance to win.

"Even with the flag back a little, I just couldn't play it too cozy," he said. "I didn't hit a bad shot; it just had no chance to check up."

The ball hit just below the pin but spun left, leaving him with 18 feet for birdie.

As the two players walked up to the green, the crowd noise was so loud that even walking right next to each other, neither could hear the other one speak. Rocco was going on about how the whole thing was "insane," but Woods couldn't hear a word he was saying.

"If I had shouted right in his ear at that moment, I don't think he would have heard me," Rocco said. "It was that crazy."

It got quiet again as they lined up their putts. Knowing Woods's penchant for doing undoable things, Rocco realized that he might have to make his birdie putt to *tie*. As soon as he saw the ball come off Woods's putter, he knew that wasn't going to be the case. It was low all the way and went about four feet past the hole.

Now Rocco's birdie putt was to win the U.S. Open championship.

"Every kid who has ever played golf has dreamed that moment," Rocco said. "Make this putt, win the U.S. Open. I'd dreamed it a million times. Now it was real, right there. I told myself, 'Whatever you do, don't you dare leave it short. Give yourself a chance.'"

He didn't leave it short. But the putt was left of the hole all the way and didn't take the break to the right Rocco thought it might when it got to the hole. When he walked down to mark, he was somewhat stunned to see he had a good three feet left. "On that green, it was anything but a tap-in," he said.

Woods's birdie putt was actually a tad longer. After talking it over at length with Williams, he calmly knocked it into the center of the hole. "I just couldn't get a read on it; I couldn't see anything. I asked Stevie what he thought [unusual; Woods usually reads his own putts], and he couldn't see anything either. So I played it dead straight and put a little bit more on it to make sure it didn't take some kind of break."

It hit the back of the hole solidly, never straying an inch.

Now Rocco had to make his putt for par to keep the match going. A miss, and Woods would win by a shot.

"I said to Matt, 'I'm not even going to read anything into this putt; I just have to make it,'" he said. "It was really a matter of making sure I didn't baby it and put break into it. I was probably more nervous over that putt than any I had all week. Three-putting the last green for bogey would have been a horrible way to lose. I just had to get that putt in the hole."

He did, looking calm, even if he wasn't. After 18 holes, they were still tied: Both men had shot even-par 71. After 90 holes, they were also tied, each of them still one under par. For all the USGA's talk about the fairness of an 18-hole playoff and the unfairness—"flukiness," as Fay called it—of sudden death, the championship would be decided in sudden death.

Before that, though, there were a couple of things that had to be done. For one, both players had to sign their scorecards. "It was a stroke play round, so they had to add up their scores and sign their cards to make it official," Mike Davis said. "We hadn't really thought about what would happen if they tied."

The scoring area was a long way off, in the clubhouse. What's more, there was no one there. So the two players sat down on the fringe of the green, added up their scores, and signed their cards.

The next step was to get them back to the seventh tee, which was where the playoff to decide the playoff would begin. The USGA had carts waiting. Rocco was ready first and he hopped into one of them and headed for the seventh tee, which wasn't very far from the 18th green, one of the reasons the USGA had selected it as the place to begin sudden death if it was needed.

He was on his way to the tee, when Woods finished his card and said to Mike Davis, "I need to go to the bathroom."

Uh-oh. The USGA hadn't really thought about that either. The locker room was a hike from the 18th green. The public porta-johns nearby would be jammed, and to get Woods to and from one would be chaotic. Davis jumped on his walkie-talkie and, fairly desperately, said, "Anyone have an idea where I can take Tiger to go to the bathroom?"

David Fay was listening up in the NBC booth. He grabbed his walkie-talkie and responded. "You're only a few yards from the NBC tower," he said. "There's a porta-john there at the bottom of the stairs. Use that."

Brilliant solution. Davis had one other concern. The porta-john was convenient and private, since it was inside the ropes, but it was still, well, a porta-john.

"Tiger," Davis said gingerly, "are we talking number one or number two?"

Woods laughed. "Number one," he said.

Davis breathed a sigh of relief and escorted Woods to the NBC tower. Both men were feeling better when Woods and Steve Williams were carted out to the seventh tee, where Rocco was waiting.

The seventh was not an ideal hole for Rocco to play sudden death. It is a 461-yard dogleg right. Woods could hit a high cut off the tee, aim at the corner, and shorten the hole considerably. Rocco can play an occasional cut, but his shot is the high draw, meaning the hole didn't set up well at all for him.

"I'd been hitting a big hook off the tee all week," he said. "Start it out right and have it come back to the center of the fairway as close to the dogleg as possible. I pulled it off a couple days, but I also landed in the first cut a couple times and in the left-hand bunker. It wasn't a good driving hole for me."

So much so that Mike Davis actually got angry e-mails and letters from people claiming the USGA had chosen number seven as the playoff hole because it wanted Woods to win. But the playoff hole had been decided on the previous Wednesday.

"Our thinking was twofold," Davis said. "First, it was close to the clubhouse and the 18th green, which would make it easy to get the players back there and relatively easy for fans to walk over there to watch, since they'd have a few minutes in between. Second, seven-eight-nine are a par-four, a par-three, and a par-five. We liked having three different pars on the first three holes if it went that far. The last thing we were thinking when we made the decision was who might be in a sudden-death playoff."

Woods, hitting first after his birdie at the 18th, hit a perfect shot, cutting the dogleg, the ball rolling to a halt just in the fairway on the right side, leaving him with a relatively simple shot to the green. Rocco tried to hit his high hook again but—a little bit like at 18—started it too far left. This time, though, he was way left, and the ball hopped into a bunker to the left of the fairway.

"Right away," he said, "I knew I was in trouble."

He knew he was in bigger trouble when he got to the ball and saw that it was in the front of the bunker, almost up against the lip, meaning he had virtually no chance to get the ball over the lip and still get it to the green. He had to give it a try, though, because he knew the likelihood that Woods was going to make anything worse than par was slim.

"I swung really hard and just flipped it," he said. "That's why the ball went so far left."

It was *way* left, up against the grandstand, short and to the left of the green. Woods, seeing where Rocco was, didn't try anything fancy, hitting a nine-iron safely onto the front of the green, leaving himself about 20 feet for birdie.

Because the grandstand was an artificial, immovable hazard, Rocco was entitled to relief. The grass in that area was so thick that the USGA had marked off a drop circle for any player who had to take a drop away from the grandstand. Davis showed Rocco the drop circle after he had picked up his ball. He walked over to it, held his arm up as the rules prescribe, and dropped the ball.

It landed in the circle, but the ground was hard enough that it hopped a little bit and rolled outside the circle. Instinctively, seeing the ball leave the circle, Rocco bent over to pick up the ball and drop again. Fortunately for everyone, Davis had not turned away but was looking right at Rocco at that moment.

"I saw him reach down for the ball and I thought, 'Oh, my God!'" Davis said. "I screamed, 'Rocco, ball's in play, the ball's in play!'"

Which it was, the instant it came to rest. "I just blanked on the rule," Rocco said. "I forgot that the ball just has to *land* in the circle to be in play and for a second thought it had to *end up* in the circle. Thank God Mike screamed at me."

If Rocco had picked up the ball, the championship would have been over at that instant. He would have been disqualified for picking up a ball that was in play. Woods would have been required to putt out to make it official, but it would have been the worst possible ending to one of the great days in the history of golf.

As soon as he heard Davis screaming, Rocco stood up, thanked him, and regrouped. "All I really wanted was to get the ball somewhere on the green and give myself a putt at it," he said. "That was my only hope. When the ball bounced out of the circle, I didn't have a very good lie at all. I actually hit a hell of a shot from there."

He lofted the ball onto the green, and it rolled to a halt 18 feet past the pin, just inside the distance Woods had from below the hole. Woods had 20 feet for birdie to win. If he missed, Rocco would have to make his putt for a tying par.

Woods cozied his putt up close to the hole— no need to take any chances—and tapped in. Rocco took his time over his par putt, read it a couple of balls outside right, and gave it a good run. "For one second I thought maybe," he said. "But then I could see it was going to go above the hole. I knew then it was over."

If Woods has one bad habit on the golf course—other than the occasional thrown club—it is that he does not first congratulate his opponent after the final putt has dropped or not dropped. After one of his victories in the U.S. Amateur—also in sudden death—he ran to his father while his vanquished opponent stood waiting for him to come and shake hands.

This time he went and hugged Williams first. When he got to Rocco, who was standing and waiting for him, he put out his hand.

"No, I don't think so," Rocco said. "I think this calls for a hug."

Woods got it instantly, and the two men hugged. "Great fight," Woods said in Rocco's ear above the cheers raining down on both of them.

"Thanks," Rocco said. "You too."

That was a perfect description of the day. It had been a great fight, the two of them repeatedly knocking each other down and getting up from a punch to deliver another one. Both were exhausted and exhilarated, Woods by the victory, Rocco by the battle.

It had been a week that would change both their lives for entirely different reasons. And one that those who watched would remember for a long, long time.

16

Suddenly Famous

IN THE HOUR AFTER HE HUGGED WOODS on the seventh green, Rocco had little chance to even begin to grasp what had happened.

As soon as Rocco missed his final putt, Cindi had made a beeline for Matt, in part because she was looking for comfort, but also to make certain she didn't get swallowed by the crowds. There had been very little security of any kind on the sudden-death hole, since the marshals who had worked the hole earlier in the day were long gone. Fans had spilled into the fairway once Rocco and Woods made their way onto the green.

"I felt so proud of him for the way he played but also sad about it all," she said. "I don't think I've ever wanted something so badly for someone in my life. He was *so* close, played *so* well. Tiger has won how many—fourteen majors? For Rocco there may be other chances, but there may not be. He's forty-five. It could happen again, but it might not."

In fact, had Rocco won, he would have been the oldest Open champion in history, a few months older than Hale Irwin was when he won the Open—on the 91st hole—in 1990.

The notion that his best chance might have just passed hadn't hit him as he rode on the cart along with Cindi and Matt back to the 18th green for the awards ceremony. "I was still pumping adrenaline," he said. "The whole day and week had been such a high. The cheers were still ringing in my ears at that moment."

It was during the awards ceremony that the sadness Cindi felt began to hit him. "I always wanted to be part of that awards ceremony," he said. "I'd seen it a million times. I remember standing there when Lee won and thinking how cool the whole thing was. So there I was, finally a part of it, but they gave Tiger the big trophy. I got a silver medal. It wasn't what I had been shooting for. I didn't even want to touch the trophy. It wasn't mine; it was his. Touching it, even looking at it, would have made it even harder."

He and Woods again went through the gauntlet of media interviews: TV, the interview room, then one-on-one with various national TV outlets.

Woods was a gracious winner. When he was asked again about struggling through the week on his surgical knee, he talked about Rocco's struggles with injuries throughout his career. "I think we saw what kind of player and competitor Rocc is this week," he said. "When he's healthy, he's a great player."

Woods was his usual circumspect self when the subject of his immediate future came up. He said he was going to "shut it down for a while," adding that he had no idea when he would play again.

British Open? "I hope so," he said. Had he hurt the knee more by playing? "Maybe," he said.

He called it his greatest victory ever, which took in a lot of territory. Dealing with the injury, having to make birdie twice on 18 to stay alive, and the way Rocco had competed combined to make it number one on his lengthy list.

In a sense it was Rocco's greatest victory too. "If you think about where I was going into the Memorial and where I was when that day ended, it was pretty amazing," he said. "I had made no money before Memorial; in fact I was hurting financially with everything that was going on in my life, and I didn't know when or if I would find my game again.

"Then I finish sixth at Memorial, make it through the playoff to get into the Open, and go 91 holes head-to-head with the greatest player alive, I'd say it was a pretty good couple of weeks."

In truth, he had no idea how good those couple of weeks had been. As he left his golf outing in Michigan, Frank Zoracki's cell phone began exploding. People had been calling his office in Greensburg and had gotten his cell number.

"One minute there was a call from Leno's show, the next Letterman. Then the *Today* show," he said. "It seemed as if every news outlet in the country was calling. There was no way I could return all the calls in any kind of timely way. I just did the best I could."

As he was leaving the interview tent, Rocco was unaware of all this. He knew he had played well, knew how close he had come, but he didn't really understand that most of the country had been riveted by the playoff or that the prime-time ratings for NBC on Sunday had been off the charts. He had no idea that people who knew nothing or almost nothing about golf now knew his name.

When he had finally done the last of the interviews, he and Cindi drove to the hotel to pack for the trip back to Los Angeles. The lobby was jammed with people who had watched the playoff, then walked over for a drink or to get something to eat.

"When we walked in the door, someone spotted me and yelled my name," Rocco said. "Then a few more people. Then it became completely insane, like I had walked into a pep rally or something. People were just going nuts, clapping and screaming and patting me on the back. That was when I first realized what was going on. I'd never seen anything quite like that."

The realization began to hit home even more when he finally had a chance to call Zoracki, who began ticking off the media requests. "I only gave him the highlights," Zoracki said. "There wasn't time to go through all of them and there was no way he was going to be able to do all of them, even though I knew he'd be willing to try."

Doing the network morning shows would mean getting up at 3 A.M. on the West Coast, but Rocco knew he couldn't afford to say no. Leno wanted him to come on the next night as a surprise guest. That sounded like fun. In fact, a lot of it sounded like fun.

"I enjoy all of that," he said. "I like performing and I like talking and I like people, so I'm fine with it most of the time. Plus, to be honest, I knew there was an opportunity here. I hadn't exactly been on the front burner in the public's mind for a while. I knew that even if I didn't want to do all of this, I would need to do it. Fortunately, even though I was exhausted, almost all of it was fun."

Rocco continued to charm America in all his interviews. He joked about how ridiculously good Woods was, about how amazed he was that he'd had a chance to beat him. He kept saying the whole thing was "a blast, the most fun I've had in my life."

Woods was long gone from the public eye by Tuesday. Once he finished his interviews on Monday afternoon, he headed straight to a private plane to go home to Florida. He would not be doing any morning shows or making surprise appearances on Leno. In fact, the day after the playoff, it was announced that he was going to be "shutting down" for a long time — the rest of the year.

It turned out that he had been playing on a knee that needed more surgery. He had a torn ACL in his knee and two stress fractures in his leg. The doctors had told him he could play in the Open but that he might damage the knee further. Regardless, he was going to need the surgery.

Knowing he was going to be out for a while and knowing he probably had as good a chance to win another Open at Torrey Pines as any place on earth, Woods had gambled that he could get through 72 holes — or 91 holes, as it turned out —and had won the gamble. He had hobbled away with the Open trophy, a feeling of amazing satisfaction, and a knee that he hoped surgery would repair once and for all.

The news that Woods had a torn ACL made his victory even more legendary in the minds of the golfing public. But it would not have been as special to most had he not been pushed so hard for so long by Rocco.

"If he had won going away, the way he does so often, a lot of people would have said, 'He's just that much better than everyone else that he can still whip everyone even when he's hurt,'" Lee Janzen said. "But the fact that he had to fight his way through it, play another round even though he was clearly in pain, and battle Rocco right to the finish, well, that just made it an even bigger deal. It's hard to imagine that Tiger could become even more larger-than-life than he already was, but this did it for him. And Rocco was a big part of it."

All the buzz about Woods and his impending surgery only made people want to hear more from Rocco. His appearance on *The Tonight Show* was a huge highlight. After Leno had gone down the guest list for the evening, he said he had one more guest, a surprise guest, someone the entire country had been watching over the past several days. When he introduced Rocco, the entire audience was on its feet, giving Rocco a standing ovation.

"Insane," he said, repeating his favorite word. "It was completely insane — just like the whole week."

He did one interview after another, spending the entire day Wednesday in a Los Angeles studio cranking them out, somehow sounding cheerful and enthusiastic throughout, even though he was hitting a wall.

There was more, though, than just media. Before Rocco and Cindi left the grounds on Monday, Cindi had received a text message from Tony Renaud, the Skins Game promoter she had talked to at the Memorial. "Where do I send a contract?" the text said. All of a sudden, Rocco had gone from a likable journeyman to a star who could perhaps save the Skins Game.

Offers to do outings were also pouring in. Because of his personality, Rocco had always done well as a golf celebrity at corporate outings. Outings are the unseen financial perk that golf pros enjoy. Fees can range from $1,000 a day for someone on the Nationwide Tour to $5,000 for tour rookies to $250,000 for a Phil Mickelson to well over $1 million on those rare occasions when Woods might do an outing.

Rocco's fee was in the $25,000 range, and if he did more than one Monday — outings are almost always on Mondays because pros are available on most Mondays — in a month, that was a very good month. After the Open, his fee doubled—and occasionally went higher—and he had offers stacked up well into 2009 and even 2010.

All of that was important because Rocco's finances had been in tough shape prior to the Open thanks to the divorce, the fact that the house in Naples still hadn't sold, and his poor play the first half of the year.

After taking the week off—from golf but not from off-course work—following the Open, Rocco went to Flint, Michigan, to play in the Buick Open. More insanity.

"I couldn't move most of the time," he said. "I did a Tuesday press conference, but everyone in the media wanted their own 'five minutes' with me. I had never said no to any of those guys before; I didn't want to start now. I didn't want people to think because I had one great week I was a different guy. So I tried to do everything."

He had always been popular with golf fans, but now he had gone to a whole new level. No one in the field drew bigger galleries during the week. No one had more people waiting for autographs when he walked out of the locker room, off the driving range, or out of the scorer's tent.

"It just never stopped," he said, "By the end of the week, for the first time I was starting to feel a little bit tired."

He played reasonably well, especially given the circumstances, finishing in a tie for 28th place. From there, it was on to Washington—specifically Congressional Country Club in Bethesda—for what is formally known as the AT&T National Pro-Am but is called by everyone on tour "the Tiger."

The tournament had been launched a year earlier, with Woods as the host, when the tour event in Denver lost its corporate sponsor and Commissioner Tim Finchem saw its demise as a way to get back into the nation's capital, bringing Woods—who wanted his own event, à la Palmer and Nicklaus—along with him. The presence of Woods opened the doors of Congressional, a past and future (2011) U.S. Open site that had previously been lukewarm to hosting a weekly tour event. With Tiger's name on it, that changed.

Except that the host was nowhere to be found in 2008. Not only was he not in the field, he wasn't there at all, saying that getting on an airplane, even a private one, was too tough a week after his knee surgery. In his absence, Rocco was asked by the tournament organizers to stand in for him at the pre-tournament sponsor party. This was normally the night that those who put up big bucks got to shake the Great One's hand and have their picture taken with him. They may have been disappointed that Woods wasn't there, but they were charmed by Rocco, who did the glad-handing and picture-taking and told funny stories all night.

"I was happy to do it for him," Rocco said. "He's been my friend for a long time and I genuinely like the guy. If I could help out, why not?"

He played well again in Washington, coming back after an opening-round 73 to shoot 68–67–66 and finish in a tie for 18th place. Two weeks later, he was tied for the lead after one round of the British Open and had people murmuring that maybe he could do it again. But a very tough, windy golf course—Royal Birkdale—wore him out the last couple of days, and he finished tied for 19th. In all, a very solid run.

Which was important for one reason: He desperately wanted to make the Ryder Cup team. In the past, he had been on the fringe of contention for Ryder Cup and Presidents Cup teams but had never been on one. With Paul Azinger as captain and with four captain's picks available—as opposed to two in the past—the consensus was that Rocco would be an ideal pick even if he didn't finish in the top eight in the standings and earn one of the automatic spots.

"I think I can help this team," he said. "It's going to be a little bit younger than in the past and I'm, well, older. I'm not going to be intimidated by anything the Europeans do or by any of their guys. I'll go into the room and raise some hell and say let's go kick some butts. If I keep playing well, I would think Zinger will pick me."

Azinger wanted to pick Rocco for his experience, his enthusiasm, and his competitiveness. This would be a different U.S. team than the one that had lost the last three Ryder Cups, if for no other reason than the fact that Woods wouldn't be there. Many people in golf thought this might be a good thing for the U.S. because Woods had never liked playing in the Ryder Cup much, and his relatively mediocre (10–13–2) record was a reflection of that.

With Woods hurt and Davis Love III and Fred Couples not playing well enough for various reasons (age, injuries) to be on the team, the only player with a lot of experience was Phil Mickelson, who had played on six Ryder Cup teams with mixed success. What's more, Mickelson wasn't going to be a vocal "Let's go kick some butts" kind of leader. Rocco could play that role.

"Basically, Zinger has said to me I need to just keep playing well and not worry about standings or anything else," Rocco said the week before the PGA Championship. "That's what I'm trying to do. Problem is, right now I'm really tired."

The schedule made taking a break impossible. In addition to playing almost every week, he was doing outings almost every Monday, posing for magazine covers, still responding to all the interview requests, and trying to help Linda and the kids get settled in Seattle. Linda had started dating someone who lived there and decided to make the move to the Pacific Northwest. Rocco was delighted, since he was spending most of his time in Los Angeles and the flight from there to Seattle was a lot easier than flying from there to Naples.

"It's great," he said of the family's move. "I met the guy and he's terrific. I think this is a good thing for everybody."

CINDI HAD FLOWN EAST for the World Golf Championship event in Akron—which brought back memories for Rocco because he had first met Tom Watson at Firestone Country Club twenty-seven years earlier—and for the PGA Championship, which was at Oakland Hills, outside Detroit.

Rocco played a good first round in Akron but again wore out as the week went on. He also played solidly in the first two rounds of the PGA, making the cut easily by shooting 73–74.

Cindi woke up Saturday morning prior to the third round of the PGA not feeling well. She was running a low-grade fever and looked and felt weak. "It's something that happens to me fairly often," she said. "It can be an infection, it can be fluid on the kidneys, it can be a lot of things."

Rocco knew Cindi wasn't feeling good when she told him she just didn't have the energy to go to the golf course that day. "When she says she can't make it to the golf course, I know it's bad," he said. "I wanted to withdraw and stay with her, but she wouldn't hear it. She said, 'It's a major and you have to try to play well because of the Ryder Cup. I'll be fine; just go and play well. That will make me feel better.'"

Reluctantly, he agreed. He called his friend and then-agent, Tom Elliott, and asked him to come over and keep an eye on Cindi while he went to play. "If anything happens, text me," he said.

On the 14th hole, he got a text. Elliott and Cindi were on the way to the hospital. He was *not* to leave the golf course. He finished the round—shooting 72 to put himself in respectable position in a tie for 22nd place—and went straight to the hospital.

Cindi's fever was spiking. This had happened before, but it was still frightening. Rocco spent the night in the hospital and never slept for a minute. Cindi was feeling a little bit better in the morning and told him he had to go and play. He did, but the combination of exhaustion and concern made it impossible to focus or to play well at all. He shot an embarrassing 85—embarrassing if you didn't know the circumstances—and finished in 72nd place. Then he went straight back to the hospital.

Cindi was there for a week. By the time Rocco got her home to Los Angeles, he had only forty-eight hours there before he flew on a red-eye to New Jersey to play in the Barclays championships—the first of the so-called playoff tournaments created by the tour a year earlier to add a post-majors climax to the season. There was a lot of money on the table—$10 million to the FedEx Cup winner—but in spite of endless promotional gambits by the tour, there just was not that much interest, with baseball closing in on the climax of its season and the college football and NFL seasons beginning.

Rocco missed the cut at Barclays, the first cut he had missed since the Byron Nelson in late April. He played respectably the first day, shooting a 70, but was completely gassed the next morning and shot 77 to miss the cut. The sensible thing to do at that point would have been to take it easy for a couple of days and then head to Boston, the next playoff spot and, more important, the last tournament before Azinger would name his Ryder Cup team.

"I called Paul to tell him what was going on with Cindi," he said. "I didn't want him to think by flying back to L.A. I wasn't aware of the fact that it was important that I play well in Boston. He had said all along that he was going to take into account your entire body of work, but he also wanted guys who were playing well down the stretch. Other than New Jersey, I'd been playing pretty well all summer. Paul knew what had happened on the last day of the PGA, so I wasn't worried about that. I said to him, 'Hey, I hope you understand why I need to go...'

"Before I finished the sentence he said, 'Are you kidding? Get your butt on a plane and get out there.'"

So he did. Cindi had rallied. She was ready to go with him to Boston the next week, which was important to Rocco. He wanted her with him on the golf course and with him when Azinger named his team on Tuesday, September 2, the day after the Boston tournament ended. (It finished on Monday because it was Labor Day weekend.)

In a way, Boston was a repeat of Detroit. Rocco played well the first two days, shooting 69–70, which put him in a tie for 18th place. But Cindi was sick again on Sunday and had to go back to the hospital, this time Massachusetts General in downtown Boston. Again, she told Rocco he had to play and that he *had* to get his rest so there wouldn't be a repeat of the 85. He tried. He shot a respectable 71 on Sunday in the third round but simply had nothing left on Monday, shooting 74. That dropped him into a tie for 69th place. Again, under the circumstances, it was pretty good golf.

He went back to the hospital as soon as he was finished playing on Monday. Cindi was still too weak to even think about traveling. The next morning he was sitting next to her bed shortly after nine o'clock when his cell phone rang. As soon as Rocco saw the number come up, he knew it was bad news.

"It was Zinger," he said later. "The press conference to announce the captain's picks was at ten. If I was on the team, he wouldn't need to call me to keep me from hearing bad news at the same time everyone else heard it. Before I even answered the phone, I knew I wasn't on the team."

He was right. Azinger was almost apologetic. "I just have to go with what my gut tells me is the best thing," he said. "I can't even really explain to you why you're out and these other guys are in."

The other guys were Hunter Mahan, J. B. Holmes, Chad Campbell, and Steve Stricker. Only Campbell had any previous Ryder Cup experience. He had played well in Boston, tying for sixth, and that seemed to have swayed Azinger in his direction.

As soon as Rocco hung up the phone and told Cindi the news, she began to cry. "I just thought it was unfair," she said. "Zinger knew what was going on in his life, the distractions he'd had, and he *still* hadn't played badly. He missed one cut [New Jersey] all summer."

Even though he was crushed when he wasn't chosen, Rocco tried to be philosophical about it. The U.S. won the matches with a dominant performance at Valhalla Country Club outside Louisville in late September, and Azinger was lauded for his selections and his leadership. The next time Rocco saw Azinger was in the parking lot at the TPC of Summerlin prior to the start of the tournament in Las Vegas in October. He walked over to him, congratulated him on the win, and gave him a hug.

"I was thrilled that they won," he said. "I really was. Hey, Zinger's been a friend for years and the guys on the team were my friends. He did a great job; he made the right choices. Was I disappointed? Sure, of course. But he had to do what he thought was best for the team and he was proven correct by the results."

Did he watch that weekend?

"Not much. I had other things to do."

Enough said.

CINDI'S HEALTH CONTINUED TO BE AN ISSUE throughout the fall and into the winter. A kidney transplant was not a viable option.

Rocco played in two more official tournaments before the end of the year. He shot an opening-round 71 in Las Vegas before withdrawing because his knee was sore. "Being honest, I could have played if I'd had to," he said. "But I just didn't feel quite right, and there was no need to take any risk."

A week later he finished tied for 29th in Scottsdale, then flew to Florida to tape the ADT Skills Challenge, a postseason unofficial event that is part of what is known in golf as "the Silly Season." (The PGA Tour prefers "Challenge Season," which is a lovely euphemism.) The tournaments have no meaning and are basically hit-and-giggle events in which players load up on extra cash.

Because he had received so much attention at the Open and

after the Open, Rocco had been invited to almost every Silly Season event that existed: the Skills Challenge, the Wendy's 3-Tour Challenge in Las Vegas, the Skins Game, and the Shark Shootout. Even though a rest might have been a good thing, these were events with guaranteed money and the chance to make more if you played well. So he accepted all the invitations.

Cindi was scheduled to go to Florida with Rocco for the taping of the Skills Challenge and for the final official tournament of the year at Disney World. But she was in the hospital again. As a result, Rocco withdrew from the Disney event after the Skills Challenge.

A week before Thanksgiving—and the Skins Game, which was Thanksgiving weekend—Cindi went back into the hospital for tests and more treatment. The doctors were hoping to find that her left kidney was not functioning at all and that the right kidney was working well enough to keep her going on its own. The plan, in that case, would have been to remove the left kidney, reducing the chances of infection.

"Unfortunately, they found it was still working at about eleven percent," she said. "I need every little bit I can get, so they decided to leave it in."

Cindi was as sick the week before Thanksgiving as she had been all year. Her fever, which had often gotten to 102 in the past, spiked at 105 and stayed there for more than a week. The doctors could not figure out what was wrong. Finally, they discovered a severe blood infection that they were able to treat, and the fever came down. By Thanksgiving Day she was sitting up in bed, still weak but feeling much better.

It was just prior to that hospital visit that Cindi was introduced to Rocco's three boys, who came to Los Angeles to visit their dad and meet her. When they came back for the Skins Game, Rocco took the three of them to see Cindi in the hospital, where the beginnings of a friendship were formed.

Rocco was the star of the Skins Game even though he finished fourth, winning one Skin and $140,000. With K. J. Choi (who won), Phil Mickelson, and Stephen Ames the other three players, Rocco's humor was desperately needed to lighten the mood. He kept up a constant chatter (the players are miked) throughout the event even though his mind was 150 miles to the west of Palm Springs, in Cindi's hospital room.

"That was a tough two days," he said later. "I had to put on this happy Rocco face the whole time and I was very, very worried. Thank God she was doing better by then. If she'd still been running 105, I don't know if I could have even played at all."

Cindi got out of the hospital the following week and felt better and stronger than she had in months. She calculated that from August 11, the Saturday of the PGA, until November 30, she had spent almost half her time in hospitals. "I've seen some of the best," she joked. "I'd really like not to see any more."

She and Rocco flew to New York the week before Christmas, in part so that Rocco could participate in Bob Costas's year-end special on HBO, in part to do some sightseeing and relax.

On the show, Rocco was in the studio with Costas while Woods was on satellite hookup from California, where he had flown to host—but not play in—the Chevron World Challenge, the final Silly Season event of the year.

It was the only Silly Season event Rocco wasn't invited to play in. Which bothered him—not as much as the Ryder Cup bothered him, but it bothered him nonetheless. There were sixteen players in the field, chosen largely based on world ranking, but not entirely. Since the event was unofficial, Woods and his staff could select anyone they wanted to play.

"Hey, it's his event and he can choose who he wants," Rocco said diplomatically. "I'll admit I was surprised when I heard the field. I thought I'd be asked."

The Costas show was the first time Rocco and Woods had "spoken" since the Open. The segment was lengthy and a bit awkward. Woods wasn't used to sharing a spotlight with anyone, much less someone who was funnier than he was. He clearly wasn't happy when Costas brought up the fact that the crowd had been for Rocco on the back nine on Monday.

"I thought the fans were great," he said. "They just wanted to see good golf."

Rocco was a little bit put off when Costas asked him about his "poor" play after the Open and brought up the Sunday 85 at the PGA.

"In one sense it isn't his fault, because he didn't understand the circumstances," he said. "Obviously I wasn't going to sound like I was making excuses, but the fact is I didn't play badly. I was nineteenth at the British Open, I played well in Washington, and I missed one cut. That isn't bad."

Instead of disputing Costas's point, Rocco just shrugged in reply and said, "I guess I'm getting old."

He turned forty-six on December 17, the same day as the Costas show. There was a bittersweet feel to the end of the year. In one sense, 2008 had been a dream year: He had lived out his fantasies of competing for a U.S. Open championship and of going toe-to-toe with the world watching against the greatest player in history. He was overwhelmingly happy with Cindi, and he was relieved that he and Linda had reached an understanding about how to go forward as parents and that the boys were dealing with all the changes in their lives.

But there were still the ongoing concerns about Cindi's health. "She's been through so much," he said. "She's a young woman [forty-three], but the pain she's gone through is unbelievable. I just hope she's going to be okay."

There was also a sense of loss when he thought back to Torrey Pines. Even though he still talked publicly about how wonderful the experience had been—and meant it—he couldn't help but what-if on occasion. What if the delay at 15 hadn't happened on Sunday, what if the putt had dropped on 17, what if Woods's putt had stayed an inch outside the hole rather than just dropping in, what if there hadn't been a seven-shot gap on the par-fives.

"There are moments when I think back to a shot, a hole, a moment, and I wish it had been just that much different," he said. "Don't get me wrong, I wouldn't trade that week for anything. But I would have loved to have held that trophy. Just that one time.

"The way people responded to it all was beyond unbelievable. They treated me like a champion. There were times when I had to say to people, 'Look, I'm proud of the way I played, but I didn't win. The other guy won.' I was close, I played as well as I could possibly have played, but I didn't win."

But that didn't stop Rocco from setting high goals for 2009: He wanted to lose some of the weight he had put on over the past six months. His plan was to go back to the workout regimen that had been successful for him before. He wanted to contend in more majors, make the Presidents Cup Team, and make it back to the Tour Championship.

"As soon as we get back to L.A., I start," he said the day after the Costas show in New York. "I'm not going to play until Phoenix [at the end of January]—that gives me six solid weeks to be home, to rest, to get in shape, and to take a breather. I haven't had one at all since the Open."

Even though the house in Naples was still unsold, the Open had helped put him back on solid financial footing. He had ended up making $1,420,875 in official money for 2008, a little bit more than $1 million of it at the Memorial ($201,000) and the Open ($810,000). He had earned another $410,000 in Silly Season prize money, in addition to the guarantees he had been paid for some of those events. He had made a good deal of money on outings, with more to come in '09, and after worrying he might lose his Callaway deal (up at the end of '08), he had re-signed for two years and twice the money—$500,000 a year—as on the previous contract.

By finishing second at the Open, he had earned exemptions into the 2009 Masters and the 2009 Open, which would be held at Bethpage Black, a course Rocco loved. That was the good news.

The bad news was what he would have earned had he won the Open: a ten-year exemption to play in the Open through 2018; a five-year exemption on the tour, meaning he would not have to worry about the money list until he was ready for the Champions Tour at the age of 50; and five-year exemptions into the other three majors.

"All that would have been nice, very nice," he said. "But I've never been one to worry about things like that. I mean, who in the world would have thought I would be sitting here with twenty-three years in on the tour, the only time missed being because I was hurt. I've had an amazing time. I've lived my dream and more. Anything from here on in is gravy."

He paused. "I would love one more shot at a major, though. One more shot."

Regardless of what the future holds, Rocco Mediate will be remembered for those five extraordinary days at Torrey Pines in June of 2008. He will be remembered for his golf, for his humor, for his boundless enthusiasm, and for his grace under pressure and in defeat.

"On my wall at home I've always had a poster from *Rocky*," he said. "It says, 'He was a million-to-one shot.' Well, I think in all I was probably a billion-to-one shot."

He smiled. "People forget; Rocky lost the first fight. Then he came back and won the championship. Maybe there's a sequel out there for me too."

ACKNOWLEDGMENTS

WHEN ROCCO MEDIATE AND I AGREED to do this book together, the last thing he said to me after all the details were worked out was, "Hey, we're going to have a blast."

I would like to think, in spite of the emotional roller coaster he was on during the second half of 2008, that Rocco had a blast doing the book. I know I did.

The people close to Rocco all went out of their way to make me comfortable and to help me understand what makes him tick—a special challenge, since I think he would admit there are times when he isn't exactly sure what makes him tick.

That list includes Cindi Hilfman, Tony and Donna Mediate, and Linda Mediate, who could not have been more gracious under very trying circumstances. Many others were extremely helpful, including Dave Lucas, Arnie Cutrell, Jim Ferree, Rick Smith, Jimmy Ballard, Charlie Matlock, Jim Carter, Curtis Strange, Raymond Floyd, Davis Love III, Paul Azinger, Lee and Bev Janzen, Tom Watson, Arnold Palmer, Doc Giffin, and Matt Achatz. Thanks also to the folks at the USGA: David Fay, Mike Davis, and the ever-patient Dave Fanucchi, and to

Tim Finchem, Marty Caffey, Dave Lancer, Guy Shiepers, and Denise Taylor—the MVP—at the PGA Tour.

The real star of this book—other than Rocco—was Frank Zoracki, who did everything but write it and no doubt would have given it a shot if asked. Getting to know Frank was for me one of the joys of the project.

Special thanks this time around go to Michael Pietsch, my publisher at Little, Brown, and Esther Newberg, my agent, for being willing to jump into a project that came up quite suddenly and caught them both by surprise. Thanks also to their staffs: Vanessa Kehren, Eve Rabinovits, Heather Fain, Heather Rizzo, Marlena Bittner, Katherine Molina, and Holly Wilkinson (emeritus) at Little, Brown, and Kari Stuart and Liz Farrell at ICM.

Then there are the usual suspects: Keith and Barbie Drum, Jackson Diehl and Jean Halperin, Ed and Lois Brennan, David and Linda Maraniss, Lexie Verdon and Steve Barr, Jill and Holland Mickle, Shelley Crist, Bill and Jane Brill, Terry and Patti Hanson, Bob and Anne DeStefano, Mary Carillo, Bud Collins and Anita Klaussen, Doug and Beth Doughty, David Teel, Beth (Shumway) Brown, Beth Sherry-Downes, Erine Laissen, Bob Socci, Pete Van Poppel, Omar Nelson, Frank DaVinney, Chet Gladchuk, Eric Ruden, Scott Strasemeier, Billy Stone, Mike Werteen, Chris Day, Chris Knocke, Andrew Thompson, Phil Hoffmann, Joe Speed, Jack Hecker, Dick Hall, Steve (Moose) Stirling, Jim and Tiffany Cantelupe, Derek and Christina Klein, Anthony and Kristen Noto, Pete Teeley, Bob Zurfluh, Vivian Thompson, Phil Hocberg, Al Hunt, Bob Novak, Wayne Zell, Mike and David Sanders, Bob Whitmore, Tony Kornheiser, Mike Wilbon, Mark Maske, Ken Denlinger, Matt Rennie, Jon DeNunzio,

Kathy Orton, Camille Powell, Dan Steinberg (cheap-shot artist that he is), Chris Ryan, Harry Kanterian, Jim Brady, Jim Rome, Travis Rodgers, Jason Stewart, Mike Purkey, Bob Edwards, Tom and Jane Goldman, Bruce Auster, Jim Wildman, Mike Gastineau, Mary Bromley, Kenny and Christina Lewis, Dick (Hoops) and Joanie (Mrs. Hoops) Weiss, Jim O'Connell, Bob Ryan, Frank Hannigan, Mary Lopuszynski, Jerry Tarde, Mike O'Malley, Larry Dorman, Jeff D'Alessio, Marsha Edwards, Jay and Natalie Edwards, Len and Gwyn Edwards-Dieterle, Chris Edwards and John Cutcher, Aunt Joan, Andy North, Neil Oxman, Bill Leahey, Dennis Satyshur, Steve Bisciotti, Kevin Byrne, Dick Cass, Mike Muehr, Bob Low, Joe Durant, John Cook, Brian Henninger, and Paul Goydos, who provided the second-best golf story of 2008.

Thanks as always to Mark Russell, Laura Russell, and Alex Russell (my favorite Republican family); Steve Rintoul, Jon Brendle, and the immortal Slugger White.

Basketball people: Gary Williams, Roy Williams, Mike Krzyzewski, Rick Barnes, Mike Brey, Jeff Jones, Billy Lange, Karl Hobbs, Phil Martelli, Fran Dunphy, Jim Calhoun—whose appearance at the 2008 Bruce Edwards golf outing was nothing short of heroic—Jim Boeheim, Billy Donovan, Rick Pitino, Thad Matta, Tom Brennan, Tommy Amaker, Dave Odom, Jim Larranaga, Mack McCarthy, Jim Crews, Pat Flannery, Emmette Davis, Ralph Willard, David Stern, and Tim Frank. Frank Sullivan should still be coaching. Thanks one more time to the orthopods who keep me running, Eddie McDevitt, Bob Arciero, Gus Mazzocca, and Dean Taylor, and to my personal trainer (he'd deny it vehemently), Tim Kelly.

Not to mention, except I always like to mention them, Howard

Garfinkel and Tom Konchalski — the Damon Runyon and Abe Lincoln of hoops.

Swimmers, as I attempt yet another comeback: Jeff Roddin, Jason Crist, Clay F. Britt, Wally Dicks, Mike Fell, Mark Pugliese, Erik (Dr. Post) Osborne, John Craig, Doug Chestnut, Peter Ward, Penny Bates, Carole Kammel, Magot Pettijohn, Tom Denes, A. J. Block, Danny Pick, Paul Doremus, Bob Hansen, and Mary Dowling.

The China Doll–Shanghai Village Gang: Aubre Jones, Rob Ades, Jack Kvancz, Joe McKeown (in absentia), Stanley Copeland, Reid Collins, Arnie Heft, Bob Campbell, Pete Dowling, Chris (the last Republican) Wallace, Herman (duck for everyone!) Greenberg, Joe Greenberg, Harry Huang, George Solomon, Ric McPherson, Geoff Kaplan, and Murray Lieberman. Red, Zang, and Hymie are always there.

The Rio Gang: Tate Armstrong, Mark Alarie, Clay (LB) Buckley, and Terri Chili.

The Feinstein Advisory Board: Drummer, Frank Mastrandrea, Wes Seeley, Dave Kindred, and Bill Brill, who thinks that Duke football revival is going to happen any minute now.

Last — not even close to least: Danny, Brigid, Bobby, and Jennifer, Margaret and David, Marcia, Ethan and Ben, Matthew and Brian, and the world's most patient human, Chris.

It can't possibly take this many people to get a book written and to keep me up and running. Except it does, and I continue to understand how fortunate I am.

ABOUT THE COAUTHOR

JOHN FEINSTEIN is the author of many bestselling books about golf (including *Tales from Q School, Caddy for Life, Open, The Majors,* and *A Good Walk Spoiled*); basketball (*Last Dance, Let Me Tell You a Story, The Punch, The Last Amateurs, A March to Madness, A Season on the Brink*); football (*Next Man Up* and *A Civil War*); baseball (*Living on the Black* and *Play Ball*); and other sports. He writes for the *Washington Post* and *Golf Digest* and is a frequent commentator on National Public Radio's *Morning Edition*. For more information visit www.feinsteinon thebrink.com.

. . . AND HIS MOST RECENT BOOK

Moment of Glory: The Year Underdogs Ruled Golf was published by Little, Brown and Company in May 2010. Following is an excerpt from the book's opening pages.

INTRODUCTION

Early in the evening of June 15, 2002, Butch Harmon stood on the driving range at Bethpage State Park waiting for his star pupil to arrive. It was already 7:30 and there was barely an hour of daylight left, but Harmon knew his day wasn't close to being over.

This "range" wasn't actually a range. It was part of Bethpage's Green Course—one of the five golf courses that make up the massive park—but for the week of the 2002 United States Open, which was being conducted on the park's famed Black Course, it was serving as the driving range. The real driving range, located on the other side of the parking lot, was being used to house structures like the media tent, and, given that it was normally covered by mats for players to hit off of, it hardly would have been suitable for the world's best—and most pampered—golfers.

There was no doubt that Harmon's pupil, one Eldrick Tiger Woods, would be more than happy to be hitting golf balls a parking lot away from where the media worked rather than right next to them. At that moment, though, where the range was located wasn't Harmon's concern.

He knew that once Woods finished his obligations in the media tent, he would cross the parking lot and walk onto the range in a sour mood.

"When he starts to get the club inside a little too much, he sometimes gets caught coming down," he said, the techno-talk of a swing coach coming to him easily after a lifetime of teaching. "When that happens, it's fairly simple to get him out of it, but that's not always good enough. One of the things that makes him great is that fixing a mistake isn't good enough. He wants to fix it *and* improve on what he's been doing, often all at the same time. Even for him that's not easy. But it's what he expects of himself and what he always wanted from me."

Woods had just completed his third round of the Open. He had shot an even-par 70, not a spectacular round but a solid one on a brutally tough golf course. He had started the day with a three-shot lead on Padraig Harrington and had ended it with a four-shot lead on Sergio Garcia. A four-shot lead with 18 holes to play in a major championship would send most players home with a smile on their face and a dream of kissing the trophy the next day.

If anyone should have felt good about a four-shot lead—or any lead—with one day left in a major, it was Woods. At the age of twenty-six, he had already won seven major titles, including an extraordinary stretch during which he had won four in a row. Seven times he had led a major after 54 holes, and seven times he had been the winner a day later. There was absolutely no reason to believe that his eighth such lead would be unlucky.

Woods didn't see it quite that way. All he knew as he and his omnipresent caddy, Steve Williams, walked onto the empty range that evening was that he wasn't comfortable with his swing, and he had less than an hour of daylight to figure out exactly what the problem might be. He and Harmon had worked together since Woods's days as a teenage phenom, so Harmon knew exactly what he was dealing with when the grim-faced Woods strode onto the range to the cheers of several hundred people who had packed the grandstand once they spotted Harmon. Golf fans knew that if Butch was on the range, Tiger was likely to be there shortly.

"I'm getting stuck again," Woods said as he walked up to Harmon.

Woods isn't one for small talk, especially during a major. There was no chatting about how the day had gone or any discussion of the lead or about playing the next day with Garcia. The two men were focused on one thing: Woods's golf swing.

"I know you are," Harmon said. "Let's get it fixed."

They went to work, Woods hitting shots, Harmon, arms folded, standing opposite him, watching. Every once in a while, Harmon would stand next to Woods and show him the kind of motion he wanted him to make. Woods would nod and hit more balls.

Even though the sun wouldn't set until 8:30, Woods and Harmon knew they were rapidly running out of time. The sun dropped in the western sky, and the air began to cool. Woods kept hitting ball after ball, Harmon kept watching and talking.

It was dark when they finally stopped. Harmon liked what he was seeing. "By the time we finished, he had it exactly where we wanted it to be," Harmon said. "Even so, I could tell he wasn't happy."

It is that perfectionist nature that is part of Woods's greatness. Every time he wins a major title, he celebrates for about fifteen minutes and then turns his mind to the next one. At that moment, he wasn't just thinking about winning the U.S. Open the next day, he was thinking about winning all four majors in the same year.

He had already won the Masters in April, and he was now 18 holes away from winning the Open for the second time in three years. But he wasn't especially happy with his golf swing. Harmon knew that.

"He always wants to tinker," he said. "If I say to him, 'I like what I'm seeing; that's fine,' that's not what he really wants to hear. He wants me to tell him something—anything—that's going to make him feel better about his swing.

"That day at Bethpage, I knew what was going on. It wasn't just that his swing hadn't been great that day. It wasn't bad, just not great. But he had been talking to [Mark] O'Meara and Hank [Haney] about Hank's swing theories. I got that. I know how close he and Mark are and how much he respects Mark. But I could tell he wanted to make some swing changes. I wasn't going to give him some kind of new move just to tell him something. His golf swing was good—hell, he was about to win his eighth major title and his second in a row. Why would I tell him to change *that?*"

As Woods walked to his car, followed by Williams and his security retinue, Harmon watched him. It occurred to him at that moment that he might not be Woods's teacher for very much longer.

WOODS WON THE OPEN the next day by three shots over Phil Mickelson. The only thing that could have stopped him was darkness. A rain delay kept him on the golf course until dusk, and it looked as if he might not finish until Monday morning. But, with a comfortable three-shot lead, he eagerly played the 18th hole, even in terrible light, so he could take the trophy home with him that night.

Four weeks later, Woods arrived at Muirfield, which is located outside Edinburgh in Scotland, to begin preparing for the British Open. As always, Harmon was waiting for him, ready to go through their normal premajor ritual: spend some time on the range, then walk with Woods around the golf course as he played his practice rounds. This is standard procedure for most teachers and their pupils.

When Woods spotted Harmon waiting for him on the range at Muirfield, he walked over, and the two men shook hands.

"Look, Butch. I'm okay this week," Woods said quietly. "I've got it."

Harmon understood exactly what Woods was saying, but he wanted to be sure.

"You don't need me out here," he said, making it more a statement than a question.

"No, I don't. Thanks."

"Good luck, Tiger."

"Thanks."

That was it. Eight years after they first began working together—eight major championship victories later—Woods, in a matter of about thirty seconds, had fired Harmon. Woods walked to a spot on the range that had been cleared for him to start hitting balls—without Harmon watching him.

Within forty-eight hours, the story was out that Woods and Harmon had split. That Saturday, playing in gale-like conditions, Woods shot 81 and blew himself out of contention. Within months, he would turn to Hank Haney as his new teacher and make over his golf swing.

Prior to splitting with Harmon, Woods had won seven of the previous eleven majors in which he had played. He would not win any of the next ten and would be a nonfactor in most of them. His absence at the top of the leaderboards in the majors changed the lives of many golfers because it gave them a chance—in many cases, a once-in-a-lifetime chance—to win a major championship.

During that ten-tournament stretch, seven players won their first major title. Since Woods began winning majors again at the start of 2005 when he won the Masters for the fourth time in his career, he has won six more of the golf tournaments that matter most. Of the seven players who won a first major during his "slump," only one—Phil Mickelson—has won another. Mickelson has now won three.

It was Mickelson who best described what the absence of Woods on a major leaderboard means to other players. Tied for the lead after 54 holes at the Masters in 2004, he was asked how he felt knowing that Woods was nine shots behind and, realistically, not in contention. Usually players answer such a question by saying something like, "You aren't just playing one player, you're playing the whole field. Your real competition is always the golf course."

Mickelson did none of that. Instead he shook his head, smiled, and said, "It doesn't suck."

Woods seriously contended twice during his drought. At the 2002 PGA Championship, before the remaking of his swing had really started, he chased Rich Beem to the finish line, making birdies on the final four holes on Sunday, only to fall two shots short and finish second. At the 2003 British Open he was one of a number of big names, including Vijay Singh and Davis Love III, who had a chance to win coming down the stretch. All of the big names came undone over the last few holes, opening the door for Ben Curtis to win the championship.

Yes, *that* Ben Curtis.

When he arrived at the British Open that year, Ben Curtis was a rookie on the PGA Tour and had played in a total of thirteen tournaments. He had qualified for the British Open because the Royal and Ancient Golf Club, which administers the Open, had agreed to exempt the top eight finishers at the Western Open who weren't already qualified for the championship. The Open did this to get more players from the PGA Tour to make the trip; few American golfers were willing to fly over the Atlantic Ocean, stay in a tiny bed-and-breakfast, play a 36-hole qualifier, fail, and then fly home if they didn't make the field.

Curtis had shot a four-under-par 68 on the last day of the Western to finish tied for 13th—his best finish on tour up until that point—to become one of the eight to make the British Open field. He was thrilled, and he and his fiancée, Candace Beatty, flew to England four days later. On the night before the championship began, Ben and Candace were eating dinner at a house rented for the week by the International Management Group (IMG), the management company that represented Curtis.

Curtis looked up from his food and saw Mike Weir, who had won the Masters a few months earlier, sitting down across from him with a plate of food. He introduced himself to Weir, introduced Candace, and congratulated Weir on his remarkable win at Augusta.

"Oh, thanks very much," Weir said. "So, what brings you guys over here? Did you come for the tournament?"

Curtis smiled sheepishly. "Well, actually, I'm playing in it," he said.

Weir was embarrassed. "Oh God, I'm so sorry," he said. "I didn't know..."

"Don't be sorry," Curtis answered. "I'm just a rookie. Why should you know?"

Later, Weir would laugh when he retold the story. "I had no idea who he was," he said. "Four days later, he was the British Open champion."

Four days later, Curtis's life changed forever, just as Weir's had—even though most golfers already knew Weir was a golfer—when he won the Masters.

The same thing would happen to Shaun Micheel when he won the PGA Championship in August, the first victory of his career, almost ten years after he had first qualified to play on tour. Even Jim Furyk, that year's U.S. Open champion, established as one of the best players on tour, admits that his life was different after winning the Open.

"Most of it was good," he said. "Certainly it was good financially. But I've always liked the fact that most of the time I can fly under the radar and let guys like Tiger and Phil and Vijay and Sergio be the stars. You become a U.S. Open champion, you become the number two player in the world, you can't really do that anymore."

The four major champions in 2003 were Weir at the Masters, Furyk at the U.S. Open, Curtis at the British Open, and Micheel at the PGA Championship. None of them had ever won a major before, and in fact only Furyk had finished in the *top 10* in a major. Curtis and Micheel had never won on tour prior to their victories. On the same July weekend in 2002, Curtis had been playing on the Hooters Tour, which isn't just one level below the PGA Tour but two.

Perhaps just as startling, none of the four has won another major title since his breakthrough moment. Furyk has contended on several occasions—missing playoffs at the U.S. Open by one shot in both 2006 and 2007—and Curtis made a run at the PGA Championship in 2008. Weir finished in a tie for third behind Furyk at Olympia Fields and was three shots behind Micheel and Chad Campbell after 54 holes at that year's PGA. Micheel finished second to Woods in the 2006 PGA but was five shots behind him as Woods cruised to an easy win. Micheel hasn't been in the top 20 in any of the other majors he has played in since his victory at Oak Hill.

Life doesn't just change when you win a major; it also changes when you come agonizingly close and don't win. Len Mattiace, who lost the 2003 Masters to Weir in a playoff, tore up both his knees on a skiing trip later that year and has not been the same player since. He is no longer a fully exempt player on tour and ended 2008 playing in South Africa, searching for his game. He played all of 2009 on the Nationwide Tour, hoping that would be his ticket back to fully exempt status on the PGA Tour. When the 2003 Masters comes up, he admits that, even now, it is difficult to talk about. "It's still raw," he said five years later. "There's a lot inside me I still haven't purged."

Furyk beat Stephen Leaney, a young Australian who had been trying to play his way onto the PGA Tour for several years, for his big win at Olympia Fields Country Club. Leaney's life also changed as a result of his runner-up finish, because it allowed him to move to the United States and play on the world's most lucrative golf tour. He played well enough to remain exempt through 2008 but never finished as high as second again. In 2008 he struggled with what doctors finally became convinced was vertigo due to an inner ear infection, and began 2009 with a partial exemption because he had been sick with that long-undiagnosed case of vertigo the previous year.

Thomas Bjorn was the runner-up when Curtis won. Bjorn had been one of the most successful players on the European Tour heading into that year's Open Championship (as the British Open is called everywhere in the world except the United States), and it seemed to be only a matter of time before he won a major.

But after taking three shots to get out of a bunker on the par-three 16th hole on Sunday to lose the lead, Bjorn finished second to Curtis. He did contend again at the 2005 PGA, but his career has not been the same since the near miss at Royal St. George's. Six years later, he still couldn't bring himself to talk about what had happened in that bunker. He wouldn't even answer questions by e-mail. Other players on the European Tour told stories about Bjorn "seeing demons" whenever he walked into a bunker.

Among the 2003 runners-up, the one who has been the most successful is Chad Campbell, who finished second to Micheel at the PGA. He still hasn't won a major, but he's won four times on tour, been on three Ryder Cup teams, and finished 24th on the 2008 money list. Just prior to the PGA in 2003, Campbell was chosen by his fellow pros as the next player likely to win his first major in a survey done by *Sports Illustrated*.

He came agonizingly close again at the Masters in April 2009, losing in a three-way playoff that included Kenny Perry and Angel Cabrera, the eventual winner. Still only thirty-four, he remains convinced his time to win a major will come. And yet, it is worth noting that Arnold Palmer and Tom Watson won their *last* majors at age thirty-four.

"It's one of those things where you have to play well *and* get a little bit lucky," he said. "I've been close a couple times but haven't quite gotten there yet. I still believe I will."

Of course, there's no way to know if it will ever happen for Campbell. It never did for Colin Montgomerie, Europe's best player for more than a decade but never a major champion, although he came up just short several times, twice losing playoffs, and finishing second on two other occasions. Perry has now lost two majors—the 1996 PGA and the 2009 Masters—when a par on the final hole would have made him a winner.

I FIRST THOUGHT ABOUT WRITING a book like this one in 1990, as I watched Mike Donald and Hale Irwin play off for the U.S. Open title at Medinah. Irwin was already a two-time Open champion, a future Hall of Famer who would end up winning twenty times on the PGA Tour and another forty-five times on the Champions Senior Tour. Winning was important to him, but it wasn't going to be life-changing.

Donald was having the week of his life. He was the quintessential "journeyman" pro, really a misnomer if you think about it, since *journeyman* implies "mediocre," and anyone who stays on the PGA Tour for almost twenty years (Donald played in 548 tournaments) has to be an excellent player. Donald won once on tour during his career. Winning the Open would have left him set for life financially and in the golf world. Once the words "U.S. Open champion" come before your name, there's no door that isn't open to you in golf and, for the most part, in the world.

Irwin ended up winning the playoff in sudden death, after Donald, who had led by a shot going to the 18th, made bogey and gave Irwin the chance to birdie the first hole of sudden death and win.

Two years later, Irwin was voted into the World Golf Hall of Fame. Two years after that, Donald finished out of the top 125 on the money list and was reduced to partial status on tour, forced to scramble for sponsor exemptions and to get into weaker fields later in the year when the stars went home. Donald turned fifty in 2005, making him eligible for the Champions Tour. As a past Open champion, he would have been able to play wherever and whenever he wanted to play. As a near Open champion, he has to scramble each year to get into tournaments.

Unlike a lot of players, Donald has talked candidly through the years about how different his life might have been if he had made a par putt on 18 on that Sunday or Monday in 1990.

Donald flashed through my mind in 1998 at Royal Birkdale as I watched Mark O'Meara and Brian Watts play off for that year's British Open title. O'Meara had been a star for years but had solidified his place in golf history that April by winning the Masters for his first major title. Watts was an Oklahoman who had spent most of his career playing in Japan because he hadn't been able to secure a spot for himself on the PGA Tour.

My sense was that this was Watts's moment the same way Medinah had been Donald's moment. He lost the playoff, but the money he made allowed him to come home and play the U.S. Tour. Watts had some success but never won a tournament, never contended again in a major, and was eventually knocked off the tour by a series of injuries.

But the moment when I truly knew this was a book that needed to be written came during the Weir-Mattiace playoff at Augusta. By then I had been around golf long enough that I knew and liked both men. Each had pieced together solid careers. Both were very comfortable financially by that point in their lives.

Even so, there was no doubt in my mind as they walked down the 10th fairway on that gorgeous late afternoon/early evening that their lives were about to go in entirely different directions. One would always be a Masters champion no matter what happened the rest of his life. The other would always wonder what might have been if one more putt had gone in the hole over the course of four days.

Nerves affected them both on the playoff hole, and Weir ended up winning by making a bogey.

My thought as I watched the two of them shake hands was that the book I would write would be about guys who got into contention at a major knowing this was a chance that might not come again — and how winning or losing changed their lives. At that moment, I had just agreed to do a book on my friend Bruce Edwards (*Caddy for Life*), so I tucked the idea into a corner of my brain knowing I wanted to come back to it.

As the rest of 2003 unfolded, I knew I had been handed the keys to the book I wanted to write. Jim Furyk was hardly an unknown or a one-time wonder when he won the Open that year, but the other winners and runners-up were players who had never before contended in a major. Or, in the case of Ben Curtis, had never *played* in a major. Only time would tell if they were one-win wonders.

In a very real sense this book began on the range at Bethpage on that Saturday evening in 2002 when it occurred to Butch Harmon that Tiger Woods was getting ready to fire him. The Woods-Harmon split led to the longest drought of Woods's career and opened the door for the events that unfolded in 2003.

Six years later, none of the winners or contenders in '03 has won another major — unless you want to count Vijay Singh and Woods, who finished tied for second and fourth, respectively, behind Curtis at the British Open.

What is clear after spending time with all these men is this:

their lives were never the same after their Moment in 2003. And the difference between first and second is a lot wider than the gulf between first-place money and second-place money.

On the Tuesday before the 2004 Masters, Weir hosted the annual Champions Dinner in the second-floor dining room of the Augusta National clubhouse. He sat between Byron Nelson and Arnold Palmer and listened to the two of them—and the other champions—tell stories all night.

Len Mattiace was at the Masters that year, but he was nowhere near the Champions Dinner. He was in the process of trying to come back from surgery on both knees only four months earlier.

The Masters was Mattiace's fourth tournament back after the surgery. He had rehabbed for three months—five months less than Tiger Woods would take after his knee surgery in 2008—before returning to the tour. One reason he had pushed to come back so soon was that he wanted to be ready to play at Augusta.

As it turned out, he came back too quickly. Not only did he miss the cut at the Masters, he went on to a disastrous year, playing in twenty-five tournaments but only earning $213,707, more than $1 million less than he had earned a year earlier, prior to the injury. Because he had won twice in 2002, he was still a fully exempt player in 2005, but he played even worse that year: thirty-four starts, earnings of $209,638. That sent him plummeting to 191st on the money list, which meant he was exempt in 2006 only as a past champion. In other words, he only got into tournaments *after* the top 125 on the money list from 2005, after all those who came through Qualifying School and the Nationwide Tour, even after those who finished between 126th and 150th on the money list.

Because he had a reputation as a good guy, Mattiace received a number of sponsor exemptions that year from tournament directors who liked him and remembered his close call at the Masters. On tour, players often refer to this as a one-year "good guy" extension. The good-guy extension got Mattiace into twenty-two events, but his golf got worse. He earned $66,540, making just four cuts. A year later, without the extension, he played only ten events, making zero cuts and zero dollars.

By 2008 he was playing almost as much on the Nationwide Tour as on the PGA Tour, still searching for his swing, his game, and his career.

Mike Weir also missed the cut at the 2004 Masters, which was a disappointment but nothing more. Weir knew his spot in the Masters field and in the champions locker room was secure — for life.

Mattiace has not been back to the Masters since 2004. In fact, he has not played in any of the major championships since the 2005 U.S. Open. The case can be made that the best day of his life playing golf produced the biggest disappointment, a memory he can't shake even though he played brilliantly for 17 holes.

Four days can change your life forever. And at the end, in the white-hot crucible of those final moments, one swing, one putt, one lucky or unlucky break, is often the difference between a lifetime of happy memories and telling and retelling a story that makes you smile, and a lifetime of wondering, years later, if you'll ever be able to shake that memory.

Sudden fame can mean radical life changes — for good and for bad. Seven years after fulfilling their lifelong dreams, the four major winners of 2003 have taken very different roads: Jim Furyk is still one of the most successful players in the world but wonders, as he turns forty in 2010, if that Open will be his only major title. Mike Weir, who was born on the same day as Furyk (Furyk is a few hours older), is still very successful but has been through some serious valleys in recent years.

So has Ben Curtis, who struggled to deal with going from being a golfer other golfers didn't recognize to being a major champion.

He struggled for two years, found his game again in 2006, almost won the PGA in 2008, and then struggled again in 2009.

At least the first three remain fully exempt players on the tour. Shaun Micheel ended 2009 at the PGA Tour's Qualifying School, trying to regain his status as a fully exempt player on tour but still battling to come back after having major shoulder surgery in June 2008. He came up short of the top 25, which would have made him fully exempt again, finishing in a tie for 64th place in the 170-player field.

"There are times I tell myself I should just walk away and do something else," he said one night late in 2009. "I'm forty, I'm in good shape financially, so why not give it a shot?"

He shook his head. "But then I remember how much I love golf, how much I love to compete. I've loved it since I was ten years old. I want to win again. I want something close to the feeling I had that day at Oak Hill."

He paused. "Then again, maybe that was a once-in-a-lifetime experience. If it was, well, I guess I should consider myself lucky that it happened once."

They all feel that way. All four want to win again, but they know how privileged they were to win once. And if they ever forget that, they might want to spend a few moments with Len Mattiace, Stephen Leaney, Thomas Bjorn, or Chad Campbell, in whose shoes they almost stood.